W9-BLK-994

THE BIG BOOK

OF

FLOWERS

THE BIG BOOK
OF
FLOWERS

A. Cort Sinnes

NATIONAL HOME GARDENING CLUB
Minnetonka, Minnesota

THE BIG BOOK OF FLOWERS

By A. Cort Sinnes

Copyright © 2000 National Home Gardening Club

Tom Carpenter
Director of Book Development

Jenya Prosmitsky
Book Design & Production

Michele Teigen
Senior Book Development Coordinator

Gina Germ
Photo Editor

4 5 6 7 8 / 06 05 04 03 02
ISBN 1-58159-098-9

National Home Gardening Club
12301 Whitewater Drive
Minnetonka, Minnesota 55343
www.gardeningclub.com

CONTENTS

CONTENTS

More than 35 years ago, when I was first getting into gardening, I ran across a book very much like the one you now hold in your hands. Being a new gardener, the contents of the book "wowed" me.

Until then I hadn't realized just how big the world of flowering plants was—not to mention the diversity and beauty of it all. Turning each page, I remember being pleased when I encountered a plant I recognized and could name correctly, excited when I saw a flower I had seen before but could now put a name to and, finally, the

intrigue of being introduced to plants I never even knew existed—plants that immediately went on my "buy-and-try" list.

To say the book had a profound effect on me would be an understatement. At 13 years old, I started hanging out at our local nursery so much, the proprietor finally offered me a job—a job that lasted for seven years! For the first few years behind the counter there, I know I asked more questions than I answered, but slowly I got to be on a first-name basis with most of the plants I had encountered in that book and gradually got to know their likes, dislikes and quirks firsthand.

All these years later, I experienced a similar sense of accomplishment while writing this book: I realized I wasn't just writing abstract observations; each entry was like revisiting an old friend and having the opportunity of telling their story. Completing the circle—from reading that old book to writing this new one—has been a very pleasant journey indeed.

Over the years, I've come to understand just how important it is to know the names of things that attract your attention— whether it's a bird, a china pattern, a new friend ... or a flower. Taking the time to learn (and remember) a name is not only a show of respect, it's a downright necessity if you want to have a relationship with that person or thing. It is our hope that this book will help you in the process of putting "a name to a face."

But when you're talking about plant names, the situation is somewhat more complex, because any single plant may have one common name in the South, another in the Upper Midwest, and yet another in the Pacific Northwest. Luckily, in addition to however many common names a plant might have, each plant has just one botanical name. Yes, it's true that because they're in Latin the names may be a little unwieldy, but botanical names will always be your best bet when it comes to asking for—and getting—what you want in the world of plants.

For that reason the flowering plants in this book are listed in alphabetical order by their botanical names. But we've included (page 250) a common name cross-reference chart. If you only know a plant by its common name, look that name up in this chart—you'll be directed to the plant's botanical name and the page number where it appears. Also, a botanical name cross-reference chart begins on page 253.

In addition to their botanical and common names, individual hybridized varieties will also have a specific cultivar name ("cultivar" is short for "cultivated variety"). When they appear in this book, cultivar names will have single quotes around them, such as hydrangea 'Forever Pink', or zinnia 'Border Beauty'. For plants where they existed or where warranted, we have given you some specific cultivar recommendations. In some cases, the recommendations are tried-and-true "old favorites;" in others they are new varieties which merit attention.

In addition to names, this Big Book of Flowers provides you with the basic information you need to grow each plant successfully: what kind of soil it prefers, how much water and fertilizer it needs, sun or shade, and whether or not it's bothered by any pests or diseases.

The one hazard with a book like this is that you'll see a plant that you just have to have, without really having a place in your garden that fits its needs. While there are exceptions to every rule, it's been my experience that if you ignore a plant's basic preferences, be prepared for an uphill battle. On the other hand, if you match the right plant with the right location and conditions, success is almost guaranteed.

It is my sincere hope that this book does for you what a similar book from my past did for me—namely, get you excited enough to get out there in the garden, digging and planting and caring for a whole group of new flowering friends. Mark my words: They may well become beautiful friends for life.

Good Gardening,

Cort Sinnes

ABELIA
Abelia
SHRUB, ZONE 6

This attractive, well-behaved shrub has small glossy leaves and clusters of long-lasting, small, bell-shaped, pinkish-white flowers in late spring or summer. Foliage turns a reddish bronze in fall. Left unclipped, abelia will grow 5 to 6 feet tall and about as wide. Useful in a wide variety of landscape situations, or can be sheared into formal shapes or used as a hedge.

In marginal zones, the tops of abelia bushes may be damaged by winter cold; the roots should remain alive, however, almost always returning the following spring. Plant abelia anytime during the growing season, preferably in spring or early fall, in well-drained soil, either in a full-sun or lightly shaded location.

Abelia 'Francis Mason'

ACANTHUS

Acanthus, Bear's Breeches

PERENNIAL, ZONE 8

If the fountain-like mound of spiky foliage of acanthus looks vaguely familiar, it's because its leaves are the inspiration for the decoration at the top of classic Corinthian columns. As striking as the foliage is, the tall spikes of hooded, mauve and white flowers are even more so; flowers can be used fresh or dried. Mature plants can reach 3 feet in height, with an equal spread.

Newly budding *Acanthus balanicus*

Acanthus spinosus

Plant acanthus anytime during the growing season. Will tolerate full sun, but prefers filtered shade in hot, humid climates. Plant in a well-drained garden loam, amended with plenty of organic soil amendment, such as peat moss or leaf mold. Plants usually enter a dormant period after blooming in late summer. In cold-winter areas, cover crowns with a thick layer of leaves or straw.

ACHILLEA

Yarrow

PERENNIAL, ZONE 2

Yarrow is one of those rare plants that is attractive and yet seemingly thrives on neglect. The old-fashioned variety, 'Coronation Gold', produces a plenitude of yellow-gold flowers on 2- to 3-foot-tall, sturdy stems, which can be used fresh or dried. The plant itself has finely cut, grayish-green, fern-like foliage. Newer varieties are not quite as vigorous but come in a wide variety of colors, from red to rose to creamy white. Most grow from 2 to 3 feet tall, with an equal spread.

Plant in fall or early spring, allowing 20 inches between plants. Not particular about soil—tolerating even sandy, rocky conditions—yarrow does best without fertilizer, in a full-sun location. It can withstand both drought and neglect. Propagate new plants from old by lifting and dividing the clump into smaller sections in spring; replant immediately. With the exception of occasional attacks by thrips or powdery mildew, yarrow is not bothered by pests or disease. If either appear, use an appropriate insecticide or fungicide, following all label directions.

Recommended: 'Coronation Gold', 'Moonshine', 'Cerise Queen', 'Fire King', 'Great Expectations', 'Paprika'.

Achillea 'Moonshine'

Achillea 'Beacon'

ACONITUM

Monkshood

PERENNIAL, ZONE 2

Aconitum carmichaelii 'Arendsii'

As one of the few plants with true blue flowers, the hardy monkshood has long been admired by gardeners. Plants grow from 3 to 5 feet tall, with a spread of about 2 feet, perfect for the back of flower borders. Although rich blue is the color most associated with monkshood, there are also varieties with purple or white flowers, all of which rise above the foliage on tall spikes. No matter what the shade, the flowers appear in late summer or early fall, at a time when most gardens are shy of color. The dark green, glossy foliage is attractive all season.

Set plants in the garden in fall or early spring, in a semi-shaded to shaded location. Monkshood demands a deep, rich soil amended with plenty of peat moss, compost or leaf mold. Soil should be kept evenly moist, but not soggy, throughout the growing season. Fertilize yearly in early spring. Once established, monkshood does not take kindly to being moved or having its roots disturbed.

Recommended: 'Arendsii', 'Bicolor', 'Bressingham Spire', 'Ivorine'.

Aconitum fischeri

ADENOPHORA
Lady Bells
PERENNIAL, ZONE 3

Adenophora confusa

These old-fashioned perennials are admired for their 2- to 3-foot spikes of bell-shaped flowers. Most commonly seen in deep shades of blue, this relative of campanula also includes varieties with pale blue and white flowers. Blooming time is usually late summer to early fall.

Plant lady bells in fall or early spring in a full-sun to partial-shade location. This easy-to-grow plant does best in a well-drained soil, amended with plenty of peat moss, compost or leaf mold. Requires only regular garden watering. Once established, lady bells resists being moved or divided; if you want to propagate additional plants, you'll be most successful by rooting stem cuttings.

AGAPANTHUS
Lily-of-the-Nile
TENDER PERENNIAL, ZONE 8

A common landscape plant in frost-free regions, lily-of-the-Nile is considered an exotic beauty in other parts of the country. Full-sized varieties form clumps of strap-shaped leaves, about 30 inches tall; ball-like clusters of blue or white trumpet-shaped flowers appear atop 4- to 5-foot-tall sturdy stems all summer. Dwarf forms grow about 12 inches tall with 18- to 24-inch flower spikes.

Plant lily-of-the-Nile in a full-sun or lightly shaded location. Does best in soil enriched with plenty of peat moss, compost or leaf mold. Keep plants evenly moist during the growing season; once established, can withstand periods of drought. No need for extra fertilizer. Excellent as a container plant; actually prefers being pot-bound for best bloom. In cold regions, trim off tops in fall, dig up and store roots in damp sand in a dark, dry place for the winter; replant in spring after all danger of frost has passed.

Agapanthus

AGERATUM HOUSTONIANUM

Floss Flower

ANNUAL, ALL ZONES

The common name, floss flower, is an apt description of the clusters of fuzzy flowers this annual produces. Powder blue is the color most often associated with ageratum flowers, but pink- and white-flowered varieties are also available. Older varieties grow 18 to 30 inches tall; more modern varieties tend to be dwarf, rarely exceeding 6 to 8 inches tall and about as wide, with a neat, compact habit. Like most annuals, ageratum bloom more or less constantly, from spring through early fall. Excellent for use in borders, containers and window boxes. Prefers a rather rich soil and plenty of water; cannot stand a hot, dry location.

Plant in spring, after all danger of frost has passed, in a full-sun location. Amend soil with plenty of peat moss, compost or leaf mold and keep evenly moist throughout the growing season: Ageratum will not tolerate a hot, dry location. To prolong bloom, cut spent flowers off regularly. Generally pest- and disease-free, ageratum will occasionally be attacked by caterpillars, whiteflies or gray mold. To control, use an appropriate insecticide or fungicide, following all label directions.

Ageratum houstonianum 'Capri'

AJUGA REPTANS

Carpet Bugle

PERENNIAL, ZONE 3

This low-growing perennial is primarily used as a ground-cover. Spreading by nature, when mature, ajuga produces a thick mat of green or bronzy 2-inch-tall foliage; 4- to 5-inch-tall spikes of purplish-blue, white or pink flowers appear in spring, often lasting into summer. This low-growing perennial serves a useful purpose. In difficult places that always look neglected it will spread quickly, making a thick mat that keeps out the weeds.

Plant ajuga in spring or early fall; space 6 inches apart for quick coverage. Ajuga accepts either full sun or partial shade, and ordinary garden soil, as long as it is well drained. Looks best with regular watering throughout the growing season. No fertilizer is necessary. Shear off (or mow down) flower spikes once they have finished flowering.

Recommended: 'Alba', 'Burgundy Glow', 'Caitlin's Giant', 'Rosea', 'Royalty', 'Silver Beauty', 'Variegata'.

Ajuga reptans, Ajuga reptans 'Catlin's Giant' (inset)

ALBIZIA JULIBRISSIN

Mimosa, Silk Tree

TREE, ZONE 6

This popular tree has beautiful foliage and flowers: foliage is very finely cut, resembling feathery ferns; pink, pincushion-like, fragrant flowers appear in great abundance in midsummer. Mature silk trees reach 30 to 40 feet in height, with an equal spread; with judicious pruning, can be held to about half that size. Some gardeners complain about the mess from spent flowers, but most find it a small price to pay for such beauty.

   Plant silk trees in spring or early fall in a full-sun or partially shaded location. Plant in ordinary garden soil; water regularly during the growing season for best appearance and growth. No fertilizer is necessary. If you're trying to keep a silk tree to a certain size, early spring is the time to prune.

Albizia julibrissin blossom

Albizia julibrissin

ALCEA ROSEA

Hollyhock

BIENNIAL OR SHORT-LIVED PERENNIAL, ALL ZONES

These tall—up to 9 feet—sentinels have guarded gates and doorways for many generations. Hollyhocks are also attractive planted in groups at the back of flower borders, where they are valuable as vertical accents. Summer flowers, both single and double, range through shades of rose, salmon, pink and maroon (some so dark they almost appear black), to yellow and white.

Grow hollyhocks from seed, or buy young plants; plant either about a foot apart in fall or spring. Choose a full-sun location, where they will receive some protection from wind; even so, where summer storms are common, hollyhocks will need staking. Prefers fertile, well-drained soil, and regular watering during the growing season. If, after blooming, the main stalk is cut back just above ground level and the plants fertilized, your hollyhocks may reward you with several shorter flower spikes in time to re-bloom in late fall. Hollyhocks are hardy, tough plants, able to survive occasional attacks from Japanese beetles, thrips, two-spotted spider mites, rust and leaf spot. Damage from these pests and diseases is more disfiguring than life-threatening; if extensive, use an appropriate insecticide or fungicide, following all directions.

Alcea rosea

ALCHEMILLA
Lady's Mantle
PERENNIAL, ZONES 3-7

Alchemilla mollis

ALLAMANDA
Golden Trumpet
EVERGREEN VINING SHRUB (ALSO USED AS A HOUSEPLANT), ZONE 10

In frost-free regions, this tender plant is easily grown outdoors, where it grows quickly and blooms over a long season. In other regions allamanda is grown as a houseplant, spending the summer outdoors. An evergreen scrambling shrub with bright green leaves and golden yellow, trumpet-shaped flowers, allamanda lends a tropical look to gardens. To train allamanda as a shrub rather than a climber, cut back the long shoots in summer.

In frost-free climates these plants may be set out at any season, in well-drained soil and full sun or light shade. Soil should be kept consistently moist, but not wet. Fertilize once or twice a year. If you want to grow allamanda as a vine, be sure to position it close to whatever support it is to climb on; long shoots develop quickly, clambering to a considerable height.

Recommended: 'Hendersonii'.

Lady's mantle is valued for its clusters of chartreuse summer flowers. Beautiful when combined with other bright orange, yellow or purple flowers, lady's mantle is also an excellent cut flower for small arrangements. Flowers hold their color when dried. Mature plants top out between 1 and 2 feet, with the flowers held slightly above the foliage. Can be used as an edging or planted in groups of five or more in borders and beds.

Plant transplants in spring or early fall in well-drained soil and a full-sun to partially shaded location. Water regularly during the growing season. Seeds are extremely slow to germinate. No fertilizer is necessary.

Allamanda

ALLIUM

Ornamental Onion

BULB, ZONE 4

These members of the onion family are known to flower lovers as alliums. All produce round clusters of flowers in midsummer or fall, held on a sturdy stem, from 6 inches to 5 feet tall, depending on the variety. Although their leaves

Butterfly on *Alliums*

may smell of onion when bruised, the flowers are usually without scent or smell faintly of lilac. All are excellent for cutting, and all hold their color and form well when dried. Flowers appear in many shades of blue, violet, red, yellow or white, depending on species.

Plant dormant bulbs in fall, in well-drained soil and a sunny location. Most effective when planted in groups. Water only during periods of drought, and fertilize twice—once in spring and again in mid-summer. In regions colder than Zone 4, lift the bulbs and store in a cool, dry place.

Alliums

ALSTROEMERIA

Peruvian Lily

PERENNIAL, ZONE 5 (WITH PROTECTION)

Relatively new to home gardens, Peruvian lilies grow between 2 and 5 feet tall and produce beautiful clusters of azalea-like flowers held aloft on sturdy stems, perfect for arrangements. Cut flowers are extremely long lasting. Flowers range in color from orange, yellow, red, rose, pink, purple, lavender and white. Many are attractively streaked or spotted with darker colors; some varieties are bicolored.

Plant in very well-drained soil, heavily amended with peat moss, compost or leaf mold. Plant in a full-sun location; in hot-summer regions, provide a location that receives afternoon shade. Plant seeds in spring or fall; transplants are best planted in fall. Plant where you're sure you want them, because Peruvian lilies resent being moved once established. Keep soil evenly moist until plants are finished blooming; then withhold water and allow plants to go dormant. In cold-winter regions, mulch roots heavily. With a twisting motion, pull (don't cut) flower stalks; they will separate from the underground rhizome cleanly and produce more foliage and flowers.

Alstroemeria (above), pink and yellow Peruvian lily (top)

AMARANTHUS

Amaranth, Joseph's Coat, Love-Lies-Bleeding, Summer Poinsettia, Tassel Flower

ANNUAL, ALL ZONES

These somewhat weedy plants are loved for their highly ornamental, multi-colored foliage or unusual flowers—depending on the variety. Love-lies-bleeding (*A. caudatus*) grows from 3 to 8 feet tall and is quite a coarse-looking plant. Long, drooping clusters of reddish-magenta, tassel-like flowers appear in summer. Can be used as a cut flower or dried. Joseph's coat (*A. tricolor*) grows from 1 to 4 feet tall, producing splendidly colored foliage in shades of yellow, green and red. Neither type combines easily with other flowering plants, but they are definitely eye-catching in their own right.

Plant in spring when all danger of frost has passed. All members of the Amaranth family require a full-sun location. Ordinary or even poor garden soil will give best results. Water regularly throughout the growing season. No fertilizer is required.

Recommended (*A. tricolor*): 'Early Splendor', 'Flaming Fountain', 'Molten Fire'.

Amaranthus 'Tricolor Joseph's Coat' (left), Amaranthus caudatus (right)

AMARYLLIS BELLADONNA

Belladonna Lily, Hardy Amaryllis, Magic Lily, Naked Lady

BULB, ZONES 9-10

These summer-flowering bulbs have one of the strangest growing cycles of any in the plant world: In early spring, long, strap-shaped leaves appear from underground and keep growing until early summer. Right when they are at their peak, they die down and disappear completely, usually in July. By August, thick, 2- to 3-feet-tall flower stalks will have appeared and, like magic, produce beautiful clusters of fragrant, lilac-pink, trumpet-shaped flowers.

In early spring or fall, plant bulbs in sun or semi-shade, in well-drained soil, 4 to 6 inches apart. In mild-winter regions, plant bulbs so their necks are right at the soil line; in cold-winter areas, plant bulbs 4 inches deep. Amaryllis are amazingly drought-tolerant, storing all the water they need for the growing season from winter rains. No fertilizer is necessary.

Amaryllis belladonna

AMMOBIUM ALATUM

Winged Everlasting

ANNUAL OR SHORT-LIVED PERENNIAL, ZONE 6

Ammobium alatum

If you like dried flowers, try growing this unusual flower. Its small, button-like flowers have yellow centers surrounded by stiff white petals with prominent ridges, or wings. Its long stems are excellent for arranging, either fresh or dried. Winged everlasting grows to 2 to 3 feet tall; plant in clumps of five or more for best effect. Cutting the long stems encourages the plants to produce more flowers.

Winged everlastings are easy to grow from seeds started indoors in early spring. Plant the transplants in a full-sun location as soon as the last spring frost has passed. Prefers a fast-draining, sandy soil and normal amounts of water. No fertilizer is necessary.

ANAPHALIS
Pearly Everlasting

PERENNIAL, ZONE 3

Pearly everlasting is an under-utilized flower—one that should be on the list of any gardener interested in dried flowers. Mounds of two-toned foliage—dark green above and fuzzy gray below—grow to about 3 feet tall. Mature plants will spread to form mats, attractive as an edging for the front of flower borders. Flowers appear in midsummer and are produced in clusters on erect stems; they resemble small daisies with pearly white or pale yellow, paper-like petals with yellow centers, excellent as cut flowers, fresh or dried.

Start plants from seed in late winter; plant transplants in early spring, or buy plants and plant them from spring to early summer in full sun or light shade. Any soil will suffice, as long as it is well drained. No fertilizer is necessary. Frequent cutting of flowers keeps this plant from becoming invasive. May self-sow.

Recommended: *Anaphalis magaritacea*, and *A. triplinervis* 'Sulphur Light'.

Anaphalis margaritacea

ANCHUSA

Alkanet, Bugloss, Cape Forget-Me-Not,
Summer Forget-Me-Not, Italian Bugloss

ANNUALS, BIENNIALS AND PERENNIALS, ZONE 3

Related to the common annual form of forget-me-nots (*Myosotis*), the two species of anchusa produce some of the bluest of the blue flowers in the plant kingdom, and both are easy to grow. The perennial kind (*Anchusa azurea*) produces clusters of bright blue flowers throughout summer and fall. It is an extremely hardy plant that, once estab-

lished, will spread and may become hard to remove. The biennial form, *A. capenensis*, is shorter, growing to about 18 inches with an equal spread. In cold-winter climates, it is usually treated as an annual. Summer-long, bright blue flowers have white throats.

Plant in a full-sun location in a well-drained soil, amended with plenty of peat moss, compost or leaf mold. Once established, plants are moderately drought resistant. No fertilizer is necessary.

Recommended (*A. azurea*): 'Dropmore', 'Opal', 'Little John', 'Royal Blue', 'Loddon Royalist'.

Anchusa capensis, Anchusa azurea (inset)

ANEMONE

*Anemone, European Pasque Flower,
Japanese Anemone, Pasque Flower,
Poppy-Flowered Anemone, Scarlet
Anemone, Windflowers*

PERENNIAL WITH TUBEROUS OR FIBROUS ROOTS, ZONE 6

Each flower season—spring, summer and fall—has its own anemone. There is considerable variation between the species, but all produce beautiful flowers. For the record, *Anemone blanda*, *A. coronaria* and *A. fulgens* are grown from bulbs; the other popular species, *A. hybrida*, grows from a fibrous root.

All anemones grown from bulbs produce flowers in late spring, one to a 12- to 18-inch-tall stem. There are single and semi-double forms, in a wide range of clear colors, including white, pink, purple and blue, up to 2 $^1/_2$ inches in diameter. The flowers of *A. fulgens* are brilliant scarlet with black centers, although pink and coral forms are also available. Anemones grown from bulbs are extremely tender and are usually treated as annuals in cold-winter climates. Cut flowers are long lasting and excellent in arrangements.

The so-called Japanese anemone or windflower (*A. hybrida*) blooms from September on, at a time when most gardens are in sore need of flowers. The flowers appear atop 2- to 4-foot-tall stems that sway gracefully in the wind. A dark background, such as an evergreen hedge or wall, provides shelter and also helps to show off the lovely white or pink semi-double flowers. Once established, windflower plants will spread readily, but resent being moved.

Plant the bulbs of spring-flowering anemones in late fall, 3 inches deep and 5 inches apart, in a partially shaded location. These bulbs prefer well-drained soil. Apply a dry, complete fertilizer at planting time, according to label directions.

In mild-winter climates, plant Japanese anemones (*A. hybrida*) in the fall; plant in spring in regions with cold winters. Choose a partially shaded location and amend the soil with plenty of peat moss, compost or leaf mold. Place 18 to 24 inches apart. No fertilizer is necessary. Keep soil evenly moist, but not wet, during the heat of summer; cover with a thick layer of leaves in late fall in regions with cold winters.

Anemone blanda

Anemone blanda 'White Splendour' (above), white *Anemone blanda* (top right)

Occasionally bothered by black blister beetles, cutworms, leafhoppers, slugs, snails and rust. Control with an appropriate insecticide or fungicide, following all label directions.

Recommended (*A. blanda*, *A. coronaria*, and *A. fulgens*): 'Blue Star', 'Red Star', 'Pink Star', 'White Splendor', 'Radar', 'De Caen', 'St. Brigid', and 'St. Bravo'; (*A. hybrida*): 'Honorine Jobert'.

ANTHEMIS TINCTORIA
Golden Marguerite
PERENNIAL, ZONE 3

A ready producer of cheery, clear yellow daisies, the golden marguerite is worthy of a place in any flower border or container planting. It grows and blooms freely and is surprisingly hardy. The ivory to golden-colored flowers on wiry stems are perfect for cutting. Flowers appear more or less constantly from June to September. The 2-foot-tall plants, with fern-like, aromatic foliage, are impressive when planted in groups of three or more near the edge of a flower border.

Plant in spring or fall, about 2 feet apart, in a full-sun location. Prefers a sandy, well-drained soil; once established, withstands drought well. Feed with a complete fertilizer once or twice during the growing season, following label directions.

Recommended: 'Beauty of Grallagh', 'E. C. Buxton', 'Kelwai' and 'Moonlight'.

Anthemis tinctoria 'Golden Marguerite'

ANTIGONON LEPTOPUS

Coral Vine, Queen's Wreath, Rosa de Montana

TENDER VINE, ZONE 8

This native of Mexico produces a luxuriant vine in warm climates, without demanding more than full sun and ordinary soil. It easily forms a dense screen on a fence or wall—anything to which it can fasten its tendrils. Leaves are attractively heart-shaped. The small, profuse flowers, in shades of bright pink, deep rose and white—are borne in long, drooping clusters almost continuously in the mildest of climates.

Plant anytime in mild climates; in cold-winter climates, plant in spring after all chance of frost has passed. Plant in a sunny spot, but withhold fertilizer: Fertile soil promotes leaves at the expense of flowers. Once established, withstands drought well. Be sure the support for this vine is close enough so that the tendrils can reach it easily.

Antigonon leptopus

White *Antigonon leptopus*

ANTIRRHINUM MAJUS

Snapdragon

PERENNIAL, USUALLY TREATED AS ANNUAL, ALL ZONES

Antirrhinum majus

The name snapdragon is an attempt to describe the shape of the individual flowers with their "jaws" that open wide when pressed at the base. The botanical name, *Antirrhinum*, meaning "like a nose", is another reference to the form of the flower.

Breeding efforts have produced snapdragon varieties in an array of sizes. Available in dwarf, medium and tall strains, they can make their appearance in the garden as edging plants, in borders or as tall, stately accents with other summer-flowering annuals. They bloom from about the middle of July to frost and are excellent as cut flowers.

Plant transplants in early spring in a full-sun location with good air circulation. Snapdragons prefer a well-drained garden loam, amended with plenty of peat moss, compost or leaf mold. Space tallest varieties about 18 inches apart, medium kinds 10 inches apart, and dwarf forms 6 inches apart. Twice—once in midspring and again in early summer—pinch out the growing tips of the tall varieties to produce bushy, well-branched plants. Keep soil evenly moist but not wet. Fertilize once or twice during the growing season, following label directions. Tallest kinds may require staking. Depending on where they are grown, snapdragons may be remarkably pest- and disease-free, or attacked by aphids, leafrollers, leaftiers, spider mites, woolybear caterpillars, anthracnose, leaf spot, Southern blight or Southern root-knot nematodes. Control with an appropriate insecticide or fungicide, following all label directions.

Recommended: 'Bright Butterflies', 'Dwarf Bedding Floral Carpet', 'Pocket', 'Topper', 'Double Supreme', 'Cinderella', 'Coronette', 'Kim', 'Kolibri', 'Little Darling', 'Liberty Bell', 'Madame Butterfly', 'Minaret', 'Pixie', 'Princess White with Purple Eye', 'Royal Carpet', 'Sprite', 'Sweetheart', 'Tahiti', 'Wedding Bells'.

Antirrhinum majus 'Double Azalea Pink'

Aquilegia Hybrids

Columbine

PERENNIAL, ZONE 3

Columbine are among the most graceful, elegant flowers in any bed or border, especially appropriate in woodland settings. Held 2 to 4 feet above the lacy foliage, on strong, wiry stems, columbine flowers appear in early summer. An impressive palette of colors and combinations is available:

Muted shades of yellow, blue, lavender, red and white are blended in beautiful array, the intriguing form of the flowers adding to their charm. Columbine make elegant cut flowers, combining well with roses.

Plant columbine transplants early in either spring or fall,

Aquilegia flabellata

Aquilegia canadensis

about 12 inches apart, in well-drained soil, previously improved with plenty of compost, leaf mold or peat moss. A cool, partially shaded spot is ideal for columbine. Keep soil evenly moist but not wet. No fertilizer is necessary. To prolong the flowering period, cut off all wilted flowers promptly. Columbine is generally free of pests and diseases, but may occasionally suffer attacks from aphids, columbine borers, leafminers or leaf spot. Control with an appropriate insecticide or fungicide, following all label directions.

Recommended: 'McKana Giants', 'Spring Song', 'Biedermeier', 'Dragonfly', 'Music', 'Fairyland', 'Nora Barlow'.

ARABIS
Rock Cress

PERENNIAL, ZONES 4-7

Hardy and free flowering, rock cress grows no more than a foot high, creating a mat of practically evergreen foliage covered with clusters of white, pink, or rose blossoms in spring. Rock cress spreads fast, useful for covering banks or dressing up stone retaining walls; in more formal settings, rock cress makes an excellent edging plant in beds and borders, particularly charming combined with spring-flowering bulbs.

Plant transplants of rock cress in early spring or fall, 6 to 8 inches apart. Remarkably tolerant of neglect, all rock cress asks for is plenty of sunshine and well-drained, light soil without any fertilizer. Let plants dry out between watering. To keep them tidy, shear (or mow) plants to about 3 inches right after they bloom. Every third year or fourth spring, dig up the clumps, separate into sections and replant them.

Recommended: 'Rosea', 'Rosabella', 'Pink Charm', 'Variegata', 'Flore Pleno'.

Arabis 'Spring Charm'

ARISAEMA
Jack-in-the-Pulpit, Indian Turnip
TUBEROUS-ROOTED PERENNIAL, ZONE 4

A horticultural equivalent of a "conversation piece," Jack-in-the-pulpit is a very unusual flowering plant, most at home in woodland gardens. The tuberous root produces a 2-foot-tall stem with a few leaves. Summer flowers appear atop the stems and look something like an upright calla lily, except that instead of being creamy white, the spathe is green or purple with white stripes, and instead of yellow, the spadix

Arisaema triphyllum

is green or purple. More odd than beautiful, Jack-in-the-pulpit nonetheless has its devotees. Flowers fade, eventually producing a seed pod resembling a small ear of corn with brilliant orange-red kernels.

Plant in the spring or fall in a shaded location. Jack-in-the pulpit demands a loose soil, rich with the addition of plenty of peat moss, compost or leaf mold. Soil should be kept evenly moist, but not wet, throughout the growing season. Does not require fertilizer.

Arisaema sikokianum

ARISTOLOCHIA SPP.

Dutchman's Pipe

SHORT-LIVED PERENNIAL VINE, USUALLY GROWN AS AN
ANNUAL, ALL ZONES

Aristolochia flower

This old-fashioned plant used to
screen many a front porch, creating
a cool, leafy retreat in no time at all.
The name Dutchman's pipe refers to
the small, brownish flowers—which
resemble a curved pipe—but you
have to look hard to see them amid
the lush, broad, heart-shaped leaves
of this vine. A very fast-growing
vine, Dutchman's pipe will cover an
area 15 by 20 feet or more in a single
growing season.

Plant from seed or transplant in
spring. Accepts any exposure, from
full sun to shade. Not particular
about soil, but puts on best growth
with plenty of water and monthly
applications of a complete fertilizer.
It is a rampant grower, so do not use
where it will crowd choicer plants.
Can be pruned to keep vine within
its bounds.

Aristolochia

ARMERIA

Sea Pink, Thrift

PERENNIAL, ZONE 4

This trim, compact perennial, with grass-like leaves, is evergreen in most parts of the country. Sea pinks grow in tidy clumps, about 6 inches tall; each clump will spread 12 inches or more. Small, long-lasting globular flowers appear in early summer on wiry stems 6 to 18 inches long, good for cutting. If you remove spent flowers, blooming season can extend into fall. Flower colors range from red, pink to white. This is a hardy plant that does well even in difficult seaside locations.

Plant sea pinks in early spring or fall, about 12 inches apart. Choose a full-sun location in a loose, very well-drained soil. Once established, sea pinks can withstand some drought. Does not require fertilizer. Every second or third year, dig up and divide individual clumps in early fall and replant immediately.

Recommended: 'Bee's Ruby', 'Bloodstone', 'Cottontail'.

Armeria 'Bloodstone'

Armeria

ARTEMISIA
Dusty Miller
PERENNIAL, ZONE 4

Artemisia

There are many varieties of artemisia, all of them valued for their "frosty" or silvery foliage. Experienced gardeners have long known that silver-foliaged plants work well in taming other, brighter colors in a flower border. Silver foliage is also an asset in cut flower arrangements and artemisia foliage can also be dried for use in winter bouquets and decorations. The most popular artemisias are hardy, easy-to-grow plants, ranging from 6 to 30 inches tall with a spread of 2 or 3 feet. Most produce inconspicuous yellow flowers.

Plant in early spring or early fall in a warm, sunny place. Artemisias demand a well-drained soil, but only moderate water. No fertilizer is necessary. When a clump grows too large, it may be dug up in spring or fall, separated into smaller parts, and replanted. Generally not bothered by pests or diseases, artemesias may occasionally be attacked by aphids, grasshoppers or rust. Control with an appropriate insecticide or fungicide, following all label directions.

Recommended: 'Silver Spreader', 'Silver King', 'Silver Queen', 'Powis Castle'.

ARUNCUS
Goatsbeard
PERENNIAL, ZONE 5

An impressive plant, especially for shaded woodland settings, goatsbeard will grow to a height of 6 feet with a spread of 3 feet or more (the variety 'Kneiffii', noted below, grows to only 3 feet tall). Finely divided leaves make for a soft, lush appearance. Attractive cream-colored, plume-like flowers appear in early summer.

Plant in spring or fall, in a partially shaded location; will tolerate full sun in cool-summer regions. While tolerant of varying conditions, goatsbeard performs best in a well-drained, loose soil, amended with plenty of peat moss, compost or leaf mold. Keep soil moist, but not wet, throughout the growing season. Does not require fertilizer.

Recommended: 'Kneiffii'.

Aruncus dioicus

ASCLEPIAS TUBEROSA
Butterfly Weed

PERENNIAL, ZONE 3

At least one part of the common name for this plant rings true: When in bloom, it does, indeed, attract butterflies in droves; it is not, however, a "weed." This is a very hardy, easy-to-grow plant. In cold-winter regions it dies completely to the ground, returning each spring to produce a 3-foot-tall, shrubby plant. By midsummer, masses of small, bright orange or yellow flowers make their appearance—and soon after, the visiting butterflies. Flowers persist into fall. An amazingly tolerant plant, butterfly weed withstands both harsh winters and summer droughts, and even does well in sandy, seaside conditions.

Plant in spring or fall, singly or in groups of three spaced 10 to 15 inches apart. This plant is a late starter in spring. Not particular about soil, but does best in a full-sun location. Once established, it tolerates drought. Does not require fertilizer. Does not take well to transplanting. Generally free of pests and diseases, butterfly weed may occasionally be attacked by caterpillars, leafminers or rust. Control with an appropriate insecticide or fungicide, following all label directions.

Recommended: 'Gay Butterflies'.

Asclepias tuberosa, Asclepias tuberosa seed pod (inset)

ASTER

Aster, Michaelmas Daisy, New England Aster,
New York Aster

PERENNIAL, ZONES VARY BY SPECIES

Asters have been deservedly popular for generations of gardeners. There are two distinct types: the annual types, known as China asters (*Callistephus*, see page 48), and the perennial ones, the most popular of which are *A. frikartii*, *A. novae-angliae*, and *A. novi-belgii*.

A. frikartii grows to 2 to 3 feet tall with about a 2-foot spread. An abundance of 2 $1/2$-inch flowers appear from early summer through fall, in either white or lavender blue. It is reliably hardy only to Zone 6. In mild-winter climates, this variety may bloom nearly year-round. Cut back or shear plants after flowering to promote repeat bloom. Divide every other year in spring. Plant in a full-sun or partially shaded location. Not particular as to soil. No fertilizer necessary. Relatively pest-free; may be bothered by mildew, leaf spot or rust. At the first sign of attack, spray with a fungicide; read and follow all label directions. Recommended: 'Monch', 'Wonder of Staffa'.

A. novae-angliae, commonly known as the New England aster or Michaelmas daisy, is one of the flowers most commonly associated with the fall season. Hardy to Zone 3. A sturdy-stemmed plant with hairy leaves, New England asters grow to 3 to 6 feet tall, with a 3-foot spread. From August through October, these asters put on a fine show with masses of 1- to 2-inch daisy-like flowers. Flower color ranges from shades of purple, to violet and pink; all have yellow centers. Cut back individual stalks in early summer

Aster

to produce bushier plants. Stake tallest varieties early in the season to keep them from tumbling under their own weight. Plant in a full-sun to partially shaded location. Not particular as to soil type. Keep consistently moist through the growing season; will tolerate wet areas. Occasionally attacked by aphids, Japanese beetles, lacebugs or leafhoppers. Control with an appropriate insecticide or fungicide, following all label directions. May be bothered by mildew, leaf spot or rust. At the first sign of attack, spray with a fungicide; read and follow all label directions. Recommended: 'Alma Potschke', 'Harringon's Pink', 'Treasurer', 'Hella', 'Purple Dome'.

A. novi-belgii, commonly known as Michaelmas daisy or New York aster, grows to 3 feet tall with a similar spread. Hardy to Zone 3. Unlike the New England asters, Michaelmas daisies have smooth foliage, produced on graceful, arching branches. Masses of flowers—in colors ranging from deep red, dark purple, pale lavender, pink and pure white—appear in late summer and early fall. Plant in a full-sun to partially shaded location. Not particular as to soil type. Keep consistently moist through the growing season. Relatively pest-free; may be bothered by mildew, leaf spot or rust. At the first sign of attack, spray with a fungicide; read and follow all label directions.

Plant perennial aster plants in the spring, 2 to 3 feet apart (or more for the tallest). Every other spring, divide the plants and replant immediately.

Aster novae–angliae 'Hella Lacy'

ASTILBE
Astilbe
PERENNIAL, ZONE 3

Astilbe's feathery flowers are wonderful vertical accents in woodland plantings or at the edge of a garden pool or stream. Hardy and very long-lived, astilbe plants are an almost fern-like clump of finely cut foliage, 2 to 3 feet tall, with a similar spread. The plume-like flower spikes—in shades of pink, rose, red, lavender and white—appear from June through September, depending on the variety.

Plant astilbe in spring or fall, in a loose, well-drained soil to which plenty of compost, peat moss or leaf mold has been added. Can handle full sun in cool-summer regions; most often planted in partial to full shade. Keep soil evenly moist throughout the growing season. Be aware that astilbe plants have shallow roots that dry out quickly during summer hot spells; extra irrigation may be required. No fertilizer is required. Dig clumps every third spring, discard the center part, divide the remaining pieces and replant immediately. In very cold areas some winter protection is advisable. Generally pest- and disease-free, astilbe may occasionally be attacked by aphids, black vine beetles, Japanese beetles, slugs, snails, fusarium wilt or powdery mildew. Control with an appropriate insecticide or fungicide, following all label directions.

Recommended: 'Amethyst', 'Bonn', 'Bremen', 'Bresingham Beauty', 'Bridal Veil', 'Deutschland', 'Erica', 'Fanal', 'Hyazinth', 'Koblenz', 'Ostrich Plume', 'Peach Blossom', 'Pumila', 'Rheinland', 'Superba', 'White Glory'.

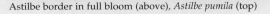

Astilbe border in full bloom (above), *Astilbe pumila* (top)

BAPTISIA
Baptisia, False Indigo
PERENNIAL, ZONE 3

Newly budding *Baptista australis*

An old-fashioned favorite, this native wildflower bears foot-long flower spikes studded with deep purple, yellow or white pocketbook flowers, resembling those of its cousin, the common pea. A willing performer and very long-lived, baptisia blooms from late spring to early summer, usually over a 3- to 5-week period. Plants reach a height of 3 to 5 feet, especially in warm climates, with a 4- to 6-foot spread. Baptisia looks best planted in clumps or drifts at the back of flower borders. If left uncut, the flower spikes eventually produce large seed pods, useful in arrangements.

Plant baptisia in spring in a full-sun or lightly shaded location. This plant prefers slightly acidic soil (amend soil with pine needles or peat moss to increase acidity). Normal water requirements. No fertilizer required. Baptisia seldom spreads far from where it is initially planted, and may be left undisturbed for several years. To increase supply of plants, dig and divide clumps in early spring and immediately transplant them.

Recommended: 'Purple Smoke'.

Baptista australis

Begonia

Begonia, Fibrous Begonia, Tuberous Begonia, Wax Begonia

ANNUAL AND PERENNIAL, ALL ZONES

The begonia family is not only extremely large, it is extremely diverse. Two types are extremely useful for summer bedding or as candidates for hanging baskets: Tuberous begonias (known as tuberhybrida hybrids) have blooms so perfect as to look unreal, and wax begonias (*Begonia* x *semperflorens*) have long been a favorite bedding plant.

Tuberous begonias produce truly spectacular flowers in shades of pink, scarlet, yellow, salmon and white. The flowers come in various forms—camellia, carnation, rose, crested or frilled, and the plants themselves are either upright or hanging. In regions of the country with cool summer temperatures, they make a spectacular showing; elsewhere they are usually grown with the protection of a lath house and frequent misting. Tuberous begonias can be grown in pots, hanging baskets or in open beds. A semi- or filtered-shade location facing east or north is best. Tuberous begonias demand a loose, well-drained, rich soil, amended with plenty of peat moss or compost. A mixture of peat moss and sand is best for container-grown tuberous begonias. Keep soil evenly moist, but not wet, throughout the growing season. Feed monthly with a liquid, complete fertilizer, following label directions. Plants die down in the fall; store tuberous bulbs in a cool, dry place (in dry sand or peat

Wax begonia

moss) for the winter and replant the following spring.

Wax begonias, with little single or double flowers, are a standby for edging and bed displays. Easy to grow, they are appreciated for constant bloom from spring through fall—and even through winter if you live in a frost-free climate or if they are dug up and brought indoors. Wax begonias have very glossy green, red, bronze or variegated leaves and pink, red or white flowers. Plants range from 6 to 8 inches tall for the dwarf varieties, to 12 inches tall for the standard varieties. Can stand full sun in areas with cool summers; elsewhere, filtered shade is preferred. Plant in spring, after all danger of frost has passed, in a loose, well-drained soil amended with plenty of peat moss, compost or leaf mold. Keep soil consistently moist, but not wet, throughout the growing season. Fertilize every other month with a liquid, complete fertilizer, following label directions. Occasionally attacked by aphids, black vine beetles, mealybugs, slugs, snails, nematodes, whiteflies, bacterial leaf spot or root rot. Control with an appropriate insecticide or fungicide, following all label directions.

Tuberous begonia

BELLIS PERENNIS

English Daisy

PERENNIAL, ZONE 4

For planting in the cracks of a stone walkway, massing at the front of a spring border, or simply sprinkling throughout a lawn, English daisies are colorful and intimate little plants. Well suited to small gardens, they are the essence of charm, especially when combined with pansies and spring-flowering bulbs. Rosettes of green leaves grow about 3 to 5 inches tall; very double flowers are held aloft on 3- to 6-inch-tall stems in spring and early summer. English daisies are available in shades of pink, rose, red and white, all with yellow centers.

Set out the plants in early spring, 6 inches apart. A full-sun location is best in all but the hottest climates, where some afternoon shade is appreciated. English daisies require a well-drained soil kept more or less consistently moist; they wilt quickly if subjected to hot, dry conditions. No fertilizer is necessary.

BOLTONIA

False Starwort

PERENNIAL, ZONE 4

Relatively new to home gardens, boltonia is a North American native that's been tamed somewhat by plant breeders. With quick growth upwards of 6 feet—with a 5-foot, or more, spread—boltonia isn't for small gardens. In large beds, or for the back of deep flower borders, boltonia is valued for its airy masses of daisy-like flowers in late summer and early fall. Bloom period lasts for 3 to 5 weeks. Flowers have yellow centers and are available in either white or lilac-pink.

Plant in spring or fall in a full-sun location. Not particular as to soil, as long as it is well drained. Once established, survives drought well, although plants may be diminished in size and flowering.

Recommended: 'Snowbank', 'Pink Beauty'.

Bellis perennis 'Smile White', *Boltonia* 'Snow Bank' (top)

BOUGAINVILLEA

Bougainvillea

TENDER SHRUB, ZONE 9

In frost-free regions this tropical vine is a spectacular grower and bloomer. It is a big, shrubby plant, sometimes reaching 40 or 50 feet in height. Growth is very dense and heavy, with spines on the stems. Brilliantly colored (almost fluorescent) flowers are borne in masses, over an extended season, sometimes completely hiding the foliage. Actually, the bracts surrounding the diminutive creamy white flower furnish the brilliant color.

Where it is adapted, bougainvillea can be planted at any time of the year. It flourishes in any soil, but demands a full-sun location. Bougainvillea can stand both drought and heavy trimming, producing a symmetrical shrub or hedge. If you prune bougainvillea, do so in midsummer. Or allow it to scramble informally over an arbor, wall, bank or up and over a porch roof. In cold-winter climates, bougainvillea can be grown in containers and brought indoors before the first fall frost. Place in a south- or west-facing window for maximum sunlight, and don't over-water.

Recommended: 'Barbara Karst', 'Crimson Jewel', 'Hawaii', 'Jamaica White', 'La Jolla', 'Lavender Queen', 'Pink Tiara', 'San Diego Red', 'Tahitian Dawn', Texas Dawn', 'White Madonna'.

Bougainvillea

BUDDLEIA

Butterfly Bush, Fountain Butterfly Bush, Summer Lilac

SHRUB, ZONE 5

Buddleia's common name comes from its extreme popularity with butterflies

There are many members of the Buddleia family; *B. alternifolia*, commonly called the fountain butterly bush, and *B. davidii*, commonly called butterfly bush or summer lilac, are two of the best. Both are extremely easy to grow and satisfying in their willingness to produce plenty of flowers, even in harsh conditions, and in their ability to attract legions of butterflies (and bees).

Buddleia alternifolia grows to a height of 12 to 15 feet with an equal spread. Its common name of fountain butterfly bush refers to its fountain-like form, with arching, graceful stems. An abundance of small clusters of lilac-purple flowers appear in spring and have a mild fragrance. Plant in spring or fall in a full-sun location. Tolerates a wide variety of soils, as long as they are well drained. Once established, *B. alternifolia* is drought tolerant. No fertilizer is necessary. Prune a few of the branches to within a couple of inches from the ground to keep plant from becoming a thicket. Alternately, prune all but 1 or 2 of the stems, remove the bottom foliage, and train *B. alternifolia* as a small tree.

Buddliea davidii is called summer lilac because of its long (12 inches or more) graceful wands of fragrant summer flowers. Flower colors include purple, lavender, red, pink, orange, yellow, blue and white. Fast growing and very vigorous, *B. davidii* will produce a large bush, to 8 feet tall (or more), with an equal spread, by midsummer. Groups of *B. davidii* make an excellent informal hedge (planted 3 to 5 feet apart) and blend well with perennials and other shrubs.

Set out the plants in early spring or fall, in any soil, as long as it is well drained. They withstand full sun or light shade, and need only enough water to sustain growth. No fertilizer necessary. In hard winters the butterfly bush is likely to die back, perhaps all the way to the ground. This is seldom fatal. Simply cut the old stems back to green wood as soon as the plants show life in spring; by summer it will have recovered admirably.

Recommended (*B. alternifolia*): 'Argentea'; (*B. davidii*): 'Charming', 'Fascination', 'Peace', 'White Profusion', 'Empire Blue', 'Fortune', 'Black Knight', 'Dubonnet', 'Nanho Blue', 'Lochinch'.

Buddleia davidii

CALADIUM

Caladium

TUBEROUS-ROOTED PERENNIAL (ALSO USED AS A HOUSEPLANT), ALL ZONES

Although the flowers of caladium are not worth mentioning, the large, flat, paper-thin leaves of caladium are so richly colored that flowers are hardly missed. Splashed and mottled, its heart-shaped leaves are available in wild combinations of white and green, pink, red, rose, silver, bronze and chartreuse. Popular for its summer-long show as a bedding or container plant, caladium may also be grown as a houseplant, in window boxes or in any shady place in the garden.

Plant the dormant tuberous roots of caladium in spring, after all danger of frost has passed and garden soil has warmed. Caladium demands a very rich, loose, well-drained soil, amended with plenty of peat moss, compost or leaf mold. Keep soil consistently moist, but not wet, throughout the growing season. Feed once or twice during the summer with a complete, liquid fertilizer, following label directions.

To grow them in pots, plant the tubers first in a box of peat moss in early spring and keep them in a warm, indoor place until they have started to grow. Then transfer each tuber to a pot of its own (not too large), filled with rich, moist potting soil, about 2 inches deep. When all threat of frost has passed, move the pots to a lightly shaded outdoor location. If you plan to plant caladiums in a garden bed or border, you can get a jump on the season using the same method: Simply transplant the started plants to the open ground as soon as the weather is warm, spacing them about 8 to 10 inches apart, but instead of planting them 2 inches deep, barely cover the tubers with soil.

Whether caladiums are in containers or the open ground, the leaves die down in late summer, signaling nap time for the tubers until next spring. To help them get the rest they need, gradually stop watering as soon as the foliage starts to droop in fall. Container-grown caladiums should then be moved to a dry, warm place until the next spring. If the plants are growing in outdoor beds, dig up the tubers and store in a dry, warm place—packed in dry sand or peat moss—for the winter. Replant the following spring.

Caladium

CALENDULA

Calendula, Pot Marigold

ANNUAL, ALL ZONES

The cheerful, daisy-like flowers of calendula—available in sunny shades of creamy white, lemon yellow, gold and orange—bloom best in the cool weather of spring but will even flower through the winter in regions with mild, frost-free weather. Very easy to grow, calendulas are available in standard sizes—18 to 24 inches tall with a spread of 12 inches—and dwarf forms, 12 to 15 inches tall with an equal spread. Taller varieties make wonderful, long-lasting cut flowers, especially pretty massed in pottery bowls. Although the majority of calendulas have a very double, daisy-like form, there are varieties with pompon centers and others with quilled petals, resembling cactus flowers.

Plant in very early spring or fall, in a full-sun location, about 12 inches apart. Calendulas need only average, well-drained soil and moderate water. No fertilizer is necessary. Remove spent flowers to increase flowering. When setting out transplants, be sure to bait for slugs and snails at the same time or else you could lose your entire planting overnight! Occasionally bothered by aphids, whiteflies, leaf spot or powdery mildew. Control with an appropriate insecticide or fungicide, following all label directions.

Recommended: 'Bon Bon', 'Dwarf Gem', 'Fiesta', 'Kabluna', 'Pacific Beauty', 'Radio'.

Calendula (left),
Calendula officinalis
'Indian Prince' (above)

CALLISTEMON

Bottlebrush

SHRUB OR SMALL TREE, ZONE 9

In regions of the country with mild winters, this tender evergreen shrub is popular for its curious flower spikes, which look just like what its common name suggests: a brilliant red bottle brush. Its flowers—loved by hummingbirds—appear from March to early summer, and are set off against narrow, dark, leathery foliage. Considered a large shrub or small tree, standard bottlebrush grows 10 to 15 feet tall with an equal spread; dwarf forms are available. A dark background shows off the plant to its best advantage. Also can be grown in a row, unpruned, as an informal, flowering hedge.

Plant anytime during the year. Bottlebrush prefers a full-sun location and ordinary garden soil. Once established, it withstands drought. No fertilizer necessary. Don't try to move well-established plants. Do any necessary pruning as soon as the flowers fade.

Recommended: 'Splendens', 'Compacta', 'Violaceus', 'Mauve Mist'.

Callistemon citrinus, close-up of *Callistemon citrinus* blossom (inset)

CALLISTEPHUS CHINENSIS

China Aster

ANNUAL, ALL ZONES

The so-called China asters are popular with both florists and home gardeners as superior cut flowers. Plants range in size from 1 to 3 feet tall, depending on the type, and there is a wide variety of flower forms. Some of the distinctive terms used to describe these showy flowers are ostrich-feathered, peony-flowered, pompon and chrysanthemum-flowered. Colors range from white to shades of pink, lavender, violet, purple, crimson and scarlet red. China asters bloom fairly late in the season, between July and October.

Plant China asters in late spring, in a full-sun location.

China asters prefer a rich, well-drained soil, amended with plenty of peat moss, compost or leaf mold. Water regularly, but don't overwater, which promotes disease organisms. Feed monthly throughout the growing season with a complete liquid fertilizer, following label directions. Space tall-growing varieties 15 inches apart; lower-growing types can do with less room. Taller varieties will be bushier and stronger if their growing tips are pinched back several times from late spring to early summer. Always favor varieties bred for wilt-resistance. Leafhoppers spread the disease; spray with an appropriate insecticide at the first sign of attack. Experienced gardeners avoid most of the problems with disease by not planting China asters in the same bed two years in a row.

Callistephus chinensis

CALLUNA VULGARIS
Scotch Heather
EVERGREEN SHRUB, ZONE 4

This, the true and only Scotch heather, has crowded, tiny, scalelike, dark green leaves and one-sided spikes of bell-shaped, rosy pink flowers. Garden varieties include dwarf groundcover and rock garden plants ranging from 2 inches to 3 feet tall. Taller varieties make good backgrounds for lower kinds and are attractive cut flowers. Flower colors include white, pale to deep pink, lavender and purple. Most bloom in mid- to late summer; a few bloom into late fall. Foliage—pale or deep green, yellow, chartreuse, gray, or russet—often changes color in winter.

Plant Scotch heather in the spring or fall. It prefers full sun and regular watering and a very well-drained soil, amended with plenty of peat moss. An application of acid-forming fertilizer (usually sold in garden centers as fertilizer for "acid lovers") in the spring and autumn will encourage plant health and bloom. To prune, shear off faded flowers and branch tips immediately after bloom.

'Red Haze' and 'Maris' *Calluna vulgaris*

CAMASSIA
Camass, Camassia
BULB, ZONE 4

Camassia

This western native produces graceful 20- to 30-inch-tall spikes of six-petaled, single, star-shaped flowers in late spring to early summer. Colors range from deep to pale blue, creamy white, to chartreuse. The grass-like foliage grows to 18 inches tall with a slightly smaller spread and disappears quickly after the plant blooms. Beautiful planted in masses of five or more, alongside garden ponds or streams, or naturalized in woodland gardens. Also attractive in a border of mixed perennials.

Plant the bulbs in the fall, 4 inches deep and 4 inches apart. Do not disturb these bulbs; they are long-lived and do not need to be moved. Can be grown in full sun or light shade. Tolerates a wide range of soils, including heavy clays. Soil should be consistently moist during the growing season; this is one of the few bulbs that will also tolerate low, damp spots in the garden.

Recommended: 'Alba', 'Plena', 'Orion', 'San Juan'.

CAMELLIA

Camellia, Japonica

SHRUB OR SMALL TREE, ZONES VARY BY SPECIES

As with so many of this country's favorite flowering plants, camellias are native to the Far East, from Indochina to Korea. Centuries ago Buddhist missionaries in China and Japan planted camellias around their temples, and in the 1700s a captain of the British East India Company brought the plant to England. By 1800 it had reached New York and 50 years later was being tried in California. The name commemorates a Jesuit missionary, George Joseph Kamel, but in the South the

plant is familiarly known as japonica.

With great age (more than 30 years old), camellias can reach 20 feet in height with an equal spread. Most often, however, they are seen grown (and pruned, if necessary) in the 6- to 12-foot-tall range, with a slightly smaller spread. Their foliage is deep green and lustrously shiny. Some kinds start flowering as early as September, although the height of their blooming season is generally regarded as between February and March. Camellias may be used in borders—beautiful combined with shrubs such as azaleas, rhododendron and holly, or with ferns and hostas—or singly, as a striking specimen plant.

The camellia family contains many species and even more named varieties. Although there is considerable variation in both plant habit and flower form, even a novice gardener would be able to recognize the flowers from any of the varieties as being a camellia. Flower color ranges from white, pink, rose, red, along with some bicolored types. Centers of some are marked with pronounced clusters of golden yellow stamens. Flower forms include single, semi-

Camellia 'Royal Velvet'

Camellia 'Lily Pons'

double, formal double, peony form, anemone form and rose form.

Oddly, camellias are dormant while they are in bloom, so that is the best time to plant them—usually between November and March. Camellias prefer locations in the garden sheltered from harsh sun and drying winds. Camellias demand a well-drained soil, rich with the addition of plenty of peat moss, compost or leaf mold. Provide regular to moderate water; somewhat surprisingly, once established, camellias can usually survive on natural rainfall alone. Use an acid-forming fertilizer (sold in garden centers as fertilizer for "acid-lovers"), following label directions carefully; do not overfertilize. When planting, make sure the base of the camellia's trunk is just at soil level—never below. Once planted, keep roots cool with a 2-inch layer of light, organic mulch, such as pine needles or shredded leaves, but do not allow mulch to come up next to the trunk of the plant. Keeping the area where camellias are grown free of spent flowers and old leaves will keep the one serious disease of camellias—petal blight—at bay. After raking up leaves and flowers, dispose of them in a covered bin and have hauled away.

A note on adaptability and hardiness: Camellias are commonly grown outdoors from southeastern Virginia along the Atlantic into Florida, along the Gulf Coast, and from California north to British Columbia. Dedicated gardeners raise them in and around New York City. Outside their range, camellias are a favorite of both amateurs and florists for growing in greenhouses. Neither a high nor a very low winter temperature is best for them; the ideal range is 35 to 60 degrees. High summer temperatures are not injurious provided the soil and air are moist. If you live outside this rather limited range, look for the newer hardy hybrids which can withstand winter temperatures to a surprising -15°F, as long as they are protected from winter winds and sun (usually with burlap stapled to a simple wooden frame). Hardy hybrids include: 'Polar Ice', 'Snow Flurry', 'Winter's Charm', 'Winter's Dream', 'Winter's Star', and 'Winter's Waterlily'.

CAMPANULA
Bellflower

MOSTLY PERENNIAL, SOME ANNUAL AND BIENNIAL, ZONE 3

The bellflower family is a huge one, showing great variation in size and form. There are dwarf varieties only a few inches tall, happy to spill over rock walls, and others that stand stately in the garden, to 4 feet or more. Some have flowers like open cups, some have "saucers" under the cups, some are more star-shaped, some have upward-facing bells, and some are quite double. Flower color runs the range, too, including shades of pink, white, blue and purple.

The shorter varieties are valuable in rock gardens; the taller ones, in borders, with such old-fashioned favorites as foxglove, columbine, iris and sweet William—perfect partners for creating a cottage garden look. Bellflowers bloom freely over a long season. The taller varieties make fine cut flowers. The popular bellflower known as Canterbury bells (*Campanula medium*) needs replanting each year as it sometimes behaves as a biennial and sometimes as an annual. With flower stalks up to 4 feet tall, covered with heavy cup-and-saucer type flowers, Canterbury bells should be staked early in the season to prevent them from falling over.

Plant bellflowers in early spring or early fall, in a full-sun or partially shaded location. They aren't particular as to soil, as long as it is well drained. Rock-garden kinds flourish where their roots can be in moist soil; other varieties prefer less water. Fertilize perennial kinds once during the growing season after they bloom. Plant dwarf varieties 8 to 10 inches apart; tall varieties, 15 inches apart. Divide and replant perennial kinds about every third year.

Recommended: 'Blue Clips', 'White Clips', 'Loddon Anna', 'Calycanthema', 'Telham Beauty', 'Blue Gardenia', 'White Pearl', 'Resholt'.

Campanula medium

CAMPSIS

Trumpet Creeper, Trumpet Vine

DECIDUOUS VINE, ZONE 5

Trumpet creeper is a fast-growing, climbing vine, topping out at about 30 feet tall with an equal spread, provided there's enough support for it to grow that large. Generations of gardeners have grown trumpet creeper for its showy display of trumpet-shaped, yellow, orange or scarlet flowers in midsummer. The vine fastens itself easily to any rough surface—brick, stone or wood—and will quickly cover a post or arbor.

Plant trumpet creepers in early spring, close to the support on which they will climb. These are very easy-to-grow

Campsis radicans 'Madame Galen'

plants, preferring a full-sun location, but they are not particular about soil type or water, accepting either wet or dry condition. No fertilizer necessary. Prune in late fall or very early spring to keep vine to the desired height and to promote blooming. Recommended: 'Morning Calm', 'Flava', 'Madame Galen', 'Crimson Trumpet'.

CANNA
Canna, Flags
TENDER BULB, ZONE 8

Cannas are plants that don't hold back: They're big, bright and bold and not afraid to call attention to themselves. These very easy-to-grow, tender bulbs quickly produce tropical-looking foliage, eventually reaching a height of 3 to 6 feet, with a spread of 2 to 3 feet. Foliage can be rich green to bronze, depending on the variety. Tall—up to 6 feet—spikes of showy flowers appear in summer and continue through the first frost in fall. Flower colors include creamy white, yellow, orange, pink, apricot, coral and red. Some varieties produce bicolored, variegated or spotted blossoms. Cannas are so big and so bright they are widely planted in parks and other public places where they make an impressive display. Because they tolerate wet feet, cannas are also good choices for poolside planting.

After all possible danger of frost is past, plant the tubers outdoors 4 to 5 inches deep and 10 to 15 inches apart, in a full-sun location. Or start them in pots indoors, transplanting to the garden after the weather has become consistently warm. Cannas prefer a rich soil and plenty of moisture during the growing season, with special attention to watering during hot, dry spells. Feed once or twice during the growing season with a complete fertilizer, following label directions. Generally not bothered by pests or diseases, cannas may suffer occasional attacks from Japanese beetles, leafrollers, spotted cucumber beetles or canna bud rot. Control with an appropriate insecticide or fungicide, following all label directions. In the fall dig up and store the tubers over winter in a cool, dry place.

Recommended: 'Cleopatra', 'Grand Opera', 'Pfitzer's Dwarf', 'Seven Dwarfs'.

Canna 'Tropical Rose'

CARYOPTERIS

Blue Mist Shrub, Bluebeard, Blue Spiraea

SHRUB, ZONE 5

Caryopteris

This neat, low-growing shrub is valued for its clusters of fringed, blue flowers, which appear in late summer through the first frost in fall. Only 2 to 3 feet tall, with an equal spread, it is suitable for planting in front of other shrubs or perennials, its silvery green foliage combining easily with most any plant. One variety, 'Worcester Gold', has unusual yellow foliage.

Plant caryopteris in spring, in a sunny location. Prefers a loose, very well-drained soil and moderate water. Tolerates heat well and, once established, is quite drought resistant. Feed in spring with a complete fertilizer, following label directions. In cold winters this shrub is likely to die to the ground. Even if it is not winter-killed, hard spring pruning (almost to the ground) will help keep the plant compact and, because caryopteris blooms on new growth, promotes free flowering.

Recommended: 'Azure', 'Heavenly Blue', 'Dark Knight', 'Longwood Blue', 'Worcester Gold'.

CATANANCHE CAERULEA

Cupid's Dart

PERENNIAL, ZONE 4

This easy-care perennial forms a clump of 8- to 12-inch-long, narrow, gray-green leaves. By midsummer, 18- to 24-inch-tall wiry stems appear, topped with loose clusters of lavender-blue flowers that resemble bachelor's buttons. Cupid's dart is very free-flowering and, once planted, you'll probably have it forever as it self-sows freely. The flowers are favorites of flower arrangers and dry easily, retaining their color.

Plant cupid's dart in early spring, 12 inches apart, in a full-sun location. Not particular as to soil, as long as it is well drained. Moderate water. No fertilizer necessary. Not bothered by pests or diseases. Dig up, divide and replant every year or two, in spring.

Catananche

CELASTRUS SCANDENS

Bittersweet

DECIDUOUS WOODY VINE OR SHRUB, ZONE 5

This North American native vine is extremely hardy and vigorous, reaching a height (or spread, depending on what it is growing on) of more than 20 feet. Bittersweet has long been admired for its clusters of orange and red berries, popular for fall bouquets and decorations. The rope-like vine twists tightly around any support and should not be grown

Celastrus berries 'American Bittersweet'

on valued trees or shrubs, for it can strangle them. Best used as a rampant climber for retaining walls, on sturdy trellises or as a cover for rocks and old stumps. To secure berries, it is necessary to have a male and a female plant in close proximity to each other (plants will be designated male or female at the nursery). There is also a self-fertile form of one species of bittersweet, *celatrus orbiculatus*, although it is considered a noxious weed by many states.

Set out the plants in fall or spring, in a full-sun location. Not particular as to soil type or water requirements. No fertilizer necessary. Once established, pruning may be needed every third or fourth year if the vine starts to take too much space. Prune in early spring. Bittersweet rebounds quickly from even severe pruning, so don't be timid.

Autumn *celastrus*

CELOSIA

Cockscomb, Chinese Woolflower

ANNUAL, ALL ZONES

Two quite different forms of this old-fashioned plant are commonly grown—the crested and the feathered cockscomb. Both are extremely showy, with big heads of bloom on both tall and dwarf plants. Brilliant, almost fluorescent, colors are the hallmarks of these flowers, including magenta, cerise, yellow, orange, pink, salmon and crimson. Flowers appear through summer and autumn, and are easily dried for winter decorations. Best grown in their own bed, both forms of celosia are so distinctive they're hard to combine with other flowering plants.

The so-called "crested cockscomb" celosia produces crinkled heads like great roosters' combs made of thick velvet. Dwarf forms grow to about 10 inches tall; standard forms grow up to 3 feet, wonderful for cutting. The other type of celosia, usually referred to as "plume cockscomb," produces pyramid-shaped, feathery plume-like flowers. Dwarf forms grow about 12 inches tall; standard varieties from 30 to 36 inches.

To dry the flowers, cut the flower heads before they are fully developed. Strip off the leaves and hang the blooms upside down in a warm, dark, dry room for 2 or 3 weeks.

Celosia spicata

Plant in late spring, after soil has warmed. Celosia thrive in full-sun, hot locations, but are not particular as to soil type. Moderate to low water requirements. No fertilizer needed. Generally not bothered by pests or diseases, celosia may suffer occasional attacks from spider mites, leaf spot or Southern root-knot nematodes. Control with an appropriate insecticide or fungicide, following all label directions.

Celosia

CENTAUREA

Bachelor's Buttons, Blue Bottle, Cornflower, Ragged Robin

PERENNIAL, ZONES 3-10; ANNUAL, ALL ZONES

Centaurea is a very large, diverse group of plants, the most popular for home gardeners being the annual *Centaurea cyanus*, commonly called cornflower or bachelor's buttons. Cornflowers are extremely easy to grow and a very satisfying producer of cobalt blue, pink, maroon or white flowers. Standard varieties grow about 30 inches tall; dwarf varieties to 12 inches. The blue flowers are the traditional choice for boutonnieres.

Seed can be sown directly in the garden in almost any season with more or less guaranteed success. Cornflowers grow quickly and easily. If sown outdoors in October, with a light cover of leaves over winter, plants will sprout in early spring and bloom for Memorial Day. Seed sown in March will flower in midsummer; or make a planting in late June for autumn bloom. Thin out the plants so that they stand 9 inches apart. They like ordinary soil and will thrive in either full sun or part shade. Cornflowers flower in such profusion that some inevitably go to seed, with the result that once you plant them you are almost sure to have succeeding generations of corn-

Centaurea

Centaurea cyannus

flowers, from one season to the next. Occasionally attacked by a variety of pests and diseases, including aphids, cutworms, scale, leafhoppers, leaftiers, aster yellows, downy mildew, powdery mildew, rust or Southern blight. Control with an appropriate insecticide or fungicide, following all label directions.

Recommended: 'Jubilee Gem', 'Polka Dot'.

CENTRANTHUS RUBER

Red Valerian

PERENNIAL, ZONE 5

Considered a weed in the far West, where it self-sows prolifically—even blooming between the cracks in concrete sidewalks. Valerian forms a bushy clump with upright stems to 3 feet high bearing 4-inch-long dusty green leaves. Small crimson, rose-pink or white flowers form clusters in late spring, early summer. It has a long, showy period of bloom, even in difficult situations. Good as a cut flower.

Will grow in poor, dry soil; accepts almost any condition except damp shade. Cut off old flowering stems to shape plants and prolong bloom.

Centranthus ruber 'Albus'

CERCIS
Redbud, Judas Tree

SHRUB OR SMALL TREE, ZONE 5

A familiar early spring sight from one end of the country to the other, redbud's purplish-pink flowers appear before the foliage, about the same time dogwood (*Cornus*, page 74) trees come into bloom. Many gardeners plant redbud and dogwood near each other, along with spring-flowering shrubs and bulbs to complete the picture. Redbud grows to about 25 to 30 feet tall, though often it is more like a large shrub. Its heart-shaped leaves turn yellow before they fall. The common name "Judas tree" refers to the story that Judas is said to have hanged himself on a variety of cercis.

Plant in fall or early spring, in ordinary soil, in sun or light shade. A very low-maintenance plant, seldom bothered by any pests or diseases. Keep newly planted trees well watered until they are established. Prune only to shape trees.

Cercis chinensis (above), *Cercis chinensis* blossoms (top)

CHAENOMELES

Flowering Quince

DECIDUOUS SHRUB, ZONE 4

Producing a dense thicket of spiny branches, flowering quince's claim to fame are the colorful, waxy flowers that are produced in very early spring—even before the leaves appear. Bare branches, brought into a warm bright room and placed in water, will burst into bloom as early as January. Single red flowers are most familiar, but there are also varieties with double blooms, in all shades of red, pink, coral and white. Depending on the variety, quince grows between 4 and 8 feet tall with an almost equal spread. Once out of flower, the shrub is unremarkable. The greenish yellow fruit that comes in the fall is not beautiful, but it can be used for making excellent jelly and tarts.

Plant in spring or fall in full sun, in any type of soil. Moderate water requirements; once established, quince is quite drought tolerant. No fertilizer is necessary. If you want to prune to improve the shape of this shrub, do so right after flowers have faded.

Recommended: 'Apple Blossom', 'Cameo', 'Enchantress', 'Jet Trail', 'Minerva', 'Pink Beauty', 'Red Ruffles', 'Rowallane', 'Snow', 'Super Red', 'Texas Scarlet', 'Toyo Nishiki'.

Chaenomeles

CHIONANTHUS VIRGINICUS

Fringe Tree

DECIDUOUS SHRUB OR SMALL TREE, ZONE 5

This lovely native of the eastern United States has large, glossy leaves that turn golden in autumn. Its real claim to fame, however, are its fleecy white clouds of feathery, fragrant flowers, borne in late spring or early summer. Fringe trees may reach 12 to 20 feet or more in height, with an equal spread, and should be given adequate space in the garden. There are male and female forms of the fringe tree; male trees produce the larger flowers of the two. If both male and female trees are present, the female tree will produce dark-blue berries, attractive to birds. Be aware that the fringe tree is one of the last plants to leaf out, so be prepared for bare branches well into spring.

Plant in either spring or fall, in a full-sun location. Fringe tree prefers a well-drained, acid soil, amended with plenty of peat moss or leaf mold, but will tolerate most any soil. Regular to moderate water requirements. Feed once in spring with an acid-forming fertilizer (sold in garden centers as fertilizer for "acid-lovers"), following label directions.

Chionanthus virginicus (above), *Chionanthus* flower close-up (top)

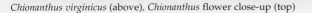

CHIONODOXA

Glory-of-the-Snow

BULB, ZONES 3-8

With the first breath of spring, these sky-blue flowers make a lovely picture combined with those other "early-risers," snowdrops and crocuses. These hardy bulbs, related to lilies, often bloom just as the snow is leaving the garden. Tubular, star-shaped flowers, in various beautiful shades of blue or white, are produced in loose clusters atop 4- to 6-inch spikes.

Plant the bulbs from September through October, 3 inches deep and 3 inches apart, in groups of at least five. Glory-of-the-snow does best in well-drained soil that is not too heavy. They are at home in either a full-sun or semi-shaded location. Regular watering during growing period. No fertilizer necessary. Don't cut the foliage before it dies down and, if you don't disturb the bulbs, they will live for years, spreading into impressive drifts over time.

Chionodoxa

CHRYSANTHEMUM COCCINEUM

Painted Daisy, Pyrethrum

PERENNIAL, ZONE 4

Chrysanthemum coccineum 'Roseum'

Gardeners and florists alike prize the painted daisy for its ability to produce large quantities of flowers for cutting. Its long, stiff stems are excellent for that purpose, and the white, red or pink flowers add a cheerful note to any bouquet. Single, double or with crested centers, painted daisies bloom in June and early July. Fine-textured, fern-like foliage adds to the attractiveness of this 1- to 3-foot-tall plant, with a 2-foot spread.

Plant in either spring or early fall in a full-sun or partially shaded location. For the best effect, plant in groups of at least three, about 15 inches apart. Accepts average garden soil, as long as it is well drained. Keep well watered, particularly during hot, dry periods. Feed at planting time with a complete fertilizer, following label directions. Cut the plants to the ground after they bloom, and fertilize again; this will encourage new growth and later flowering. Every third or fourth year, dig up the clump in late summer and divide it into smaller pieces. Replant individual pieces; protect with a 2-inch layer of peat moss for the first winter.

CHRYSANTHEMUM FRUTESCENS

Marguerite, Paris Daisy

TENDER PERENNIAL, ZONE 9

Chrysanthemum frutescens 'Marguerite'

This mounding, shrubby perennial is a real workhorse, both in the garden and in containers. Marguerites grow to 3 feet tall with a similar spread. The dense, finely cut, bright green foliage is very attractive. Great quantities of $1\,^1/_2$- to $2\,^1/_2$-inch daisies are produced on stiff, wiry stems, held slightly above the foliage, perfect as cut flowers. Flowers come in white, yellow or pink, both single and double, and some with crested centers. They bloom in June and early July. Great for mass planting, in groups of three or more, 30 inches apart, where a quick effect is desired.

Plant marguerites in spring in a full-sun location. Tolerant of a wide range of soil types and summer heat. Regular water requirements. Feed at planting time with a complete fertilizer, according to label directions. Shear plants back after flowering, removing approximately one-third of the overall plant, to encourage new growth and later flowering. Make a second application of fertilizer after shearing. Watch for leaf miners and thrips; control with an appropriate insecticide. Read and follow all label directions.

CHRYSANTHEMUM MAXIMUM

Shasta Daisy

PERENNIAL, ZONE 4

These large daisies belong to the chrysanthemum clan. Growing 2 to 4 feet tall on good, sturdy stems, they are valuable for cutting as well as for planting in a group with other hardy perennials. Their white petals and gold centers make it possible to use them with any other flowers, and they are fine blending material in a mixed bouquet. Blooms freely from midsummer through fall. Breeding has greatly increased the diversity of this once simple flower: Flower forms now include single, double, quilled and fringed or shaggy-petaled varieties. The plant itself makes a leafy crown close to the ground, which remains green all winter.

Shasta daisies can be planted in spring or early fall. Prefers a full-sun location, but will accept light shade, particularly in regions with hot summers. Tolerant of most soil types, as long as they are well drained. Regular water requirements; do not allow them to go dry during droughts. Feed at planting time with a complete fertilizer, according to label directions. Make a second application of fertilizer after initial flush of flowers fades. In cold-winter areas, mulch with a thick layer of peat moss or leaves, making sure not to let it mat on the crown of the plant, where it can cause rot. Every second or third year, when the flowering season is past, dig up the plant, divide it into smaller clumps and set them out separately. Discard the center of the original clump and use only the outside pieces.

Recommended: 'Esther Rea', 'Marconi', 'Alaska', 'Horace Read', 'Majestic', 'Thomas Killin', 'Cobham's Gold'.

Chrysanthemum maximum

CIMICIFUGA

Bugbane, Black Snakeroot

PERENNIAL, ZONE 3

Bugbane produces large, compound, shiny leaves to 2 feet tall with a spread of 3 or 4 feet. From midsummer to fall, extraordinary spires appear—up to 8 feet in height—covered with small white flowers. Planted in drifts, set 12 to 18 inches apart, bugbane's majestic flowers are good exclamation points in any garden, but are particularly well suited to woodland settings, combined with ferns, *Pieris japonica* and *hostas*. They also make striking accents at the back of any flower border.

Plant in early spring or fall in a partially shaded location. Bugbane does best in well-drained but moist soil, enriched with plenty of peat moss, compost or leaf mold. Don't let the soil dry during hot spells and don't disturb the bugbane's shallow roots with too-close cultivation. Feed with a complete fertilizer as growth commences in spring, following label directions.

Recommended: 'White Pearl', 'Elstead Variety'.

Cimicifuga racemosa (above), flower details (top)

CLARKIA
Clarkia, Farewell-to-Spring, Godetia, Mountain Garland

ANNUAL, ALL ZONES

This attractive annual was discovered in the Rocky Mountains by members of the Lewis and Clark Expedition, from which it derived both its botanical and one of its common names. There is considerable variation within the family, but all are very free-flowering, low-maintenance plants. *Clarkia amoena* (which includes the plant commonly sold as godetia or farewell-to-spring) comes in both a low-growing form (approximately 5 inches tall) and a tall form that grows to 30 inches tall. Both produce masses of 2-inch, single, cup-shaped flowers in shades of lavender, pink, cerise and white. Excellent as a cut flower, especially when cut in the bud stage. *Clarkia unguiculata*, commonly known as clarkia or mountain garland, grows from 1 to 4 feet tall. The 1-inch, single flowers are available in purple, white and rose. Double-flowered varieties are available in shades of orange, red, rose, pink, pale yellow and white.

Best grown from seed, sown in spring or fall (in mild-winter regions), planted where you want them to grow in the garden. Thin seedlings to 12 inches apart. Pinch out growing tips to make the plants bushier. Not particular about soil type, as long as it is well drained. Keep soil consistently moist throughout the growing season. Prefers a full-sun location, but accepts partial shade, particularly in regions with hot summers. Fertilizer is not recommended.

Recommended: 'Dwarf Gem', 'Tall Upright'.

Clarkia

CLEMATIS

Clematis, Old Man's Beard, Traveler's Joy, Virgin's Bower

HARDY VINE, ZONE 4

One of the most beautiful of all flowering vines, clematis offers gardeners ease of growing along with a great variety of flower color and form. Flower shapes include bell, urn, saucer and star, and range in size from 1 to an astounding 10 inches across. Flower color runs the gamut, too, wine red to pure white, shades of blue and violet to pink and even yellow varieties.

The vines reach a height of 5 to 50 feet, depending on the variety. They cling by twisting their tendrils about a support. Some bloom in late spring and early summer, while others wait until late summer and early fall. Their fruits are often borne in feathery masses. The most vigorous growers are useful for screening porches, arbors and fences, but the large-flowered hybrids are better displayed on a trellis or twining up a post. Cut blooms last up to 10 days in the house and are very desirable for flower arrangements.

In cold-winter regions, spring planting is most success-

Clematis 'Ramona'

ful; where winters are mild, fall planting is advised. Clematis demands a well-drained, loose loam soil, amended with plenty of peat moss, compost or leaf mold. If your soil is acidic, use agricultural lime (incorporated into the soil

Clematis paniculata

A clematis vine

CLEOME HASSLERANA
Spider Flower
ANNUAL, ALL ZONES

This extremely easy-to-grow plant puts on an amazing show for very little effort. In a single season, cleome can reach 4 to 6 feet in height with an almost equal spread. Starting in midsummer and continuing right through the first frost, cleome produces open clusters of pink, purple, mauve or white flowers with attractive, arching stamens. Big, but not dense, cleome is best in the back row of flower borders, grouped with cosmos and hollyhocks. Be careful when working around cleome as the stems have hard-to-see, nasty thorns. Because spider flower is such a quick grower it is particularly valuable for temporary effects. Unfortunately, the rather elegant-looking flowers do not hold up well when cut for arrangements. Plants self-sow, so once you've had them in your garden, you're likely to have them again—whether you want them or not.

Plant in spring, after the threat of frost has passed, either from seed or nursery-grown transplants. Space or thin plants to 24 inches apart. Excellent for hot, dry locations, cleome will also endure considerable shade. Not particular about soil type. Regular water requirements. For the best effect, plant lower-growing plants in front of cleome, to hide its somewhat rangy appearance. Rarely bothered by insects or diseases, cleome may suffer occasional attacks from aphids and leaf spot. Control with an appropriate insecticide or fungicide, following all label directions.

Recommended: 'Cherry Queen', 'Mauve Queen', 'Pink Queen', 'Purple Queen', 'Rose Queen', 'Ruby Queen', 'Helen Campell'.

according to label directions) to "sweeten" it. Old-timers say that clematis "like to have their feet in the shade and their heads in the sun." Good advice, but not always easy to accomplish. A thick layer of mulch will help keep clematis roots cool, as will the strategic placement of flat stones over the rooting area. Clematis simply won't grow if the roots are subject to hot, dry conditions. Keep soil consistently moist during the growing season and feed monthly with a complete fertilizer, following label directions. After planting, carefully guide the new stems with string until they reach the wall or trellis on which they will climb—gently, though, as clematis stems tend to be brittle. Clematis are rarely bothered by pests or diseases.

Varieties that bloom in spring need little pruning; if any is done, it should be after the blooming season. Those that flower in summer and autumn should be cut back rather severely in early spring.

Recommended: 'Belle of Woking', 'Comptesse de Bouchaud', 'Duchess of Edinburgh', 'Flore pleno', 'Hagley Hybrid', 'Hendersonii', 'Madame Edouard Andre', 'Mrs. Cholmondeley', 'Niobe', 'Candida', 'General Sikorski', 'Nellie Moser', 'Ramona', 'Dr. Ruppell', 'Lasurstern', 'Miss Bateman', 'The President', 'Betty Corning', 'Ernest Markham', 'Lady Betty Balfour', 'Madame Julia Correvon', 'Purpurea', 'Ville de Lyon', 'Jackmanii'.

Cleome hasslerana

CLETHRA

Japanese Sweet Shrub, Pepperbush, Summersweet, Sweet Pepperbush

DECIDUOUS, EVERGREEN SHRUB, ZONE 5

This attractive, accommodating shrub grows 10 to 15 feet tall, depending on the variety, with a spread of 12 feet. Can be kept smaller with judicious pruning. Starting in midsummer, clethra produces 4- to 6-inch-long spike-like clusters of sweetly fragrant flowers in shades of pink and white. Just one bush will perfume an entire garden. The black seeds that follow look like peppercorns, hence the common name "pepperbush." Clethra's glossy leaves turn soft yellow-gold before dropping in the autumn. This shrub is hardy anywhere in the United States; in fact, it grows wild from Maine to Florida.

Plant clethra in spring or fall, preferably in a partially shaded location. Clethra does best in a well-drained soil, slightly acid in reaction. Best bet is to amend the soil where these shrubs are planted with plenty of peat moss. Keep consistently moist throughout the growing season; clethra will even tolerate low, wet spots in the garden. Because this plant is also resistant to salt spray, it's an excellent choice for withstanding difficult seaside conditions. Fertilize in spring with an acid-forming fertilizer (sold in garden centers as fertilizer for "acid-lovers"), following label directions.

Recommended: 'Hummingbird', 'Paniculata', 'Pink Spire', 'Rosea', 'Ruby Spice'.

Clethra alnifolia

CLIVIA MINIATA

Kafir Lily

TUBEROUS-ROOTED PERENNIAL, ZONE 9

This relative of amaryllis is native to South Africa. It is a striking plant that forms a clump of glossy evergreen, strap-like leaves, about 18 inches long. Impressive clusters of trumpet-shaped flowers are produced atop thick stems, from 18 to 24 inches tall. Flower colors range from deep red-orange to pale yellow, and all the shades in between, along with orange-and-yellow bi-colors. Flowers appear between late winter and early spring and are very long-lasting.

In frost-free regions, clivia is often grown outdoors, where it forms a big clump, but in other parts of the country it is better off as a container-grown specimen (where it can be brought indoors for the winter). Whether in the ground or in a container, clivia prefers a protected location with filtered sun. Plant the tubers in a rich, well-drained soil, amended with plenty of peat moss or compost, with the top of the tuber just above soil level. Regular water requirements. Feed monthly with a mild, organic, liquid fertilizer from spring through fall. If grown in a container, clivia will bloom best if you allow the plant to become somewhat root-bound.

Recommended: 'Flame', 'Solomone Hybrids'.

Clivia miniata

COBAEA SCANDENS

Cup-and-saucer Vine

ANNUAL VINE, ALL ZONES

Cobea scandens

This rapid-growing annual climber is native to Mexico. Wherever you want a mass of foliage in a hurry—plus flowers—to cover a trellis or wall, this is a vine to consider. It grows as much as 25 feet in a single growing season, until frost cuts it down, attaching itself to any rough surface with twirling tendrils. In frost-free regions, it may grow to 40 feet or more. Freely produced cup-shaped flowers start out a greenish shade and then turn violet. Commonly called the cup-and-saucer vine because the flowers rest in a green "saucer." The flowers are followed by plum-shaped fruits.

Best grown from seed sown indoors about March. Nick the tough outer coating on the seeds with a knife (a process known as "scarification," intended to help hard-shelled seeds germinate) and place them on edge in 4-inch containers filled with moist potting mix; barely cover the seeds with soil. Place containers in a warm, sunny windowsill. Transplant into the garden when weather has thoroughly warmed, in a full-sun location, close to whatever it is they are to grow on. Not particular as to soil, as long as it is well drained. Fertilize once or twice during the growing season with a complete fertilizer, following label directions.

COLCHICUM

Meadow Saffron, Autumn Crocus

BULB, ZONE 4

A horticultural oddity, this hardy bulb of the lily family produces strap-shaped leaves about a foot tall in spring, which
completely disappear by mid- to late summer, and then in
autumn, seemingly from out of nowhere, large crocus-like
flowers appear, sans foliage. Flowers are 4 inches or more
across and available in shades of violet, lavender, mauve
and white. They are held aloft on somewhat floppy stems;
to avoid having them fall over in the height of bloom, consider overplanting the bulbs with a groundcover such as
Vinca (page 243) or *Ajuga* (page 16). Attractive in rock gardens. The compound colchicine is produced from the bulbs
(used as a medicine for treating gout); all parts of the plant
are extremely poisonous if eaten.

Plant the bulbs in August in groups of at least three. Set
them 3 to 4 inches deep and 4 to 6 inches apart. Bulbs bloom
later that fall, with the foliage, somewhat surprisingly, making an appearance the following spring. Does best in a full-
sun location, but accepts partial shade. Not particular as to
soil type. Tolerant of heat and drought, but performs best
with regular water during the growing season. Do not disturb the bulbs or take them up over winter. Let the foliage
die naturally without being cut.

Colchicum 'Sissinghurst' (above), *Colchicum cilicicump* (top)

COLEUS (SOLENOSTEMON)

Coleus

ANNUAL, ALL ZONES

There are few plants with more extravagantly patterned and brilliantly colored foliage than coleus. These tender plants will reach about 18 to 24 inches in height, but most gardeners pinch out the growing tips regularly to keep the plants low and bushy. Maximum spread is about 24 inches. Coleus plants produce rather inconspicuous lavender-blue flowers, but they are primarily grown for their intricately detailed leaves, available in color combinations of green, chartreuse, yellow, cream, salmon, orange, magenta, red, purple and brown. Color patterns appear as streaks, splashes, spots or splatters. For an exotic look, combine coleus of several different patterns and color combinations in a single bed or container.

Plant in spring when all danger of frost has passed. Does best in partial shade, but will accept full sun, particularly in regions with cool summers. Prefers a loose, well-drained soil, amended with plenty of peat moss or leaf mold. Keep soil consistently moist, but not wet, throughout the growing season. Fertilize monthly with a liquid, organic fertilizer, according to label directions. Occasionally bothered by mealybugs (cottony white insects) or whiteflies. Control with an appropriate insecticide, following all label precautions. New coleus plants are very easy to start from 2-inch-long cuttings placed in a glass of water; after roots form in a week or two, transfer cuttings to containers filled with a lightweight soil mix.

Recommended: 'Dwarf Midway', 'Giant Exhibition', 'Oriental Splendor', 'Salicifolius'.

Coleus 'Dwarf Midway'

CONSOLIDA AMBIGUA

Larkspur

ANNUAL, ALL ZONES

If you're looking for an easy-to-grow annual that produces masses of blue flowers, look no further than larkspur. This is the annual form of *Delphinium* (page 87), which is likely to spring up in your garden, year after year, because the seed sows itself readily. Larkspur produces 3- to 4-foot-tall, airy spires of flowers, most commonly in shades of blue, but also available in lilac, pink, rose, salmon and red. Excellent as a cut flower. Larkspur may have a rather short blooming season if the weather turns hot.

Broadcast larkspur seed in late fall or very early spring where you want it to grow in your garden (it's even possible to scatter the seed on top of snow in late winter, in order to have it reach the soil at the earliest possible moment when the snow thaws). Prefers a full-sun or partially shaded location and needs a humus-rich soil amended with plenty of peat moss or leaf mold. Keep soil consistently moist, but not wet, throughout the growing season. Does not require fertilizer. Transplants are also available at garden centers in spring. Thin seedlings, or plant transplants, 6 to 8 inches apart. Once planted, don't move larkspur plants because their long tap roots makes successful transplanting almost impossible.

Consolida 'Frosted Skies'

Consolida

CONVALLARIA MAJALIS
Lily-of-the-Valley

PERENNIAL GROWN FROM A RHIZOME, ZONE 2

The diminutive, arching stems of lily-of-the-valley, hung with fragrant bell-shaped flowers, are the very picture of old-fashioned charm. Wonderful for perfuming a corner of the garden, or as a quaint, small bouquet, this plant is also a workhorse of a groundcover in shady locations. Even under trees it readily forms a very long-lived, dense cover and blooms freely in April and May. The broad, pointed leaves, 8 to 10 inches tall, are ornamental even when flowers are absent.

Plant outdoors in fall, in a loose, well-drained soil, amended with plenty of peat moss, compost or leaf mold. Plant the rhizomes (called pips) 4 to 6 inches apart and $1\frac{1}{2}$ inches deep. Fertilize yearly, in spring, with a complete fertilizer, according to label directions. Average water requirements. After foliage has died down in fall, cover the bed with a 1- to 2-inch layer of shredded leaves or pine needles for winter protection. Rarely bothered by pests or diseases; may suffer occasional attacks from slugs, snails or Southern blight. Control with an appropriate insecticide or fungicide, following all label directions.

Convallaria (above), hanging flowers (right)

73

COREOPSIS

Coreopsis, Calliopsis

PERENNIAL AND ANNUAL, ZONES VARY BY SPECIES

Coreopsis

The various members of the coreopsis family, along with its annual cousin, calliopsis, are dependable bloomers over a long period from early summer to frost. For the border—and for a profusion of long-stemmed cut flowers—it is hard to find a more satisfactory producer of yellow, orange and reddish-brown daisy-like blossoms. Calliopsis flowers often sport a band of contrasting color on the single or semi-double flowers. Depending on the variety, they grow 9 inches to 2 $1/2$ feet tall, with a spread more or less equal to their height. The ability to withstand drought and some neglect endears coreopsis to busy gardeners.

All members of the coreopsis family may be grown in the same way—sown either in October or in early spring. Simply scatter the seed and rake in lightly, making sure it is in a full-sun location. Ordinary soil is good enough; in fact, the seeds can endure a rather hot, dry place. No fertilizer is necessary. Once established, it usually sows, returning year after year. Coreopsis, if sown in fall or early enough in spring, will bloom later that summer; or nursery-grown plants may be purchased and set 12 to 18 inches apart. For continuous bloom, keep spent blossoms cut. Toward the end of the season, let some flowers go to seed for next year, and to attract birds, which love the seeds of all coreopsis.

Recommended: 'Golden Showers', 'Moonbeam', 'Zagreb'.

CORNUS

Dogwood

TREE, ZONES 2, 4-5

It's hard to imagine a more picturesque tree than dogwood. A hillside where their snowy blooms stand out from the darkness of big sheltering trees, not yet in leaf, is a sight you won't soon forget—the very picture of springtime. Dogwood earns high marks in every department: These hardy shrubs and small trees are ornamental in flower, foliage, fruit and even branch. The largest grow to about 30 feet or more in height, while some are shrubby in character. Besides the spring flowers, there are colorful autumn berries; many kinds have foliage that turns beautiful shades before it falls,

Cornus florida

or branches that show color all winter. They grow rapidly and are long lived.

Dogwoods are widely planted in home gardens as lawn specimens and additions to shrub borders. They look best in association with larger trees, similar to the way they grow in the wild. An evergreen background provides a beautiful setting. They are especially appropriate to combine with spring-flowering shrubs and bulbs. Creamy white is the most common flower color, but dogwoods are also available with pink, rose to darkish-red blossoms.

Early spring is the best time to plant, although fall is also a possibility. Ordinary garden soil, slightly acid, is adequate; dogwoods prefer a location with filtered sun or light shade. No fertilizer is necessary. Dogwoods are vigorous and hardy, and therefore require little care. Cut out any dead or broken branches in late summer rather than spring.

Recommended: 'Cherokee Chief', 'Cherokee Princess', 'Cloud Nine', 'Milky Way', 'Pendula', 'Pink Flame', 'Rainbow', 'Rosabella', 'Rubra', 'Summer Stars', 'Welchii'.

Cornus florida flower 'Cherokee Princess'

CORYDALIS

Fumaria

PERENNIAL, ZONES 5-7

Both the foliage and flowers of fumaria add a grace note to partially shaded, woodland gardens. Depending on the type, fumaria grow 8 to 15 inches tall. The foliage is finely cut, looking much like a maidenhair fern. Fumaria flowers, which appear in spring, resemble a miniature version of bleeding heart, but in shades of yellow, white or blue. Where content, fumaria may self-sow.

Plant in spring or fall in a partially shaded location. Prefers a loose, well-drained soil, with a neutral to alkaline pH. Keep soil consistently moist, but not wet, throughout the growing season. No fertilizer necessary. Although seeds (especially old ones) may be somewhat difficult to germinate, fumaria readily self-sows, returning year after year.

Recommended: 'Blue Panda', 'Pere David'.

Corydalis solida

COSMOS
Cosmos

ANNUAL, ALL ZONES

It's hard to beat cosmos for a fast-growing, graceful background plant. Best planted in groups of five or more, preferably against a dark background where its feathery foliage and big daisy-like flowers are accentuated. Cosmos produce flowers—and lots of them—from summer through fall, especially if you're faithful in keeping dead flowers trimmed off. The most common flower colors are pink, red and white but yellow and orange are also seen. Cosmos grows between 2 $^1/_2$ and 5 feet tall, with a spread slightly smaller than its height. Excellent cut flowers.

Cosmos grow easily from seed sown outdoors after the weather (and soil) have thoroughly warmed. Any soil, even quite poor, will do, as long as it is in a sunny location. Once seedlings have germinated, thin to 18 to 20 inches apart. Alternately, buy nursery-grown transplants and plant in late spring. Moderate water needs. Fertilize once in early summer with a complete fertilizer, according to label directions. Occasionally bothered by aphids, aster yellows, Japanese beetles, spider mites or spotted cucumber beetles. Control with an appropriate insecticide, following all label directions. Tallest kinds may need staking. Any spindly plants may be pinched back to encourage bushiness.

Recommended: 'Dazzler', 'Radiance', 'Candystripe', 'Seashell', 'Klondike', 'Dwarf Klondike', 'Sonata', 'Gloria', 'Purity', 'Ladybird Scarlet', 'Versailles Carmine', 'Versailles Tetra'.

Cosmos

Cosmos 'Versailles Carmine'

COTINUS COGGYGRIA

Smoke Tree, Purple Fringe Tree

DECIDUOUS SHRUB OR SMALL TREE, ZONE 3

Cotinus coggygria

An old-fashioned garden favorite, the smoke tree gets its name from the hazy appearance of its fine, silky flowers. Pinkish flowers appear in summer and last over a long period; foliage, dense green in summer, becomes red and yellow in autumn. A bushy, wide-spreading shrub (or small tree), smoke trees grow to about 15 feet in height, and make a fine specimen for lawns.

Plant in spring or fall, in a full-sun location. Easy to grow in well-drained, even rather poor, dry soil and a sunny location. Water consistently during dry spells the first summer after planting. No fertilizer necessary.

CRAMBE

Colewort, Sea Kale

PERENNIAL, ZONE 6

There's nothing subtle about this cabbage relative. In spring, crambe produces a 3-foot-tall mass of 12-inch-wide leaves, with about a 3-foot spread—but wait—you haven't seen anything yet. Sometime in summer, crambe sends forth many flowering stems which eventually create an enormous cloud of fragrant, starry white flowers, reaching 8 feet in height and a width of 5 feet or more. Not a plant for small gardens, but when planted in the right place, crambe is very effective. Sea kale (*C. maritima*) is edible and produces much smaller clusters of flowering stems—about 18 inches tall, and as wide. Does well in seaside locations.

Plant in spring in a full-sun location. Accepts almost any soil, as long as it is very well drained. Regular water needs. No fertilizer necessary. Occasionally bothered by the same pests as any cabbage-family member, especially caterpillars; treat with an appropriate insecticide. Read and follow all label directions.

Crambe cordifolia

CRATAEGUS
Hawthorn
DECIDUOUS TREE, ZONE 3

There is a lot to be said for these small trees: They have attractive, dark-green foliage, beautiful clusters of late spring flowers in shades of rose, red and white, followed by bright-red fruits resembling miniature apples. Some hawthorns are broad and spreading, some more shrublike, but all have long thorns and are easy to grow. The berries are a favorite food of wild birds.

Hawthorns are small enough (18 to 25 feet tall and about as wide) to be very desirable as lawn trees, especially on small lots. They are also good as accents in a shrub border. Because of their thick habit of growth, not to mention their thorns, hawthorn also makes an excellent protective hedge. Will withstand hard pruning.

Plant in spring or fall in a full-sun location. They prefer a humus-rich soil, amended with plenty of peat moss or leaf mold. Regular water needs. No fertilizer necessary. Prune in winter to keep these bushy trees from becoming too overgrown, cutting out the weakest, smallest branches.

Crataegus (above), 'Hawthorn' *Crataegus* (top)

CROCOSMIA
Montbretia
CORM, ZONE 5

Crocosmia

Red *Crocosmia* 'Lucifer'

Although the flower stems are branched, montbretia looks like a minature version of gladiolus. Like gladiolus, monbretia is an extremely long-lasting cut flower. Plants grow to a height of $2\frac{1}{2}$ to 3 feet, with sword-shaped leaves; flowers appear in late summer, in sparkling yellow, gold and orange-red tones. Because the stems are so stiff, they make nice accents when combined with other softer-foliaged plants.

Plant the bulbs in early spring in groups of at least six, 3 to 4 inches deep and 5 inches apart. Montbretia will accept almost any soil, as long as it is well drained. Prefers a full-sun location. Very little water required. No fertilizer necessary.

CROCUS

Crocus

BULB, ZONE 3

Even the smallest doorstep garden has enough room for a cluster of crocuses. And as one of the bravest of all flowers—often blooming while there is still snow on the ground—no flower of the entire gardening year is more appreciated. Flowers are available in shades of gold, blue, purple and white, often striped.

Crocuses are sometimes scattered in lawns, but this is not very practical because the grass will usually need to be mowed before the bulb foliage is ready to be cut. Better to place these diminutive beauties on the edge of a flower border, under shrubs and trees, or in rock gardens, in groups of a dozen or more. Plant bulbs in fall in a full-sun or slightly shaded location, 2 to 3 inches deep and about as far apart. Accepts almost any soil, as long as it is well drained. Regular water needs. No fertilizer needed. Rarely bothered by pests or diseases; occasionally attacked by bulb mites or dry rot. Control with an appropriate insecticide or fungicide, following all label directions. Don't cut off the foliage until it has completely died down. The bulbs may be left undisturbed for years.

Autumn crocus (above), spring crocus (top)

Cyclamen

Cyclamen

Tender bulb (usually grown indoors), Zone 6

In winter, when flowers are few and far between, cyclamen are especially valued. Truth be told, with their elegant, recurved petals, cyclamen flowers would be appreciated at any time of the year. In shades of pink, rose and white, they rise above interesting heart-shaped leaves marked with silvery-white patterns.

As befits plants that bloom in winter, cyclamen don't like heat. Keep in a room not over 60 to 65°F, where they receive light but not strong sunshine. Cyclamen will languish quickly if placed in a warm room. Keep the soil consistently moist, but not wet. It is best to water from below, by placing pot in a saucer of water. To maintain the moist air needed by these plants, some gardeners place the pots on top of a pebble-filled, low tray. Keep the tray filled with water, barely to the top of the pebbles.

After your cyclamen has bloomed, gradually stop watering it. Leave the tuber in the pot over summer, in a cool, protected place either indoors or out. About August, repot in fresh potting soil. Do not cover the tuber by more than half. Water from below, and keep the pot in a cool, bright room.

Cyclamen

CYNOGLOSSUM

Chinese Forget-Me-Not

ANNUAL, ALL ZONES

This annual looks like a tall forget-me-not, with upright, 18- to 30-inch-tall branching stems, filled with blue flowers. Makes a stunning effect when grown in masses. Blue is the most popular color, but there are types with pink or white flowers, as well. Excellent as a long-lasting cut flower.

Sow seed outdoors in early spring and barely cover it. Already-started plants, ready for transplanting, are also available in garden centers in spring. Thin or move the little plants to allow 8 to 9 inches between them. Chinese forget-me-not prefers full-sun but accepts light shade. Tolerant of almost any soil, as long as it is well drained. Regular water requirements. No fertilizer necessary. Once established, it often self-sows, returning to your garden, year after year.

Cynoglossum (above), *Cynoglossum* flower details (top)

DAHLIA

Dahlia

TENDER BULB, ALL ZONES

Dahlias

Dahlias are real workhorses in the garden: Available in a dizzying array of plant and flower forms, it can truthfully be said there's a dahlia for everyone, from dinner-plate-sized blossoms to diminutive dwarf dahlias, perfect for edging. Flowers appear in every color and shade except for blue. Along with chrysanthemums and asters, dahlias help to bring down the curtain on the flowering season—blooming right up until the first hard frost in fall.

So many flower forms exist that about a dozen categories are necessary to describe them, such as decorative (formal and informal), cactus (straight, semi- and incurved), pompon, ball, collarette, orchid-flowered, peony, anemone and single. For the longest-lasting cut flowers, cut in late afternoon or early morning and hold for several hours in water in a cool, dark place.

To plant dahlias, wait until spring weather (and soil) has thoroughly warmed. They require a soil that is rich and deep, amended with plenty of leaf mold, compost or peat moss before planting. Choose a full-sun location, although

dahlias will tolerate a little shade. Dig a hole 5 inches deep. Next to the hole, drive a sturdy stake (4 or 5 feet tall for tallest varieties, shorter for low growers). Lay the tuber flat in the hole, being careful not to break off the sprout, and cover with 2 or 3 inches of soil. As the sprouts emerge, gradually fill up the hole with loose soil. Tie the plant to the stake with soft string. Allow 2 feet between plants. If you're growing dahlias from seed, start it indoors in March and set out the young plants 18 inches apart after the soil is warm.

Never let the ground dry out. A 2-inch layer of straw around the plants will help keep the soil moist. No fertilizer

Dahlias in a cut flower garden (above), *Dahlia* 'Fascination' (top right)

is necessary. Occasionally bothered by European corn borers, earwigs, Japanese beetles, tarnished plant bugs or mildew. Control with an appropriate insecticide or fungicide, following all label directions. After the first killing frost, cut off the stalks just above ground and carefully dig up the clump of roots. Dry them out in the air for a few hours, then wrap in newspaper and keep in a cool, frost-free place over winter. Before planting again the next season, divide the root clump into parts, being sure to have at least one eye or growing spot on each section. Plant these roots separately.

DAPHNE

Daphne

SHRUB, ZONE 4

Daphne is treasured for its intensely fragrant flowers, which make their appearance very early in the year. A single shrub of daphne in full bloom can perfume an entire garden. These low-growing shrubs are especially good in foundation plantings when seen against a background of dark evergreens.

Plant in spring or fall in a full-sun or lightly shaded location (morning sun and afternoon shade is also acceptable). Daphne must have a humus-rich soil and excellent drainage. It does not do well in hot, dry conditions and prefers to always have cool roots. To help hold moisture in the soil during hot summers, mulch with a layer of peat moss or pine needles. Keep soil moist, but not wet, throughout the growing season. Fertilize once or twice during the growing season with a complete fertilizer, following label directions. A light covering of straw or evergreen branches will provide winter protection from wind and sun.

Daphne 'Aureomarginata'

DELPHINIUM

Delphinium

PERENNIAL, ZONE 3

Delphinium may not be the easiest perennial to grow, especially where summers are hot and humid, but it puts on such a magnificent show that many gardeners consider it worth the extra care it demands.

The immense spikes, as much as 4 to 6 feet tall, make the stateliest accents imaginable in a border, where they lend distinction to the entire garden. Although most people associate the color blue with delphinium, a wide range of shades is available, from purple through lavender and mauve to light blue—not to mention pink and white varieties.

Plant delphinium transplants in spring or fall in a full-sun location, approximately 18 inches apart, with the crown just at soil level. Choose a spot with good air circulation, where they will not be crowded by other plants. Prefers a loose, well-drained soil. In waterlogged soils, delphinium are subject to rot. They prefer soil slightly on the alkaline side; check your soil's pH and, if necessary, add a little agricultural lime (available at garden centers) to "sweeten" the soil. Regular water needs. Fertilize at planting time, with a complete fertilizer, following label directions. When cultivating around plants, take care not to damage delphinium's shallow roots. Occasionally bothered by aphids, common stalk borers, cyclamen mites, leafminers, spider mites, slugs, snails or bacterial leaf spot. Control with an appropriate insecticide or fungicide, following all label directions. Bait for slugs and snails just after planting.

Provide stakes for the tallest kinds early in the season. After they flower in early summer, cut flower spikes back partway to encourage a second crop of blossoms. An additional, light application of fertilizer around the plant at this time will encourage new growth. When the new flowering stems have grown a few inches, cut the old ones down to the ground. In autumn, cover the crown of the plants with an inch or two of sand (to promote fast drainage) and, after the ground freezes, add a 2- or 3-inch layer of straw or shredded leaves for winter protection.

Recommended: 'Pacific Hybrids', 'Mid-Century Hybrids', 'Giant Imperial Series', and 'Connecticut Yankee Series'.

Delphiniums

DENDRANTHEMA GRANDIFLORUM

Chrysanthemum

ANNUAL AND PERENNIAL, HARDINESS DEPENDS ON CULTIVAR

Without a doubt, chrysanthemums dominate the fall flower garden. Plant breeders have worked wonders with "mums," with the result that there are now a bewildering number of varieties to choose from, in every color but blue, with a wide range of blooming times. By choosing varieties carefully, home growers may have blooms from early August to hard frost.

Besides producing a breathtaking outdoor flower show, mums are wonderful for cutting; it's doubtful whether any cut flower is as long-lasting in bouquets. By breaking off an inch or two of the stem and changing the water daily, you will help cut chrysanthemums last up to 2 weeks. This trait has endeared mums to home gardeners who desire prolonging summer for as long as possible with bouquets fresh from the garden.

Plant chrysanthemum transplants in the garden in spring, when both the weather and the soil have warmed, in a full-sun location. Prefers a loose, well-drained soil, amend-ed with plenty of peat moss, compost or leaf mold, along with some dried manure. Space approximately 18 inches apart. Do not plant where there is competition from tree or shrub roots, and never plant close to a hedge. Regular water requirements. Fertilize once a month until the end of July, using a complete fertilizer, according to label directions. Occasionally bothered by aphids, lacebugs, leafminers, thrips, two-spotted spider mites, aster yellows, botrytis blight, leafspot, powdery mildew, ray blight or rust. Control with an appropriate insecticide or fungicide, following all label directions. When plants are 6 inches or more tall, pinch off the very tip of each shoot to make the plants bushier. Pinch back all the growing tips every three weeks, until the middle of July.

Where severe winters occur, cut back the stalks to 5 or 6 inches after a hard frost has finally killed them. Cover the plants with a layer of straw or evergreen branches. The purpose is not to protect them from low temperatures but to keep the soil from alternately freezing and thawing, which causes the plants to be heaved up out of the ground. In the spring, remove this cover gradually. Divide mums every other spring. Dig up the plant, separate it into smaller pieces, throw away the center and replant the others.

Dendranthema grandiflorum 'Grenadine', *Dendranthema grandiflorum* 'Shelly' (inset)

DEUTZIA

Deutzia

SHRUB, ZONE 4

This old-fashioned favorite contributes its share of brilliant white blossoms to the spring garden at the same time that mock oranges, lilacs, tulips and Dutch iris are in flower. Deutzia produces a bushy shrub, 3 to 8 feet tall (depending on the variety), with spread roughly equal to its height. Long sprays of bloom are carried on the dense plant in such quantities that the leaves are almost completely hidden. After this outstanding show, deutzia quietly retreats to the background for the rest of the year, being somewhat drab when not in bloom.

Plant in spring or fall in a full-sun to partially shaded location. Prefers a loose, well-drained soil, amended with plenty of peat moss or leaf mold. Regular water requirements. Fertilize plants once a year in spring, using a complete fertilizer, according to label directions. As soon as the flowers have faded, cut back some of the flowering stems at the base to encourage new growth.

Recommended: 'Codsall Pink', 'Nikko', 'Peek-a-Boo', 'Pride of Rochester', 'Rosealind'.

Deutzia x *lemoinei* 'Compacta'

Deutzia gracilis

DIANTHUS BARBATUS

Sweet William

BIENNIAL, ZONE 3

Old-fashioned flowers are always in fashion when they are as pretty as this one. The colorful and fragrant flower clusters of ruby and pink, crimson and white—often zoned or starred—are long-lasting when cut. They are good massed in a garden border where they bloom in early summer. Varieties in the 12- to 18-inch range make a great show when combined with taller plants like delphinium and foxglove; dwarf dianthus are commonly used for edging. While not long-lived, they may persist from one year to the next, or self-sow where winters are relatively mild. They are of the same family as pinks and carnations.

Plant in spring or fall in a full-sun location. Prefers a well-drained soil, with a slightly alkaline reaction. Test your soil pH; if it is acid, make an application of agricultural lime (available at garden centers) to "sweeten" it. Regular water requirements. Fertilize monthly with a liquid, organic fertilizer, according to label directions. Cut the plants back after they bloom to encourage repeat bloom. A light winter cover-

ing of shredded leaves is advisable in severe climates. Recommended: 'Excelsior Mixed', 'Indian Carpet Mixed', 'New Era Mixed'.

Dianthus barbatus 'Telstar Pink' (above), *Dianthus barbatus* 'Telstar' (top)

DIANTHUS PLUMARIUS

Cottage Pink, Grass Pink, Pink

PERENNIAL, ZONE 4

These old-fashioned relatives of the carnation have dainty single, semi-double and double, often fringed, flowers in solid colors or with contrasting centers. Flowers have wonderful, spicy fragrance. In the garden they make a fine edging or mass planting at the front of a border, and they are also prized in rock gardens; as cut flowers, they are charming in mixed bouquets. They are easier to raise than carnations. All of the family like cool rather than hot dry summers.

Plants grow about 9 to 18 inches tall. Annual pinks are less fragrant than the perennial ones, but even so they are nice, bushy plants that often live over winter and bloom again early the next spring. Perennial pinks have a delicious spicy scent and live many years.

Plant in spring or fall in a full-sun location. Prefers a loose, well-drained soil, with a slightly alkaline reaction. Test your soil pH; if it is acid, make an application of agricultural lime (available at garden centers) to "sweeten" it. Regular water requirements. Fertilize monthly with a liquid, organic fertilizer, according to label directions. Occasionally bothered by cutworms, spider mites, bacterial leafspot or rust. Control with an appropriate insecticide or fungicide, following all label directions. Cut the plants back after they bloom to encourage repeat bloom. A light winter covering of shredded leaves is advisable in severe climates.

Recommended: 'Dad's Favorite', 'Essex Witch', 'Musgrave's White'.

Dianthus plumarius

DICENTRA
Bleeding Heart

PERENNIAL, ZONE 3

It's hard not to fall for the charms of this old-fashioned perennial favorite. Bleeding heart is very easy to grow, reaching 2 feet in height and breadth, and blooming at the peak of spring. The slim, arching flower stems seem to bend with the weight of the pink-and-white, or all-white "hearts." Flowers are relatively long-lasting; finely cut, light green foliage dies down and disappears with the heat of summer.

Plant in very early spring or fall in a partially shaded location. Prefers a loose, well-drained soil, amended with plenty of peat moss or leaf mold. Keep soil consistently moist, but not wet, throughout the growing season. Fertilize once in spring with a liquid, organic fertilizer, according to label directions. Occasionally bothered by various scales, slugs, snails or stem rot. Control with an appropriate insecticide or fungicide, following all label directions. Clumps may be left without dividing for several years.

Recommended: 'Adrian Bloom', 'Alba', 'Bountiful', 'Snowdrift', 'Luxuriant'.

Dicentra spectabilis

Dicentra eximia

DICTAMNUS

Fraxinella, Gas Plant

PERENNIAL, ZONE 3

A hardy, long-lived perennial of the highest order, gas plant is a bold and vigorous grower. It makes a bushy specimen more or less like a shrub in appearance, about 3 feet in height and width. The glossy dark foliage with a lemony scent is attractive all season, and in early summer the flower spikes provide a good accent in the garden and in bouquets. Loose spires of flowers are available in pink, lilac and white.

On still evenings it is possible to ignite the vapor from the flowers if you hold a lighted match under them—hence the common name "gas" plant.

Plant in spring or fall in a full-sun or partially shaded location. Space plants 2 to 3 feet apart. Prefers a loose, well-drained soil, amended with plenty of peat moss or leaf mold. Keep soil consistently moist, but not wet, throughout the growing season. Fertilize once in spring with a liquid, organic fertilizer, according to label directions. Established plants do not take well to being transplanted.

Recommended: 'Albiflorus', 'Rubra', var. *purpureus*.

Dictamnus albus

DIGITALIS
Foxglove

BIENNIAL OR PERENNIAL, ZONE 4

Easy to grow and long on charm, foxglove produce 3- to 6-foot-tall, tapered spires of flowers in early summer, at the same time as Canterbury bells and early lilies. Beautiful at the rear of any flower border, they are also attractive when allowed to naturalize in woodland settings. Their sturdy

Digitalis

Digitalis x mertonensis

stalks, encircled with speckle-throated white, yellow, salmon, pink, purple and rose flowers, are good accent points and a favorite of hummingbirds.

Plant in spring or fall in a lightly shaded location, 8 to 10 inches apart. Prefers a loose, well-drained soil, amended with plenty of peat moss or leaf mold. Keep soil consistently moist, but not wet, throughout the growing season. Fertilize in spring with a liquid, organic fertilizer, according to label directions. Occasionally bothered by thrips, foxglove anthracnose, fusarium wilt or verticillium wilt. Control with an appropriate insecticide or fungicide, following all label directions. Plants are likely to be short-lived but readily self-sow.

Recommended: 'Alba', 'Apricot', 'Excelsior', 'Foxy', 'Silver Fox'.

DIMORPHOTHECA
African Daisy, Cape Marigold
ANNUAL, ALL ZONES

This annual, native to South Africa, has dark-centered, daisy-shaped flowers, 2 1/2 to 3 inches in diameter, carried on good cutting stems 18 inches long or more. Foliage is

Dimorphotheca sinuata

grayish green. In full sun the plant will bloom all summer and fall, until frost cuts it down. At the front of a border it makes a nice showing when planted in a mass.

Plant in spring or fall (in mild-winter regions) in a full-sun location, approximately 12 inches apart. Prefers a loose, well-drained soil. Moderate water needs; let soil dry slightly between waterings. Fertilize once in spring with a liquid, organic fertilizer, according to label directions.

DORONICUM
Leopard's Bane
HARDY PERENNIAL, ZONE 4

Leopard's bane produces big yellow daisies—2 to 3 inches across—in early spring. Plants grow 1 to 3 feet tall (depending on the variety), with a spread roughly equal to its height. Classically combined with blue and lavender-colored spring flowers, such as violas, tulips and forget-me-nots, leopard's bane also makes a wonderful cut flower. After the blossoms fade, the bright green, heart-shaped leaves also disappear. Plan ahead for its absence by planting annuals in among these plants, or a later-flowering perennial to fill their place.

Plant in very early spring or fall in a partially shaded location, 8 to 10 inches apart. Prefers a somewhat heavy soil, with the ability to retain moisture through the hot summer months. Because it is shallow-rooted, leopard's bane will suffer quickly during hot, dry weather if the soil is not consistently moist. Fertilize once in the spring with a liquid, organic fertilizer, according to label directions. Every second or third year dig up the clump after the blooming period, divide it into sections and replant.

Recommended: 'Excelsum', 'Magnificum', 'Finesse', 'Mme. Mason' (sometimes sold as 'Miss Mason'), 'Spring Beauty'.

Doronicum orientale

Echinacea Purpurea

Coneflower, Purple Coneflower

Perennial, Zone 4

This big, coarse-leaved plant, extremely sturdy and easy to grow, is good for furnishing color in late summer. It reaches about 3 to 5 feet in height with a 2- to 3-foot spread. Flowers appear over a long season, with a single row of drooping petals surrounding a pronounced pinecone-like, dark center. Colors range from pink, purple and white, along with a rare yellow variety.

Use coneflower singly, or in a group toward the back of a border, or wherever its vigorous growth will not crowd less rampant plants. One of its most valuable features is that it withstands drought conditions well, blooming in full sun through the heat of late summer. Individual flowers last a long time, and the blooming season continues for 2 months or more. Flowers are good to use as heavy material in a mixed bouquet.

Plant in spring or fall in a full-sun location. Not picky about soil type, as long as it is well-drained. Moderate water requirements; once established. No fertilizer necessary. Occasionally bothered by Japanese beetles, powdery mildew or Texas root rot. Control with an appropriate insecticide or fungicide, following all label directions. Cut the flowers freely and don't let them go to seed. Every third spring the clump should be dug up, divided into sections and replanted.

Recommended: 'Bright Star', 'White Swan'.

Echinacea purpurea

Echinacea purpurea 'White Swan'

ECHINOPS

Globe Thistle

PERENNIAL, ZONE 3

Globe thistle is a coarse plant with grayish, prickly leaves and sturdy stems. The globe-shaped, blue flowers appear in midsummer and are very long-lasting when cut. This is a bold plant that calls attention to itself; with equally showy neighbors, it can be used in the midsection or rear of a flower border, or elsewhere as a singular specimen plant.

Plant in spring or fall in a full-sun location, allowing 12 to 15 inches of space between plants. Prefers a loose, well-drained soil, amended with plenty of peat moss or leaf mold. Regular water requirements; once established, tolerates drought fairly well. No fertilizer necessary. This sturdy perennial may be left alone for many years without any special care.

Recommended: 'Taplow Blue', 'Vietch's Blue'.

Echinops ritro

ELAEAGNUS ANGUSTIFOLIA
Russian Olive
DECIDUOUS SHRUB OR SMALL TREE, ZONES 3-8

A vigorous, fast grower, Russian olive can reach about 20 feet at maturity. It is dependably hardy even into southern Canada. Long, narrow leaves make dense growth in summer; when they drop in autumn the shredding bark adds interest to the dormant garden. While not very showy, the small, yellow flowers are intensely fragrant, perfuming the entire garden—sometimes even entire neighborhoods. The yellow-orange berries that follow are not to be confused with edible olives.

Plant in spring or fall in a full-sun location. Accepts ordinary garden soil, provided it is well-drained. Regular water requirements. No fertilizer necessary. If cosmetic pruning becomes necessary, do it in the spring.

Elaeagnus angustifolia (above), leaves and berries (top)

EPIMEDIUM

Barrenwort

PERENNIAL, ZONE 5

Epimedium x *perralchicum*

Barrenwort belongs to the select group of plants recommended as groundcover for shady places, increasing when given the cool, moist soil it craves. Although it will be less vigorous, barrenwort will also grow in full sun, particularly in areas with cool summers. Invaluable in rock gardens and tucked into stone walls. Reaching 9 to 12 inches in height and width, it blooms with early spring bulbs and continues for several weeks. Flowers are produced on thin, wiry stems in loose clusters, in shades of pink, violet, red, orange, pale yellow and white. The heart-shaped leaves have bronze tints in spring, which become purplish or darker red and remain even into winter. Both flowers and leaves are nice for cutting.

Plant in spring or fall in a partially shaded location. Prefers a loose, well-drained soil, amended with plenty of peat moss or leaf mold. Keep soil consistently moist, but not wet, throughout the growing season. Fertilize once or twice during the growing season with a liquid, organic fertilizer, according to label directions. Leave the plants alone as long as they do well. After several years they may have to be dug up in spring, separated into smaller pieces and replanted. Old leaves should be left on the plant as protection over winter.

Recommended: 'Ellen Wilmott', 'Frohnleiten', 'Pink Queen', 'Rose Queen', 'Snow Queen', 'White Queen'.

EREMURUS

Desert Candle, Foxtail Lily

BULB, ZONE 5

Quite unlike any other plant, eremurus needs a special spot in the garden. It starts by growing a large, imposing clump of sword-like leaves. In early summer, dramatic flower spikes make their appearance, growing to a height of 3 to 9 feet, depending on the variety. The tapering spikes are completely covered with small, $1/2$-inch flowers in shades of yellow, orange, pink and white. Because the spikes grow so tall, the plant must have a location sheltered from the wind.

Plant in spring or fall in a full-sun location. Eremurus grows from large, fleshy roots; they are easily broken, so handle carefully. In mild-winter regions, set crowns just below soil surface; in cold-winter regions, plant 4 to 6 inches deep (and provide a protective 2- to 3-inch layer of shredded leaves in winter). Prefers a loose, fast-draining soil, amended with plenty of peat moss or leaf mold. Moderate water requirements; allow soil to dry out somewhat between waterings. No fertilizer required. Once planted, it's best not to disturb these beauties.

Recommended: 'Cathedral Mixed', 'Shelford Hybrids'.

Eremurus

ERICA

Heath, Heather

EVERGREEN SHRUB, ZONE 4

These evergreen shrubs—6 to 18 inches tall, according to variety—have foliage-like scales, sometimes very colorful, and tiny pink, white, red or lavender flowers in upright spikes. Where it grows wild in Europe these spikes are short, but garden forms have been developed with blooms 6 to 8 inches long, borne in summer. This plant makes a dense green mat for use in rock gardens, on banks and as a groundcover. Branches may be used for indoor decorations as dried bouquets.

Heath is a close relative to heather. Often the two are confused, but heath has needle-like foliage and flowers like little bells very early in the spring or even late in the winter. This plant is especially popular in the Northwest, and some varieties can be grown in New England. It spreads fast in poor soils and has the same growing requirements as heather.

Set out the plants in spring or fall, allowing 12 inches between them. Full sun produces the best bloom. Mix peat moss or leaf mold into the soil, but no fertilizer. Prefers soil with a slightly acid pH; to increase the acidity of your soil, add additional amounts of peat moss or pine needles. Keep well watered through hot weather until established. Heather should be cut back to the ground in very early spring to make the plants thicker. In cold-winter climates, give these plants a loose winter covering of straw or evergreen branches.

Erica carnea 'Porter's Red'

ERIGERON

Fleabane, Mexican Daisy,
Santa Barbara Daisy

PERENNIAL, ZONE 2

Erigeron as a groundcover between stair steps

Erigeron

Two forms of erigeron are planted in home gardens: *E. karvinskianus* and *E. speciosus*. Both freely produce aster-like flowers in later summer through early fall, in shades of pink, blue, lavender, violet and white—all with yellow centers. *E. karvinskianus* has a trailing habit, wonderful for rock walls and hanging baskets, while *E. speciosus* is an erect grower to 2 feet tall, with a similar spread.

Plant in spring or fall in a full-sun or partially shaded location. Prefers a loose, well-drained (even sandy) soil, amended with peat moss or leaf mold. Moderate water requirements. Fertilize once in spring with a liquid, organic fertilizer, according to label directions. Recommended: 'Blue Beauty', 'Darkest of All', 'Dimity', 'Forester's Liebling', 'Moerheimii', 'Pink Jewel', 'Schneewittchen', 'Strahlenmeer'.

ERYNGIUM

Sea Holly

PERENNIAL, ZONE 5

These spiny-foliaged, multi-branched plants look a little like they might have come from another planet. Growing from 16 to 36 inches tall (depending on the variety), sea holly is best compared to a thistle, except that sea holly has grayish-blue foliage and blue or purplish flowers, surrounded by spiny blue bracts. Sea holly calls so much attention to itself, it is hard to combine with other plants, but its strange flowers dry easily and are wonderfully weird in any cut flower bouquet. Bloom time is mid- to late summer. May self-seed.

Plant in spring or fall in a full-sun location. Accepts almost any soil, as long as it is well drained. Moderate water requirements. Fertilize once in spring with a liquid, organic fertilizer, according to label directions. Cut plants back after flowering. Once established, sea holly does not take well to transplanting. Small rooted divisions taken from the outside of mature clumps can be cut off and transplanted in either spring or fall.

Recommended: 'Blue Star', 'Opal', 'Superbum', 'Amethyst', 'Miss Wilmott's Ghost'.

Eryngium variifolium (above), *Eryngium planum* 'Blaukappe' (top)

ESCHSCHOLZIA CALIFORNICA

California Poppy

ANNUAL, ALL ZONES

Drifts of this well-known annual give a casual, bright look to any garden, especially pretty when combined with blue-flowering plants like lupine or cornflowers. California poppies produce airy-looking, 12- to 15-inch-tall plants with finely cut, gray-green foliage. Individual flowers, single and also double, are short-lived but are produced steadily and profusely all summer. In addition to the traditional clear-orange hue, California poppies are available in shades of scarlet, pink, orange, yellow and white. Somewhat surprisingly, California poppies make a lovely cut flower.

This plant needs space to spread. It is easy to grow in a hot, dry spot in loose, well-drained soil. Seed can be scattered on the ground around spring-flowering bulbs, to provide color after the bulbs are gone, or in fall for earliest spring bloom the following year. Often self-sows. Moderate water needs. No fertilizer necessary. Because of their long tap roots, California poppies do not transplant well.

Recommended: 'Sunset', 'Mission Bells', 'Ballerina'; the Silk strain which includes: 'Cherry Ripe', 'Milky White', 'Purple-Violet'.

Eschscholzia californica

EUPATORIUM

Boneset, Mist Flower, Joe Pye Weed

PERENNIAL, ZONE 5

Of the 600 or so species of eupatorium, many of which are native to North America, only a handful are valued as ornamental. Even among these, they are more prized by the English than here, in their own country. Although they vary widely in size—from 16 inches to 9 feet tall—all are noted for the billowy clusters of tiny flowers in shades of blue, pink, purple or white during late summer and fall. These are big, back-of-the-border plants, best used where you want to make a bold statement. Can be quite stunning when used as a cut flower in mammoth bouquets.

Plant in spring or fall, in full-sun or, in regions with hot summers, partially shaded locations. Accepts a wide variety of soil types, as long as it is well-drained. Keep soil consistently moist, but not wet, throughout the growing season. Fertilize once in spring with a liquid, organic fertilizer, according to label directions.

Recommended: 'Album', 'Cori', 'Gateway', 'Plenum', 'Wayside Form'.

Eupatorium fistulosum

EUPHORBIA MARGINATA
Snow-on-the-Mountain
ANNUAL, ALL ZONES

This old-fashioned annual, with its white-edged, light green foliage, is a showy highlight throughout the summer. Reaching 2 to 2 $^1/_2$ feet in height, the strong, well-branched plants are attractive in borders. Snow-on-the-mountain is often used as a filler in mixed bouquets. They grow easily from seed and often self-sow; in many parts of the United States they grow wild.

Sow the seed in the open ground in early spring, and thin out the young plants 9 to 12 inches apart. Plant in spring or fall in a full-sun or partially shaded location. Accepts any garden soil. Moderate water needs. No fertilizer necessary. Be sure to sow seed where the plants are wanted, as snow-on-the-mountain does not transplant well. When cut or bruised, stems produce a milky juice poisonous to some persons.

Euphorbia marginatap (left), *Euphorbia marginata* 'White Top' (right)

EUPHORBIA PULCHERRIMA

Poinsettia

EVERGREEN, SEMI-EVERGREEN OR DECIDUOUS SHRUB,
ZONES 10-11 (ALSO USED AS A HOUSEPLANT)

This flower, which has become completely associated with Christmas, is raised in great quantity by florists, primarily because so few people have luck keeping it alive from one year to the next. In Zones 10 and 11, poinsettias grow year-round outdoors, often to great size, astonishing visitors from colder climates.

Indoors, keep the plant away from drafts, and see that it gets good light but no direct sun. It needs moisture in the air as well as in the soil; setting the pot on a tray of wet pebbles

A mix of white and red *Euphorbia pulcherrima*

Euphorbia pulcherrima

will help. Night temperatures should not go below 65 degrees.

As the leaves begin to turn yellow and drop off, gradually stop watering the plant. Keep it dry and cool until about the end of April. Then prune it quite hard and give it more light, heat and water. When the weather is warm and settled, sink the pot in the ground outdoors. Supply the plant with liquid fertilizer from time to time throughout the summer, and bring it indoors in the early fall, before the first frost. To have it bloom for Christmas you'll have to trick it into thinking it's receiving the long nights it needs to trigger blossoms. Starting in October, move the poinsettia into a totally dark closet for 14 hours a night. Bring out into sunlight for 10 hours each day. Keep this schedule for 10 weeks, and you'll have blossoms right on schedule for Christmas.

EXOCHORDA
Pearlbush
HARDY DECIDUOUS SHRUB OR TREE, ZONE 4

Young flower buds that look like pearls have given the common name to this vigorous, fast-growing shrub. The "pearls" appear in late April or May and develop into pure white flowers, similar to spiraea, but larger. The upright, 8- to 10-feet-tall plants are extremely hardy and easy to grow. Useful in combination with other shrubs as a border or screen, or as a single, bushy specimen plant.

Plant in spring or fall in a full-sun location. Prefers a loose, well-drained soil, slightly acid, amended with plenty of peat moss or leaf mold. Regular water requirements. Fertilize every other spring with an acid-forming fertilizer (sold in garden centers as fertilizer for "acid-lovers"), according to label directions. Pruning away some of the inner branches after the flowers fade will improve the plant.

Exochorda 'Northern Pearls'

107

FORSYTHIA

Forsythia

DECIDUOUS SHRUB, ZONE 4

Practically everyone knows forsythia, one of the true harbingers of spring. Its bright yellow, scentless, bell-shaped flowers are borne all along the arching branches in very early spring, even before the leaves appear. Its earliness, hardiness and willingness to grow in almost any situation make forsythia among the most popular of all flowering shrubs.

Give forsythia plenty of room to reach its

Forsythia flower close-up

mature size. Individual specimens should not be planted closer than 8 feet to walks and driveways, as forsythia's greatest beauty is realized when it is permitted to achieve its own natural form, rather than being pruned into some geometric shape. Sprays of forsythia are easily forced into bloom indoors from January on, merely by placing them in a water-filled vase in a warm, bright room.

Plant in spring or fall in a full-sun location. Accepts any garden soil. Moderate water needs. No fertilizer necessary. When forsythia gets straggly, some of the older stems may be cut back to the ground immediately after the blooming season, to encourage new shoots to grow and replace the older ones.

Recommended: 'Beatrix Farrand', 'Fiesta', 'Goldzauber', 'Lynwood', 'Meadowlark', 'New Hampshire Gold', 'Northern Sun', 'Spectabilis', 'Tetragold', 'Vermont Sun'.

Forsythia x *intermedia* 'Beatrix Farrand'

Freesia

Freesia

Bulb, Zone 9 (also used as a houseplant)

These sweetly fragrant flowers, in white, orange, yellow, lavender and rose, are carried at right angles on their wiry, 12- to 18-inch-tall stems. Hardy outdoors only to 20°F, in most parts of the country they are best raised in pots.

In containers, plant freesia bulbs (called corms) 2 inches deep and 2 inches apart in lightweight potting soil. Place containers in a sunny window, preferably in a room kept on the cool side, especially at night. As they grow, keep soil evenly damp, but not wet. No fertilizer is necessary. Freesias should bloom about 3 months after planting. After the bulbs have bloomed, keep them growing as long as possible. When the foliage withers and dies, let the bulbs dry out until the next fall and then repot them in fresh soil.

In mild-winter regions, plant freesia bulbs in fall in a full-sun or partially shaded location, 2 inches deep and 2 inches apart. Prefers a loose, well-drained soil, amended with plenty of peat moss or leaf mold. Keep soil consistently moist, but not wet, throughout the growing season. No fertilizer is necessary. Where adapted, freesias will multiply on their own. Recommended: 'Alba', 'Tecolote' hybrids.

Freesia

FRITILLARIA IMPERIALIS
Crown Imperial
BULB, ZONE 5

Fritillaria imperialis

Some people say if Dr. Seuss were to design a flower, it would look like the crown imperial. Others would say that such an observation is disrespectful to this elegant native of Persia, introduced with great fanfare into England in the days of Elizabeth I. It is a showy, 3- or 4-foot-tall plant with yellow, orange or red flowers in midspring. The large head of strong-scented, bell-shaped flowers is crowned by a fringe of leaves at the top of the stalk. Best grown in groups in a sheltered spot in a border.

To ensure good root growth during the autumn, plant the bulbs in late August or early September, 6 inches deep and 8 inches apart. Prefers a sunny location and a loose, well-drained soil, amended with plenty of peat moss or leaf mold. Keep soil consistently moist, but not wet, throughout the year. Fertilize once, after blooming, with a liquid, organic fertilizer, according to label directions. After flowers fade, let foliage grow undisturbed until it withers and dies. A 1- or 2-inch layer of shredded leaves will help these exotic bulbs survive in cold-winter regions.

FRITILLARIA MELEAGRIS
Checkered Lily, Guinea Hen Flower, Snake's Head
BULB, ZONE 5

Although this bulb is related to the imposing crown imperial, it is easier to grow. As a clump in a rock garden or grouped under a tree where it gets a little shade, it soon becomes established. The patterned, nodding, bell-shaped flowers appear in April atop 10- to 12-inch stems, in intricately patterned shades of purplish-bronze and creamy white. Plant checkered lilies where they can be admired up close.

Midautumn is the time to plant the bulbs, 3 inches deep and 6 inches apart. A small group is needed to make a good effect. Plant in a full-sun or partially shaded location in a loose, well-drained soil, amended with plenty of peat moss or leaf mold. Keep soil consistently moist, but not wet, throughout the growing season. After flowering, fertilize once with a liquid, organic fertilizer, according to label directions. The bulbs resent being moved so, once planted, do not disturb them.

Fritillaria meleagris

FUCHSIA

Fuchsia

TENDER EVERGREEN SHRUB, ZONE 9
(ALSO USED AS AN INDOOR-OUTDOOR PLANT)

In relatively frost-free regions, this tender shrub is grown outdoors, sometimes trained against a wall or fence. In less benign climates, fuchsias are grown in containers and treated as indoor-outdoor plants, for use on porches and patios and especially in hanging baskets and window boxes. Container-grown fuchsias can also be plunged in the ground with other bedding plants for the summer, and then returned indoors during cold weather. Fuchsia's graceful, drooping blossoms, single and double, are as beautiful as they are profuse. Available in a wide variety of colors and combinations, including purple and rose, violet and crimson, magenta and cream; there is also a dizzying array of both plant and flower forms.

Whether planted in a container or in the ground, the vast majority of fuchsias cannot tolerate frost; don't put outdoors until spring weather has thoroughly warmed. Filtered sun (or morning sun and afternoon shade) suits them best. Prefers a loose, well-drained soil, amended with plenty of peat moss or leaf mold. Keep soil consistently moist, but not wet, throughout the growing season. Fertilize monthly with a liquid, organic fertilizer, according to label directions. In regions with hot summers, mist plants frequently to approximate the cool weather fuchsias love. Occasionally bothered by whiteflies. Control with an appropriate insecticide, following all label precautions.

If you grow fuchsias in containers and want to overwinter them, bring the plants indoors in the fall and gradually give them less water. The leaves will drop as the plants go into their resting season. Store them over winter in a cool place, keeping the soil just damp. The following spring, cut all the branches back to two or three growing buds and start watering again. Feed with a liquid fertilizer, and move back outdoors.

'Royal Purple', 'Checkerboard' and 'Marinka' are the most cold tolerant of all the varieties, able to withstand temperatures slightly below freezing.

Fuchsia details

Fuchsia

GAILLARDIA
Blanket Flower

ANNUAL, BIENNAL OR PERENNIAL, ZONE 3

Dashing color combinations make this native American daisy a bold addition to a hardy border. Looks best in a massed planting, near blue or white flowers. Baby's breath softens its strong colors, which are mainly red, orange and yellow. Plants grow 2 to 2 1/2 feet tall and are profuse bloomers from June to September. They do well even in heat and drought, providing plenty of flowers for cutting. There are also annual varieties in showy colors, both single and double-flowered.

Plant in spring in a full-sun location, approximately 12

Gaillardia 'Kobold'

inches apart. Prefers a loose, well-drained soil. Moderate water requirements. Fertilize once in the spring with a liquid, organic fertilizer, according to label directions. Pick the flowers freely. The plants may need replacing after a year or two.

Recommended: 'Baby Cole', 'Goblin', 'Dazzler', 'Monarch Strain', 'Burgundy'.

GALANTHUS
Snowdrop
BULB, ZONE 4

Snowdrops are one of the classic precursors of spring. Delicate stems hold the drooping bell-shaped flowers among narrow, dark green leaves. Best planted under trees, at the edge of an evergreen hedge, in rock gardens or at a doorstep where their diminutive charms can be enjoyed up close. Wherever they are used, plant them in sufficient quantity to make an effect. Excellent for planting in a lawn, as the foliage of snowdrops dies back even more quickly than that of the more commonly planted crocus. This hardy small bulb grows 6 to 8 inches high in almost any soil, in sun or cool damp shade. Set out the bulbs in very early autumn, 3 inches deep and 3 inches apart or closer. Left alone, snowdrops form a colony that will be enjoyed for many years. Fertilize once, after the flowers have faded, with a liquid, organic fertilizer, according to label directions.

Galanthus elwesii

GARDENIA

Gardenia

EVERGREEN SHRUB OR TREE, ZONE 8

Where winters are virtually frost free, gardenias are grown outdoors like other evergreen shrubs. They reach 4 to 6 feet in height and bloom through the summer. The glossy, dark green leaves and sculptured, waxy white, sweetly scented flowers are equally attractive. The flowers are among the most popular of all for use in corsages, and potted plants are commonly offered in early spring.

To grow a gardenia successfully indoors it is necessary to keep the plant in a sunny place away from drafts, at a temperature of about 60 degrees day and night. Do not let the plant stand in water but keep the soil moist. Spray the foliage often to humidify the air. Set the pot outdoors for the summer. Before cold weather, bring it indoors, and let the plant rest for several months in a cool, bright room. Give it less water than in the summer.

In regions where gardenias can be grown outdoors, plant in spring or fall, preferably in a location with filtered sun, or with morning sun and afternoon shade. In areas with cool summers, gardenias can be grown in full sun. They demand a loose, well-drained soil, amended with plenty of peat moss or leaf mold, with a slightly acid pH. Keep soil consistently moist, but not wet, throughout the growing season. Feed every 4 to 6 weeks throughout the growing season with an acid-forming fertilizer (sold in garden centers as fertilizer for "acid-lovers"), according to label directions.

Recommended: 'August Beauty', 'Chuck Hayes', 'First Love', 'Golden Magic', 'Klein's Hardy', 'Mystery', 'Radicans', 'Veitchii', 'White Gem'.

Gardenia jasminoides

GAURA

Gaura

PERENNIAL, ZONE 6

Gaura

A relative newcomer, gaura has earned itself a loyal following for its impressive ability to perform in hot, dry conditions. Gaura produces large clumps of willowy leaves and quantities of tall, airy flower spikes, each individual white blossom tinged with pink. A real workhorse in any garden, gaura blooms continuously throughout the spring and summer.

Gaura requires only a well-drained soil and a full-sun location. Some gardeners report that plants may take a year or two before they really put on a show. Remove spent flowers to prolong bloom.

Plant in spring or fall in a full-sun location. Prefers a loose, well-drained soil, amended with plenty of peat moss or leaf mold. Moderate water requirements; once established, gaura is very drought tolerant. No fertilizer necessary.

Recommended: 'Whirling Butterflies'.

GERANIUM

Cranesbill

PERENNIAL, ZONE 3

What we in America call "geraniums" are really pelargoniums (page 185). Geraniums are hardy perennials, long favored by the English, who really know and relish their perennials. A widely adaptable genus with over 400 species and many cultivars, geraniums offer mounding forms and long-blooming pastel flowers—in shades of rose, blue, purple, pink and white—for sunny and partially shaded locations.

Plant in spring in a full-sun or partially shaded location, especially in regions with hot summers. Prefers a loose, well-drained soil, amended with plenty of peat moss or leaf mold. Keep soil consistently moist, but not wet, throughout the growing season. Feed once in spring with a liquid, organic fertilizer, according to label directions; too much fertilizer encourages foliage at the expense of flowers. Remove spent blossoms to prolong flowering.

Recommended: 'Ann Folkard', 'Birch Double', 'Cambridge', 'Claridge Druce', 'Johnson's Blue', 'Kashmir White', 'Lancastriense', 'Lawrence Flatman', 'Max Frei', 'Mrs. Kendall Clark', 'New Hampshire', 'Prostratum', 'Wargrave Pink', 'Vision'.

Geranium 'Johnson's Blue'

GERBERA JAMESONII

Gerbera, Transvaal Daisy

PERENNIAL, OFTEN GROWN AS AN ANNUAL, ZONE 9

Hardly for the beginner, gerbera is nevertheless such a graceful and refined member of the daisy family that it is especially treasured and worth the painstaking care it demands. Either on the plant or when cut, the single or double flowers on long, slim stems are elegant and long-lasting. Their fashionable colors include soft pastels in shades of coral, yellow, orange, rose and white.

This tender perennial from South Africa is a specialty plant grown outdoors in mild, frost-free climates; elsewhere they are relegated exclusively to greenhouse culture. The hairy leaves grow in a big rosette-shaped cluster on the ground, and if conditions are not "just right" (as in perfect drainage) the plant may rot in the center. Gardeners find gerbera daisies to be a challenge worthy of their best effort.

Plant in spring in a full-sun location, protected from damaging winds and summer storms. Gerbera daisies require a loose, very well-drained soil, amended with plenty of peat moss or leaf mold. If your soil is not well-drained, grow gerberas in containers filled with a lightweight soil mix. Don't plant too deep: Keep the crown of the plants slightly ($1/2$ inch) above soil level to discourage crown rot. Keep soil consistently damp, but not wet, throughout the growing season. Fertilize once or twice during the growing season with a liquid, organic fertilizer, according to label directions. In the fall, cover plants with a 3-inch-thick layer of straw, or in September transfer them to pots and bring them indoors for the winter. Indoors, they're not what you'd call a "low-maintenance" plant: They need good air circulation, plenty of sunshine and regular watering, misting and fertilizing.

Recommended: 'Happipot', 'Double Parade', 'Blackheart', 'Ebony Eyes'.

Gerbera jamesonii

GEUM
Avens
PERENNIAL, ZONE 4

These old-fashioned, open-faced flowers are carried on sturdy but graceful stems well above the foliage. Their color range is limited to yellow through orange to red, but they combine beautifully with white-flowering plants. Geum grows 18 to 24 inches tall and belongs in the middle of a hardy border, where it will bloom from late May through the first half of summer. The almost evergreen foliage, growing in a low tuft, is attractive in all seasons. Geum is perfectly hardy, and the flowers are excellent for cutting.

Plant in spring or fall in a full-sun location. For the best effect, use them in groups of three or more, planted 10 to 12 inches apart. Prefers a loose, well-drained soil, amended with plenty of peat moss or leaf mold. Keep soil consistently moist, but not wet, throughout the growing season. Fertilize once in spring with a liquid, organic fertilizer, according to label directions. Dig up, divide and replant the clumps every third or fourth spring.

Recommended: 'Boris Avens', 'Fire Opal', *G. coccineum*, 'Lady Stratheden', 'Georgenberg', 'Mrs. Bradshaw', 'Red Wings'.

Geum 'Boris Avens'

GLADIOLUS

Gladiolus

PERENNIAL, ALL ZONES

There is no middle ground with gladiolus: gardeners either love them or hate them. With flower spikes up to 5 feet tall, and nearly every imaginable color combination and tint, the world of "glads" provides enough depth and diversity to last a lifetime. Flowers begin opening from the bottom of the stalk; if it is cut as the first blooms show color, the remaining ones will open in water. Older flowers should be removed as they fade and the water should be changed daily. When cutting gladiolus, leave at least four leaves on the plant.

Gladiolus are so distinctive in appearance that they are hard to combine with other flowers. Most home gardeners plant glads in rows by themselves. Plant in spring or fall in a full-sun location. Prefers a loose, well-drained soil, amended with plenty of peat moss or leaf mold. Keep soil consistently moist, but not wet, throughout the growing season. Make the first planting whenever warm weather is certain; make successive plantings, about 2 weeks apart (for the longest possible season of bloom), until 2 months before frost is to be expected in your area. Dig a trench 6 inches deep, and in it set the bulbs 6 to 10 inches apart. Cover with 2 to 3 inches of soil, and fill in the remainder after the leaves show. No fertilizer is necessary. Occasionally bothered by aphids, borers, bulb mites, gladiolus thrips, tarnished plant bugs or botrytis blight. Control with an appropriate insecticide or fungicide, following all label directions. Keep down weeds by very shallow cultivation to avoid damaging bulbs and roots. In winter, store the bulbs in a cool, dark place with good air circulation.

Gladiolus

GLADIOLUS CALLIANTHUS (FORMERLY ACIDANTHERA)

Acidanthera

BULB, ZONE 7

Gladiolus callianthus 'Karen'

This late-summer, flowering bulb is grown in much the same way as the gladiolus. Five or six of the creamy white flowers with chocolate-brown centers are carried on arching, 2- or 3-foot-tall stems. They have a sweet fragrance, especially in the evening, and are fine cut flowers. The little bulbs require warm soil; they bloom in August and September. Sometimes they are planted in pots in the spring, kept outdoors all summer, and brought in before frost.

Plant in spring in a full-sun location. When all danger of frost is over, plant the bulbs 5 inches deep and 4 to 5 inches apart, in rows like gladiolus, or in groups along the edge of a border. Tolerates almost any soil, as long as it is well-drained soil. Moderate water needs. No fertilizer necessary. In mild-winter climates, bulbs may be left in the ground. In colder climates, cut off the top growth when the foliage has died down; dig the bulbs and store in a dry place where they will not freeze. Replant the following spring.

GLORIOSA ROTHSCHILDIANA

Gloriosa Lily

TUBEROUS-ROOTED PERENNIAL, ALL ZONES

This low climber with exotic bicolored flowers of red and yellow is not hardy but may be grown outdoors—even in cold-winter climates—if treated like any other summer-flowering bulb. With support, it grows 6 to 10 feet tall, blooming through summer and fall. The curled leaves have tendrils that cling to vertical wires or a trellis. Gloriosa lily's distinctive flowers have sharply reflexed petals and are carried on long stems; colors are brightest in full sun. They last well when cut and may be used for extraordinary corsages.

Plant in spring in a full-sun or partially shaded location, 4 to 5 inches deep. Best if protected from strong winds and summer storms. Demands a loose, well-drained soil, amended with plenty of peat moss or leaf mold. Keep soil consistently moist, but not wet, throughout the growing season. Fertilize monthly with a liquid, organic fertilizer, according to label directions. When frost comes, dig up the tubers, dry them and store over winter in a frostproof place.

Gloriosa rothschildiana

GYPSOPHILA

Baby's Breath

ANNUAL AND PERENNIAL, ZONE 3

Gypsophila

Few flowers are better mixers than baby's breath. In a garden its dainty white or pink flower sprays have a softening effect on bolder flowers, and, as a cut flower, it is much in demand as a filler for bouquets. The billowy, graceful flowers appear in great quantities, starting about June. Plants are from 1 to 3 feet tall, depending on the variety, with spread to match their height.

Plant in spring in a full-sun location. Accepting of most soils, as long as it is well drained and does not have an acid pH. If your soil is acid, "sweeten" it with the addition of agricultural lime, available at garden centers. Moderate water needs. No fertilizer necessary. Occasionally bothered by aster leafhoppers, crown galls, slugs, snails or aster yellows. Control with an appropriate insecticide or fungicide, following all label directions. Once established, gypsophila plants don't like being moved. Keep clipping off the dead flowers to encourage subsequent bloom. A 2-inch mulch in winter provides good insurance in the coldest regions of the country.

Recommended: 'Alba', 'Bristol Fairy', 'Compacta Plena', 'Dorothy Teacher', 'Dubia', 'Pink Star', 'Perfecta', 'Rosea'.

HELENIUM AUTUMNALE

Sneezeweed, Helen's-flower

PERENNIAL, ZONE 3

In late summer and early autumn the big flower clusters of this sturdy perennial produce masses of color, about the same time as hardy asters, but before chrysanthemums. The daisy-petaled flowers come in shades of yellow, brown and orange, with a prominent center. Older varieties had a rangy and coarse appearance, but the new varieties are more restrained and make excellent cut flowers. A native American plant, sneezeweed is hardy and easy to grow. For best effect, place plants in the background of borders. Height varies from 2 1/2 to 5 feet, depending on the variety.

Plant in spring or fall in a full-sun location, allowing at least 24 inches between plants. Accepts any garden soil, as long as it is well drained. Regular water requirements; once established, plants are quite drought tolerant. No fertilizer is necessary. Stake the plants, and pinch back the tips of new growth to encourage bushiness. Every spring dig up the clump, throw away the center and replant the outer pieces.

Recommended: 'Baudirektor Linne', 'Butterpat', 'Crimson Beauty', 'Cymbal Star', 'Dunkel Pracht', 'Gold Kugel', 'Moerheim Beauty', 'September Gold', 'Sunball', 'Waldtraut', 'Wyndley'.

Helenium autumnale

HELIANTHUS
Sunflower

ANNUAL, ALL ZONES; PERENNIAL, ZONE 3

Extremely vigorous in growth, the old-time black-centered variety reaches huge proportions—often more than 8 feet in height. Sunflowers were once a "mandatory" member of every family's vegetable garden, where its seeds were devoured by birds and its novelty admired by children. Newer, more refined varieties have been introduced for flower borders and cutting gardens. All sunflowers are very sturdy growers—some annual, some perennial—especially useful for color at the back of borders and for use as a temporary screen.

Plant annual types in spring; perennial types in spring or fall. Both forms require all the sun they can get. Prefers a loose, well-drained soil. Keep soil consistently moist, but not wet, throughout the growing season. Fertilize once in spring with a liquid, organic fertilizer, according to label directions. Occasionally bothered by aphids, sunflower beetles, tarnished plant bugs, woolybear caterpillars, powdery mildew or rust. Control with an appropriate insecticide or fungicide, following all label directions. To keep perennial plants from spreading too much, dig up the clump every other fall, divide it into smaller parts, and replant.

Recommended: 'Autumn Beauty', 'Big Smile', 'Color

Helianthus annuus 'Colour Fashion Mix'

Fashion Mixed', 'Double Sun Gold', 'Elite Sun', 'Inca Jewels', 'Italian White', 'Music Box', 'Prado Red', 'Prado Yellow', 'Sunrich Lemon', 'Sunrich Orange', 'Taiyo', 'Valentine'.

Helianthus 'Starburst Aura'

HELICHRYSUM
Strawflower
ANNUAL AND PERENNIAL, ALL ZONES

Helichrysum 'Scotch 100'

Strawflowers are sturdy, unfussy plants which produce quantities of attractive flowers in a wide range of colors—including pink, rose, red, purple, violet, yellow, burnished orange and white. One of their best attributes is the fact that the flowers retain their brilliant color when dried, making them ideal for everlasting bouquets, arrangements and holiday decorations.

To dry the flowers, cut them just as they reach their peak, taking as much stem as possible. Strip the leaves off the stems, and tie the flowers in small bunches. Hang upside down in a warm, dark place (never in the sun or in artificial heat) where there is excellent air circulation. In 2 or 3 weeks they will be fully dried and ready for use for arranging or crafts.

Plant in spring, after all danger of frost is passed, in a full-sun location. Tolerates any garden soil as long as it is well drained. Moderate water requirements. No fertilizer necessary.

Recommended: 'Bright Bikini Mixed', 'Summer Solstice', 'Tanner's Pride'.

HELIOPSIS
Heliopsis
PERENNIAL, ZONE 4

Bold and brassy heliopsis is a good filler plant in flower borders, and is useful as a screen in out-of-the-way corners. Growing 3 feet tall, it is attractive when grown near phlox and delphinium; makes a showy mass of yellow or orange from midsummer to the first frost in fall. It is extremely hardy and free blooming. The wiry-stemmed flowers, sometimes called orange sunflower, are excellent for cutting. They are heavy and somewhat coarse looking, but their very boldness is attractive. Because it is so undemanding, this native American plant is "surefire" almost anywhere—as long as you don't try combining it with anything dainty.

Plant in spring or fall in a full-sun location, 18 inches apart. Tolerates any garden soil as long as it is well drained. Moderate water requirements. No fertilizer necessary. Pick the dead flowers to prolong the blooming season. Every third autumn, dig up the plant, divide it into pieces and replant them.

Recommended: 'Golden Greenheart', 'Summer Sun'.

Heliopsis 'Golden Plume'

HELIOTROPIUM

Heliotrope

TENDER PERENNIAL, USUALLY GROWN AS AN ANNUAL,
ALL ZONES

Tight clusters of intensely violet flowers—along with their signature sweet fragrance—are the hallmarks of this old-fashioned favorite. Plants grow 14 to 24 inches tall; some dwarf forms are even lower growing. Attractive as a cut flower. It is not hardy but is often grown outdoors in warm weather and then potted and brought indoors before cold weather sets in.

   Plant in spring in a full-sun location. Prefers a loose, well-drained soil, amended with plenty of peat moss or leaf mold. Keep soil consistently moist, but not wet, throughout the growing season. Fertilize once in spring with a liquid, organic fertilizer, according to label directions.

   Recommended: 'Black Beauty', 'Mini Marine', 'Iowa', 'Atlantis'.

Heliotropium 'Atlantis'

HELLEBORUS

Christmas Rose

PERENNIAL, ZONE 3

Helleborus orientalis

Helleborus are very unusual, choice plants. Not related to roses in any way, helleborus are woodland beauties with an almost unbelievable blooming season—usually December through March. Any plant that blooms in December is considered a curiosity, but it is more than that. The flowers are innocent white cups 2 to 4 inches across, gradually turning a pinkish shade and finally green after many weeks. Some flowers are attractively streaked and spotted with contrasting colors. Plants range in height from 18 to 36 inches. The handsome evergreen foliage is thick and leathery. Even cold and snow will do the plant no harm, but a suitable location is very important.

   Plant in spring, about an inch below soil level and 12 inches apart. Choose a spot sheltered from the wind, with cool, moist shade in summer and some sun in winter, where it can be left undisturbed year-round. A good place is under a tall shrub or tree that loses its leaves in the fall, or near a protecting wall. Prefers a loose, well-drained soil, amended with plenty of peat moss or leaf mold. Keep soil consistently moist, but not wet, throughout the growing season. It is good practice to keep a layer of peat or leaf mold around the plants always, but otherwise leave them alone. No fertilizer necessary. Plants may require a year or two to establish themselves and begin blooming, but when well situated, they will spread, forming attractive drifts.

   Recommended: 'Sunrise', 'Sunset', 'White Magic'.

HEMEROCALLIS
Daylily
PERENNIAL, ZONE 3

If there is a place where this durable perennial will not grow, it hasn't yet been found. Through the untiring work of a number of plant breeders, the familiar old "lemon" or "privy" lily of yesteryear has blossomed out into a contender for the title "mainstay of the summer garden." It is planted as enthusiastically in the far South and in difficult areas of the Midwest as it is in the East and North, and to hail the daylily as the All-American perennial would not be an exaggeration.

In foundation plantings, beside steps, in front of a hedge on a terrace, even under shade trees, as well as in perennial and shrub borders, these persistent plants grow and bloom. They seem especially appropriate beside a pool or a brook, where their graceful foliage and gay trumpet-shaped flowers are reflected in the water. Foliage is narrow and arching—sometimes evergreen—and makes a good background for lower plants.

Colors now extend through many shades and combinations of red, copper, brown and pink besides the original yellow and oranges. The blooms are carried on stems with many branches. Even though an individual flower lasts only a day, it is replaced the next morning by another opening bud. There are some kinds that open in the evening and last into the next day; some are even fragrant.

Earliest varieties start blooming with iris in spring. Each kind blooms for several weeks. Others come along later in the season; by keeping flowering times in mind when choosing varieties, you can be treated to daylilies until September. Heights vary from 18 inches to 4 feet tall. The flowers tend to face in the direction of the light.

Daylilies are useful in informal bouquets for the house if a stem is cut when the buds are just starting to open. Each morning, pinch off the flowers from the previous day.

Plant in spring or fall in a full-sun or partially shaded location, approximately 24 inches apart. Accepts almost any garden soil, but does best in loose, well-drained soil, amended with plenty of compost or leaf mold. Regular water requirements, but keep well watered during hot, dry spells. Fertilize once in spring with a liquid, organic fertilizer, according to label directions. Occasionally bothered by aphids, nematodes, spider mites, thrips or bacterial soft rot. Control with an appropriate insecticide or fungicide, following all label directions. They can be left for years without any special care. When eventually a clump gets too big, dig it up in early spring or late summer and separate it into smaller pieces. Cut off part of the roots and also the leaves before replanting the divisions.

Recommended: 'Becky Lynn', 'Betty Woods', 'Caboodle', 'Chicago Scintillation', 'Condilla', 'Dragon's Mouth', 'Ed Murray', 'Fairy Tale Pink', 'Hyperion', 'Joan Senior', 'Mary Todd', 'Quaker Aspen', 'Ruffled Apricot', 'Statuesque', 'Stella D'Oro', 'Treasure Shores'.

Hemerocallis 'Caboodle'

HESPERIS

Dame's Rocket

PERENNIAL, ZONE 3

Something about the casual beauty of a mass planting of dame's rocket reminds one of an impressionist painting. Airy plants grow to 3 feet tall, producing quantities of simple, four-petaled flowers in shades of lavender and purple, swaying in the breeze. There is a rare, white-flowered variety. Flowers appear between late spring and midsummer. As an added attraction, flowers are sweetly fragrant once the sun goes down. Often self-sows.

Plant in spring or fall in a full-sun or partially shaded location. Prefers a loose, well-drained soil, amended with plenty of peat moss or leaf mold, neutral to alkaline in pH. If your soil has an acid pH, make an application of agricultural lime (sold at garden centers) to "sweeten" it. Keep soil consistently moist, but not wet, throughout the growing season. Fertilize once in spring with a liquid, organic fertilizer, according to label directions. Remove dead flowers regularly to prolong blooming.

Hespersis matronalis

HEUCHERA

Coral Bells

PERENNIAL, ZONE 3

Heuchera sanguinea

Thin, wiry stems, 15 to 30 inches tall, hold these delicate bell-shaped, nodding flowers above low-growing clumps of bronzy green, heart-shaped foliage. Flowers are available in dusty shades of scarlet, rose, pink or white, as well as coral. Depending on the variety, flowers appear between April and August. Very long-lasting as a cut flower, coral bells are also favorites of hummingbirds. Dwarf varieties are popular in rock gardens.

Plant in early spring or fall in a full-sun or partially shaded location. Prefers a loose, well-drained soil, amended with plenty of peat moss or leaf mold. Set the plants 10 inches apart, in groups of three or more. Regular water requirements. No fertilizer necessary. Generally pest- and disease-free; occasionally bothered by leaf spot, mealybugs, powdery mildew, rust or stem rot. Control with an appropriate insecticide or fungicide, following all label directions. Dig up and divide plants every third or fourth spring; replant divisions immediately.

Recommended: 'Cherry Splash', 'Frosty', 'June Bride', 'Garnet', 'Lace Ruffles', 'Palace Purple', 'Pewter Moon', 'Pewter Veil', 'Ring of Fire', 'Ruby Veil', 'Ruffles', 'Snowstorm', 'Velvet Night'.

HIBISCUS ROSA-SINENSIS
Hibiscus

SHRUB, PERENNIAL AND ANNUAL, ZONE 9

Tropical Asia is the original home of this broad-leaved evergreen shrub, but it has found its way into many warm countries. Prized for its exotic, tropical-looking flowers, hibiscus attracts great attention from visitors to Hawaii, Southern California and Florida. Hibiscus is a fast grower, reaching a height of 30 feet, with glossy dark leaves and wide, trumpet-shaped flowers—single, semi-double or double—in pink, crimson, yellow, orange and white. Summer is its blooming season, although in frost-free climates it flowers practically all year long. Where adapted, it makes a fine tall hedge. Outside of its range, hibiscus can be grown as a container plant and be kept, albeit with some effort, in a sunny window through the winter.

Plant in spring or fall in a full-sun location. Prefers a loose, well-drained soil, amended with plenty of peat moss or leaf mold. Keep soil consistently moist, but

Hibiscus

not wet, throughout the growing season. Fertilize once or twice during the growing season with a liquid, organic fertilizer, according to label directions. Prune in very early spring to keep this shrub to the size desired.

Recommended: 'Agnes Galt', 'Bridal Veil', 'Butterfly', 'Crown of Bohemia', 'Diamond Head', 'Fiesta', 'Golden Dust', 'Hula Girl', 'Kate Sessions', 'Morning Glory', 'President', 'Red Dragon', 'Ross Estey', 'Vulcan', 'White Wings'.

Hibiscus 'New Ruffles'

HIBISCUS SYRIACUS

Rose of Sharon, Shrub Althaea

DECIDUOUS SHRUB, ZONE 5

Hibiscus syriacus 'Diana'

As a screen or as a specimen in a border of tall shrubs or perennials, this plant is valued for its late-summer flowers. It grows erect, as a large shrub or small tree, to 6 to 10 feet in height. Very vigorous and free-flowering from July through September, it is grown over most of the United States (see Hibiscus, page 126, for warm-climate varieties). The large, single or double flowers of white, blue, or pink and red shades are somewhat like those of a hollyhock, which belong to the same plant family.

Plant in spring in a full-sun location. Tolerates most any soil, as long as it is well drained. Regular water requirements; once established, tolerates drought and heat. A tough, easy-to-grow plant, rose of Sharon is rarely bothered by pests or diseases. Occasionally—during hot, dry spells, may become infected with spider mites. Control with an appropriate insecticide, following all label precautions. Cut off the flowers as they fade. No regular pruning is needed, but for larger flowers, cut back the canes in early spring.

Recommended: 'Albus', 'Aphrodite', 'Blue Bird', 'Blushing Bride', 'Collie Mullens', 'Diana', 'Helene', 'Lucy', 'Minerva', 'Red Heart', 'Woodbridge'.

HIPPEASTRUM

Amaryllis

TENDER BULB, ZONE 9

The huge trumpet of the amaryllis appears in February or March, when this bulb is grown as an indoor pot plant, although it is frequently forced for the winter holidays. In frost-free regions it may be planted in light shade in the open ground, where it flowers between March and May. The sturdy, 2-foot-tall spike carries three or four bright flowers of pink, brick-red, orange, salmon or white; sometimes they are striped. Occasionally a bulb will produce a second flower spike. Usually the long, strap-shaped leaves do not appear until the flower bud is well advanced.

In early winter, plant the bulb in a lightweight, packaged potting soil. The pot should not be more than 3 inches wider than the bulb. Take care to set the bulb so that its neck and top third are left uncovered. Place in a sunny window, watering it only a little until it starts to grow; once growth commences, keep soil consistently moist, but not wet. Rotate the pot every day so that the flower spike will grow straight.

When the flowers fade, continue to water the plant so that the leaves will keep on growing. A little liquid fertilizer is recommended at this time. When warm weather comes, put the plant outdoors. Leave it in the pot and sink the pot in the ground. Before cold weather arrives, bring it indoors and let it rest in a dark place, giving it only a little water about once a month. When the neck of the bulb turns green again, new growth is about to start. It is not necessary to repot the bulb every year; in fact, they bloom better when pot-bound.

Hippeastrum

HOSTA

Funkia, Plantain Lily

PERENNIAL, ZONE 3

When it comes to providing beautiful foliage and tall spikes of flowers in the shade, nothing can beat the huge and varied hosta family. Clumps of pointed leaves range in height from diminutive dwarfs less than a foot tall, to over 3 feet tall with flower spikes up to 6 feet in height. The large leaves make a broad mass; some kinds are dark green, others bluish to gray-green. Some are variegated with white, still others are chartreuse to almost yellow. All are very ornamental and furnish a good solid background for light-textured flowers. In addition to their superlative foliage, all hostas produce sturdy spikes of blue or white flowers in midsummer. These vigorous, hardy perennials are long-lived and vigorous and essentially trouble free.

Plant in spring or fall in a partial- to full-shade location, approximately 2 $\frac{1}{2}$ to 3 feet apart. Plant so that the crown of the plant is right at soil level. Prefers a loose, well-drained soil, amended with plenty of peat moss or leaf mold. Keep soil consistently moist, but not wet, throughout the growing season. Fertilize once in the spring with a liquid, organic fertilizer, according to label directions. Occasionally bothered by scale, slugs, snails or crown rot.

Hosta albomarginata 'Lancifolia'

Control with an appropriate insecticide or fungicide, following all label directions. In cold-winter regions, cover young plants with a 2-inch layer of shredded leaves or straw to protect from winter damage.

Recommended: 'Antioch', 'Blue Angel', 'Chartreuse Wiggles', 'Francee', 'Frances Williams', 'Gingko Craig', 'Gold Standard', 'Golden Haze', 'Golden Tiara', 'Halycon', 'Mediopicta', 'Royal Standard', 'Sum and Substance', 'Variegeta'.

Hosta

HUNNEMANNIA FUMARIIFOLIA
Golden Cup, Mexican Tulip Poppy,
Tulip Poppy
PERENNIAL, USUALLY TREATED AS ANNUAL, ALL ZONES

This isn't a tulip, but a Mexican member of the poppy family. The sturdy, 18- to 24-inch-tall plants have grayish-green, fine-cut leaves. In midsummer, cupped yellow blooms, like a big California poppy, appear—especially attractive near blue flowers. If picked in the bud, they make long-lasting cut flowers.

Sow seeds in spring, after both weather and soil are warm, in a full-sun location. Once seedlings appear, thin to 9 to 12 inches apart. Prefers a loose, well-drained soil. Moderate to scant water requirements. No fertilizer necessary. Don't try to move the plants from the place where seed was sown; like other poppies, this one also resents being disturbed.

Hunnemannia fumariifolia

HYACINTHUS

Hyacinth

BULB, ALL ZONES

Hyacinthus

It's hard to imagine that so much fragrance and bright color can be stored in one rather humble-looking hyacinth bulb. Favorites of home gardeners and florists for hundreds of years, hyacinth flowers are available in rich, clear colors of yellow, blue, pink, purplish-blue and white. A bit formal and stiff in beds and borders, hyacinths are naturals for container growing indoors.

The hyacinth is one of the easiest of all bulbs to grow indoors in winter. This may be done in a pot of soil or in a glass of water. In any case, large-sized bulbs or those specially prepared for forcing must be used. For growing the bulbs indoors in water, a special hyacinth glass is convenient. Place a little charcoal in the glass, and add enough water to barely touch the base of the bulb as it rests in the cup at the top of the glass. Keep in a cool dark place until the bulb has produced a quantity of roots and then move it to a warm, sunny windowsill, where it will bloom in a couple of weeks.

For indoor forcing in a pot, start in the early fall by planting one large bulb in a 5-inch pot (with drainage) filled with

packaged potting soil. The tip of the bulb should be just peeking through the top of the soil. Water the bulb, and place the pot in a cool dark room until roots form; this takes about 8 weeks. Then gradually bring it into a warm, light window.

If you want to plant hyacinths outdoors, do so in fall. Hyacinths require a full-sun location and a loose, well-drained soil. Regular water requirements. Feed once, after flowers fade, with a liquid, organic fertilizer, according to label directions. Occasionally bothered by aphids, bulb mites, bacterial soft rot, botrytis blight, mosaic virus or nematodes. Control with an appropriate insecticide or fungicide, following all label directions. Hyacinths grown outdoors benefit from a light cover of straw over winter. If you want the flower spikes to remain large, take the bulbs up after the leaves die down, dry and store in a cool, dry place until planting time the following fall.

HYDRANGEA

Hydrangea

DECIDUOUS SHRUB OR VINE, ZONES VARY BY SPECIES

There is much to be said for hydrangeas, even if some types have been so widely planted as to be considered "common." Except for one climbing form (*H. anomala*, sometimes sold as *H. petiolaris*), these are big shrubs, with big leaves and big flowers. Depending on the variety, they grow from 3 to 15

Hydrangea petiolaris

Hydrangea macrophylia 'Mariesii'

feet tall with a similar spread. Flower clusters, in shades of pink, blue and white, can be as much as 12 inches across. Invaluable in foundation plantings—especially around older homes with tall foundations—hydrangeas are also attractive as singular specimens. In general, they bloom for many weeks, from the middle to the end of summer.

The so-called "garden hydrangea" (*H. macrophylla*) is sold in great numbers as a gift plant for Mother's Day and Easter. Outdoors, it is hardy to Zone 6 and has proved very good for use at the seashore. The large rounded flowers of pink or blue appear in late summer. Lime in the soil makes the flowers pink. Aluminum sulphate (from the garden store or drugstore), added to water at the rate of 1 tablespoonful per gallon and used every few weeks for watering the plants, will turn the flowers a beautiful cobalt blue.

Climbing hydrangea, hardy to Zone 5, clings easily to stone, brick or wood walls and to tree bark. It will not harm a tree, as some vines do. Flowering in shade or sun, it is a handsome vine with glossy, clean, dark leaves and large, flat, white flower heads in early summer.

Plant in spring or fall in a full-sun to partial-shade location, particularly in regions with hot summers. Prefers a loose, well-drained soil, amended with plenty of peat moss or leaf mold. Keep soil consistently moist, but not wet, throughout the growing season. Fertilize once in spring with a liquid, organic fertilizer, according to label directions. Hydrangeas bloom on old wood, so in cold-winter regions where plants are killed to the ground, you'll have plenty of foliage but probably no flowers. To protect above-ground growth, mound soil over the stems as winter protection; remove soil as soon as spring weather starts to warm. Prune hydrangeas right after blooming, to control size and shape.

Recommended: 'All Summer Beauty', 'Annabelle', 'Blue Billow', 'Blue Wave', 'Domotoi', 'Forever Pink', 'Goliath', 'Grandiflora', 'Pia', 'Preziosa', 'Quadricolor', 'Silver Variegated Mariesii', 'Snow Queen', 'Snowflake', 'Tricolor', 'Variegata'.

HYMENOCALLIS

Basket Flower, Peruvian Daffodil

BULB, ZONE 8

This is not really a daffodil but a summer-flowering bulb belonging to the same plant family. It has long, strap-shaped leaves, and blooms profusely from midsummer on. The very fragrant flowers are like big white lilies, sometimes tinged greenish, with the petal edges cut and fringed. Three or more appear together on each 18-inch-tall stem. Best planted in groups of five or more. A group will add interest to any summer garden. Ordinary soil will grow them, in sun or a little shade.

Plant in spring, as soon as both the weather and the soil have warmed, in a full-sun or partially shaded location. Plant bulbs with tops just 1 inch below the soil surface, approximately 18 inches apart. Accepts most any soil, as long as it is well drained. Keep soil moist, but not wet, throughout the growing season. Fertilize once, after flowers fade, with a liquid, organic fertilizer, according to label directions. Where winters are mild, the bulbs need not be disturbed, but in cold climates they must be taken indoors and stored in a warm, dry place until planting time the following spring.

Recommended: 'Advance', 'Sulfur Queen'.

Hymenocallis

HYPERICUM CALYCINUM
Aaron's Beard, St. John's Wort
PERENNIAL OR LOW-GROWING SHRUB, ZONE 5

Hypericum

For summer-long production of flowers, it's hard to beat hypericum. There are a number of varieties, all with clear-yellow, single flowers with prominent puffs of stamens in the center; one variety (*H. calycinum*) is good as a ground-cover; others are smallish shrubs from 2 to 5 feet tall. Blooming through most of the summer when there are few other shrubs in flower, this plant is useful at the front of a border and as a low hedge.

Plant in spring or fall in a full-sun or filtered-sun location. Tolerates a variety of soil, as long as it is well-drained. Regular water requirements; once established, tolerates drought fairly well. Fertilize once in spring with a liquid, organic fertilizer, according to label directions. Unless winter kills back these shrubs, they should be pruned hard in spring. When used as a groundcover, shear (or use a lawn mower set on the tallest mowing height) in spring.

IBERIS SEMPERVIRENS
Candytuft
PERENNIAL AND ANNUAL, ZONE 3

Perennial candytuft (*I. sempervirens*) is a tidy, hardy plant, favored by generations of gardeners as an edging plant. Its dark evergreen foliage is covered with snow-white flowers, early enough in the season to combine beautifully with spring-flowering bulbs. Undemanding and long-lived, it is perfect for low masses at the edge of flower borders and for rock and wall gardens. Usually not more than 10 inches tall, candytuft spreads to make a 2-foot cushion. It does well anywhere, including city gardens, and is nice to cut.

The little clusters of flowers arrive in profusion at the end of every stem, and last for about 6 weeks. Annual candytuft (*I. umbellata*) offers pink, rose, salmon, crimson, lavender and blue flowers in addition to white.

Plant in spring or fall in a full-sun location, approximately 6 inches apart. Prefers a loose, well-drained soil, amended with plenty of peat moss or leaf mold. Regular water requirements. Fertilize once in spring with a liquid, organic fertilizer, according to label directions. Occasionally bothered by diamondback moths or powdery mildew. Control with an appropriate insecticide or fungicide, following all label directions. Immediately after they bloom, cut back the plants hard, to make them grow bushy again. Divide old clumps in early fall or immediately after they have stopped blooming.

Recommended: 'Alexander's White', 'Autumn Snow', 'Dwarf Fairy', 'Kingwood Compact', 'Little Gem', 'Magic Carpet', 'October Glory', 'Purity', 'Snowflake', 'Snowmantle'.

Iberis sempervirens 'Snowflake'

IMPATIENS WALLERIANA
Busy Lizzie, Impatiens
ANNUAL, ALL ZONES

Due in large part to improvements on the part of plant breeders, impatiens have become the number one annual for shady locations. Many, many varieties exist, with great variation in plant habit and flower form and color. Dwarf varieties grow from 4 to 12 inches tall; tall varieties grow to 2 feet tall with a similar spread. Flower color includes about every shade imaginable (including some bicolors), with the exception of yellow and blue. Blooms nearly nonstop all summer, right up until the first frost in fall. The New Guinea hybrids produce large flowers with variegated, multicolored foliage.

Plant in spring in a partial- or full-shade location (New Guinea hybrid impatiens can be planted in full sun or partial shade), approximately 8 to 10 inches apart. Prefers a loose, well-drained soil, amended with plenty of peat moss or leaf mold. Keep soil consistently moist, but not wet, throughout the growing season. Fertilize once, shortly after planting, with a liquid, organic fertilizer, according to label

Impatiens walleriana 'Stardust Mix'

directions. Occasionally bothered by aphids, spider mites, spotted cucumber beetles, tarnished plant bugs, bacterial wilt or Southern root-knot nematodes. Control with an appropriate insecticide or fungicide, following all label directions.

Double impatiens

IPOMOEA ALBA AND I. TRICOLOR

Moon Flower, Morning Glory

ANNUAL, ALL ZONES

Morning glory (*I. tricolor*) and moon vines (*I. alba*) are impressive vines. In one season they can cover from 15 to 30 feet of wire fences, trellises or any handy support. Beautiful large flowers—blue, rose, red and white—are produced in great numbers over a very long season. Morning glory flowers open in the morning—in cloudy weather they stay open most of the day—but full sun causes them to close. Moon flowers open only after sundown and are wonderfully fragrant. Leaves of both varieties are heart-shaped.

Plant seed in spring, when both weather and soil have warmed, in a full-sun or partial-shade location. Before planting, soak the seed overnight in warm water to soften its hard coat, or nick it with a file or knife. Plant seeds close to whatever vertical support they are intended to climb. Thin seedlings to about 18 inches apart. Accepts any soil type. Regular water requirements. Do not fertilize; nutrient-rich soil will result in all foliage and no flowers.

Recommended: 'Heavenly Blue', 'Scarlet Star', 'Star of Yalta'.

IPOMOEA QUAMOCLIT

Cardinal Climber, Cypress Vine

ANNUAL VINE, ALL ZONES

Ipomoea quamoclit

For a quick effect, up to 20 feet in a single season, on a trellis or against a wall, this annual climber is very useful. The foliage is too fine-cut to give much shade, but the flowers make a bright display. The tubular, fiery scarlet flowers, somewhat like small morning glories, are set off by the glossy, rich green foliage. They appear about midsummer and continue until frost.

Plant seed in spring, when both weather and soil have warmed, in a full-sun or partial-shade location. Before planting, soak the seed overnight in warm water to soften its hard coat, or nick it with a file or knife. Plant seeds close to whatever vertical support they are intended to climb. Thin seedlings to about 18 inches apart. Accepts any soil type. Regular water requirements. Do not fertilize; nutrient-rich soil will result in all foliage and no flowers.

Ipomoea tricolor 'Flying Saucers'

IRIS

Iris

BULB AND RHIZOME, ZONES VARY, ACCORDING TO
SPECIES OR TYPE

Iris variegata

Irises have been cherished by gardeners in many countries
for many centuries. There are well over a hundred wild
kinds, and plant breeders in many lands have greatly
increased the types and varieties available. The names of
some of the most-planted types—Siberian, Japanese, Dutch,
English, Spanish—indicate the world-wide origin and interest in them. Because irises are so easy to grow and long-
lived, they rank with peonies as basic garden plants.

A bewildering number are offered by dealers who spe-
cialize in iris. There are low growers only a few inches tall
that bloom with other early spring bulbs, and others that
may reach over 4 feet in height and do not flower until midsummer. By far the most widely planted irises are the tall
bearded types. They grow $1\,^1/_2$ to $3\,^1/_2$ feet tall and bloom
in late spring with other perennials, such as poppies and
columbine. The upright center petals are called the stan-
dards, and the lower petals are the falls; on the falls is the
velvety beard for which this type is named.

Besides these tall growers, there are dwarf and interme-
diate bearded types. The dwarfs grow about 6 to 10 inches
tall and are ideal for rock gardens and as clumps at the front
of a border, attractive with daffodils and other spring-flowering bulbs. Intermediates average 18 to 24 inches in height,
and furnish bloom between the early dwarfs and the later

irises. All these bearded types like a dry sunny location and
a soil that is not too rich. Occasionally bothered by iris borers, slugs, snails, thrips or bacterial soft rot. Control with an
appropriate insecticide or fungicide, following all label
directions.

Japanese irises are beardless. They have wide, flat, very
large, soft-looking flowers in midsummer on a $2\,^1/_2$ to 4
foot plant. These are extremely exotic-appearing blooms that
must have rich, rather acid soil and plenty of moisture. A
low, damp location is good for them, or a place in a border
where they can have the moisture they demand.

Siberian irises, also beardless, are valuable with other
perennials in a border. Their graceful flowers, although
smaller than some types, are very freely produced and their
foliage is attractive and lasting. They prefer moist soil and
are beautiful when massed beside a pool. They bloom a little
later than bearded iris.

The Dutch irises, so popular as cut flowers, may be
grown outdoors, especially in regions with mild climates,
where they bloom in May and June. They like well-drained,
light soil and a place in the sun. These, and the less-planted
English and Spanish irises, are grown from bulbs, as is the
very fragrant, early-flowering dwarf *iris reticulata*, most
commonly planted in rock gardens.

All the bearded kinds
need very shallow plant-
ing. Allow about 12
inches between
clumps, and barely
cover with moist soil.
Cut back foliage to 6
inches at planting
time. July and
August are the
best months
to plant this
type. When
a clump of
iris gets too
large and crowd-
ed, in midsummer (immediately
following the blooming period) dig
it up carefully and divide it. Throw
away the center and keep the outer
parts. Replant them at once, about 12
inches apart. After planting, cut back
the foliage to 6 inches. This process will
only need to be done every 3 or 4 years.

Bulbous irises are planted in October,
like other spring-flowering bulbs. Set them in
groups, 4 to 5 inches deep and the same distance apart, in a sunny location with well-
drained soil. They will benefit by a light covering
after the ground has frozen.

Iris 'Sea Double'

IXIA
Corn Lily
BULB, ZONE 8

Ixia

Long popular as a cut flower in Europe, corn lily deserves wider popularity in this country. Where the weather is mild, corn lily is not hard to grow. It spreads quickly and flowers freely in early summer. Graceful, wiry stems, 12 to 18 inches tall, carry yellow, orange, rose, red and cream flowers like little six-petaled stars, each with a tiny center of a different color.

In regions with mild climates, plant the bulbs outdoors in late fall, 3 inches deep and the same distance apart. Choose a location with full sun and a loose, well-drained soil, with a slightly alkaline pH. If your soil has an acid pH, make an application of agricultural lime (available at garden centers) to "sweeten" it. Regular water requirements. No fertilizer is necessary.

To grow ixia indoors, plant the corms—six to a 6-inch pot—in fall. Cover with about one inch of soil. Keep the pot moist and cool until roots have developed. Once roots have developed, move to a sunny, warm windowsill. Blooms should appear by January. Bulbs grown indoors may be dried after they bloom and planted again the next fall.

JASMINUM
Jasmine
DECIDUOUS OR EVERGREEN SHRUB OR VINE, ZONE 6

These rambling shrubs are, for the most part, natives of tropical or semi-tropical regions, with yellow or white flowers—usually intensely fragrant. The dark green, glossy foliage is evergreen in mild-winter climates, where they are grown outdoors as shrubs or trained on walls or trellises.

One variety (*J. nudiflorum*) may be grown outdoors in protected places as far north as southern New England. Although the yellow flowers are not fragrant, they do appear very early in the spring. Called winter jasmine because, farther south, it blooms all winter long. In the North the stems are green throughout the year; the gracefully drooping branches add quite a decorative touch to gardens.

Plant in spring or fall in a full-sun location. Prefers a loose, well-drained soil, amended with plenty of peat moss or leaf mold. Keep soil consistently moist, but not wet, throughout the growing season. Fertilize once in spring with a liquid, organic fertilizer, according to label directions. Cut back hard immediately after the flowering season.

Jasminum x *stephanense*

KALANCHOE

Kalanchoe

SUCCULENT, ZONE 9 (ALSO USED AS A HOUSEPLANT)

This is a bushy little plant that does well potted or in a dish garden. It has thick, fleshy leaves and clusters of tiny flowers. Indoors it blooms over a long period, from December to April or May, and because it can withstand dry heat it is a favorite in homes too warm for many flowering houseplants. Kalanchoe needs plenty of sun and should not be given too much water. It is not hardy, but in frost-free regions, it is occasionally grown outdoors.

Keep the plant in a sunny window, and don't overwater it. Remove the flowers as they fade, to encourage more bloom. Move the pot outdoors to a shady spot for the summer; bring indoors before first fall frost.

Recommended: 'Pumila', 'Tetra Vulcan'.

Kalanchoe

KALMIA

Mountain Laurel

EVERGREEN SHRUB, ZONE 4

Kalmia latifolia

Both Pennsylvania and Connecticut have chosen the mountain laurel as their state flower, honoring this native evergreen shrub that puts on such a glorious display every spring from New England down through the Appalachians. It grows at the edge of woodlands with azaleas and rhododendrons, in the partial shade of large trees. The bushy plant grows to 10 feet tall, or more, with thick, glossy foliage all year round. Large clusters of small flowers appear in late May and June, each flower a little, soft pinkish bowl. In their natural setting the flowers gleam against the dark shady background.

Plant in spring or fall in a full-sun or partially shaded location. Plant so that the crown is just at soil level. Prefers a loose, well-drained soil, amended with plenty of peat moss or leaf mold. Keep soil consistently moist, but not wet, throughout the growing season. A layer of pine needles or peat moss on the ground will help to keep the soil cool and moist. Fertilize once in spring with an acid-forming fertilizer (sold in garden centers as fertilizer for "acid-lovers"), according to label directions. Cut off the flower heads as soon as they fade. If the plant grows too tall, it may be cut back hard after it blooms.

Recommended: 'Bay State', 'Bullseye', 'Ostbo Red', 'Sarah', 'Tiddlywinks'.

KERRIA JAPONICA
Kerria
DECIDUOUS SHRUB, ZONE 4

Kerria japonica

This hardy native of China makes an attractive shrub with arching branches. Mature height is approximately 6 feet, with a slightly larger spread. Rich yellow flowers—which look like small single or double roses—appear en masse in spring and then sporadically throughout the summer. Twigs remain green all winter, making kerria a pleasing shrub even after the flowers and leaves have faded. They start in May and continue to some extent through the summer.

Plant in spring or fall in a partially shaded location. Prefers a loose, well-drained soil, amended with plenty of peat moss or leaf mold. Keep soil consistently moist, but not wet, throughout the growing season. Fertilize once in spring with an acid-forming fertilizer (sold in garden centers as fertilizer for "acid-lovers"), according to label directions. Prune immediately after the flowers have faded, cutting the weakest branches all the way to the ground. Older stems should be pruned back to the place where new shoots are starting to grow.

KIRENGESHOMA
Yellow Waxbells
PERENNIAL, ZONE 5

This attractive, easy-to-grow perennial produces 4 1/2-foot-tall, reddish stalks and large, maple-like leaves. Shrubby, but elegant in appearance, yellow waxbells produce nodding clusters of pale yellow, bell-shaped flowers in late summer and early autumn. Wonderful in informal settings or woodland gardens. Flowers are followed by unusual seed capsules.

Plant in spring or fall in a partial- or full-shade location, protected from strong winds. Prefers a loose, well-drained soil, amended with plenty of peat moss or leaf mold. Keep soil consistently moist, but not wet, throughout the growing season. Fertilize once in spring with an acid-forming fertilizer (sold in garden centers as fertilizer for "acid-lovers"), according to label directions. Best left undisturbed for at least three to five years.

Kirengeshoma palmata

KNIPHOFIA
Red-Hot Poker, Torch Lily

PERENNIAL, ZONE 6

This exotic-looking plant, native to South Africa, is known for its clumps of long, grass-like leaves and its showy 3- to 4-foot-tall flower stalks. Very long-lasting tubular flowers of red, orange and yellow are packed in tight, poker-shaped clusters. Bloom mostly late in the summer, although some may start as early as July. Wonderful as long-lasting, unusual cut flowers.

Plant in spring in a full-sun location. Prefers a loose, well-drained (even sandy) soil. Keep soil consistently moist, but not wet, throughout the growing season. Will not tolerate cold wet feet in the winter. Fertilize once in spring with a liquid, organic fertilizer, according to label directions. In regions with cold winters, dig roots up in fall and store indoors over winter in a box of cool, dry, sandy soil.

KOLKWITZIA AMABILIS
Beautybush

SHRUB, ZONE 5

China is the original home of this graceful and free-blooming shrub, but like many other plants from the Orient, beauty bush is perfectly adapted to growing conditions in most of the United States. This is a fast-growing, vigorous shrub with a profusion of bell-shaped, lightly perfumed, pink flowers in clusters on the arching stems in late spring. Growth is dense, with the outer branches drooping over toward the ground. It makes a handsome specimen 8 to 10 feet tall, with a spread of about 6 feet.

Plant in spring or fall in a full-sun or partially shaded location. Not fussy about soil type, as long as it is well drained. Regular water requirements. Fertilize once in spring with a liquid, organic fertilizer, according to label directions. Beauty bush grows so vigorously that it is likely to get unkempt and scraggly, taking up too much space. If that happens, cut some of the older stems down to the ground to encourage new shoots to grow. Do this pruning just after the flowers have faded in late spring.

Kniphofia (top), *Kolkwitzia amabilis* (above)

LABURNUM

Golden Chain Tree

DECIDUOUS LARGE SHRUB OR SMALL TREE, ZONE 5

Laburnum

The golden chain tree is quite a sight when in full bloom: Its 12- to 18-inch-long clusters of deep-yellow flowers appear in late spring, hanging like great golden chains of wisteria all through the foliage. When the flowers have gone, it is still an attractive upright tree, growing 15 to 20 feet tall, with smooth bark and leaves shaped like clover. As a companion for tall shrubs in a border or as a specimen on the lawn, especially where space is limited, the golden chain tree is an excellent choice. It gives light shade all summer and is long-lived and easy to grow. While hardy, this tree does not do well in the high heat and humidity of the South. Plant in spring or fall, in full sun or semi-shade, in well-drained garden soil. Regular water needs. No fertilizer necessary. Drive a sturdy stake next to the trunk and keep the tree tied to it until well established. After flowers fade, seedpods appear. If possible, remove them, as they not only sap the strength of the tree, but are poisonous.

Recommended: 'Pendulum', 'Vossii'.

LAGERSTROEMIA INDICA

Crape Myrtle

SHRUB OR SMALL TREE, ZONE 7

This native of China has been enthusiastically embraced by gardeners in relatively mild climates. With its impressive early summer through fall display of flowers—clusters of crinkled and fringed, pink, white, lavender or red blossoms—it's easy to understand crape myrtle's popularity. It is so easily grown in either shrub or tree form that it is sometimes called the lilac of the South—although it performs well in other regions, as well. It cannot be depended on to survive the winter much north of Maryland, but if given a sheltered location it is worth trying in colder parts. It makes a large lawn specimen, and may be combined with other shrubs in hedges and borders if given enough room. Standard varieties produce shrubs, or single-stemmed trees, in the 12- to 20-foot range. Dwarf forms are also available.

Plant in spring or fall in a full-sun location. Tolerates any garden soil, as long as it is well drained. Regular water requirements; once established, tolerates drought. No fertilizer necessary. Older varieties may occasionally be bothered by mildew. Control with an appropriate fungicide, following all label precautions. Most newer varieties are mildew-resistant. Cut off the flowers as soon as they wither, to prolong the blooming season. In the South, prune in late winter, to encourage new flowering shoots to grow. If the top growth gets killed in cold-winter regions, cut back and allow to grow up again from the base. Flowers will appear on this new growth.

Recommended: 'Acoma', 'Centennial', 'Glendora White', 'Hopi', 'Muskogee', 'Natchez', 'Petite Red Improved', 'Queen's Lace', 'Seminole', 'Sioux', 'Tonto', 'Tuskegee', 'Yuma', 'Victor', 'Zuni'.

Lagerstroemia indica

LANTANA

Lantana

EVERGREEN SHRUB, ZONE 7

Lantana

In frost-free regions this 2- to 3-foot-tall shrub is popular because it blooms so freely—practically all year round—and because it thrives in the poorest of soils. Flowers of yellow and orange, red, lavender and white are carried in neat little round clusters against the evergreen foliage. In areas with cold winters, lantana is used as a summer bedding plant. In frost-free regions, it is a spectacular trailing plant for sunny locations and may also be used as a groundcover or as a screen if trained against a wire fence. Florists grow lantana in standard or tree form, as well.

Plant in spring, after weather and soil have thoroughly warmed, in a full-sun location. Tolerates any garden soil, as long as it is well drained. Moderate water requirements; once established, tolerates drought. Keep soil consistently moist, but not wet, throughout the growing season. Feed every other month throughout the growing season with a liquid, organic fertilizer, according to label directions. May occasionally be bothered by mildew. Control with an appropriate fungicide, following all label precautions.

Recommended: 'Confetti', 'Dwarf Pink', 'Dwarf White', 'Dwarf Yellow', 'Gold Rush', 'Irene', 'Lemon Swirl', 'Radiation', 'Spreading Sunset', 'Spreading Sunshine', 'Sunburst', 'Tangerine'.

LATHYRUS ODORATUS

Sweet Pea

ANNUAL OR PERENNIAL VINE, ALL ZONES

Few flowers evoke as much emotion as sweet peas: Their fragile, pastel-colored blossoms are the essence of beauty and their haunting fragrance is memorable, to say the least. One of the world's favorite cut flowers. They grow 4 to 7 feet high, although there is also a bush form. Although they have some special needs—one of the most important being their love of cool weather—once you get the hang of growing sweet peas, you can count on continued success with these wonderful flowers. A favorite subject of plant hybridizers, sweet peas are now available in shades of rose, blue, purple, scarlet, salmon, lavender and white.

Sweet peas must be planted just as early in spring as the ground can be worked. Choose a full-sun location. Soak the seed in water overnight. Dig a trench a foot wide and deep, and in the bottom put a 6-inch layer of organic fertilizer (dried manure) and rich loam. Press down well. Position presoaked seeds 1 to 2 inches apart on top of the loam. Cover with 2 inches of soil. As they grow, gradually fill up the trench with soil. When the plants are 6 inches high, provide support—netting, wire fencing, brush or strings. Don't try to transplant them (they resist mightily), and never let the soil dry out. Grass clippings spread on the ground around them will help keep it cool and moist. Occasionally bothered by leaf rollers, leaftiers, bacterial fasciation, botrytis blight, damping off or powdery mildew. Control with an appropriate insecticide or fungicide, following all label directions. Keeping the flowers cut increases the number of new flowers and the duration of bloom.

Recommended: 'Annabelle', 'Anniversary', 'Anthea Turner', 'Bijou', 'Chatsworth', 'Cream Southbourne', 'Cupid', 'Firecrest', 'Jet Set', 'King Size Navy Blue', 'Knee-Hi', 'Lilac Shades', 'Little Sweethearts', 'Louise', 'Maggie May', 'Matucana', 'Memories', 'Midnight', 'Mollie Rilestone', 'Pip Tremewan', 'Orange Dragon', 'Orange Surprise', 'White Supreme', 'Wiltshire Ripple', 'Wings'.

Lathyrus odoratus

LAVANDULA
Lavender
EVERGREEN SHRUB OR SUBSHRUB, ZONES VARY BY SPECIES

Reminiscent of the Mediterranean, where it is native, lavender is a satisfying garden inhabitant in both looks and fragrance. With its finely cut, gray-green foliage and thin spikes of lavender blossoms, it is attractive at the front of a flower border, on a dry bank or in a rock garden. Most varieties grow 1 to 2 feet tall, with a 2- to 3-foot spread. This whole plant is fragrant, particularly on warm days. These flowers are the source of oils used in perfumes, and it is an easy matter to dry them for sachets. If cut as the center buds begin to open and hung in a protected but airy place to cure, they will retain their fragrance for months.

Plant in spring or fall in a full-sun location. Tolerates a variety of soil, as long as it is very well drained. Moderate water needs; once established, tolerates drought. No fertilizer necessary. Trim plants after flowers fade to maintain their compact good looks.

Recommended: 'Alba', 'Compacta', 'Grey Lady', 'Hidcote', 'Jean Davis', 'Lavender Lady', 'Munstead', 'Otto Quast', 'Rosea', 'Twickel Purple'.

Lavendula (above), *Lavendula* 'Munstead' (top)

LAVATERA TRIMESTRIS
Lavatera
ANNUAL, ALSO SOME SHRUB FORMS, ALL ZONES

When the flowers of spring become ragged in late summer, lavatera takes the stage. These bushy 2- to 3-feet-tall plants become covered with large, hibiscus-like flowers, and bloom nonstop for as long as warm weather lasts. Blossoms may be pink, white or light lavender, usually in loose clusters on bushy stems.

Plant seeds in spring in a full-sun location. Thin seedlings to about 12 inches apart. Lavatera does not like to be transplanted, so it's best to sow the seeds where the plants will grow. Prefers a loose, well-drained soil. Moderate water needs. Feed once in summer with a liquid, organic fertilizer, according to label directions.

Recommended: 'Loveliness', 'Mont Blanc', 'Mont Rose', 'Ruby Regis', 'Silver Cup'.

Lavatera trimestris 'Pink Beauty' (above), *Lavatera trimestris* 'Silver Cup' (top)

LEUCOTHOE

Leucothoe

SHRUB, ZONE 4

Leucothoe fontanesiana 'Girard's Rainbow'

This 3- to 6-foot plant—native to woodlands from Virginia to Georgia—deserves wider popularity. In May, waxy white flowers are borne in drooping clusters along the lower side of the branches. Leucothoe's leathery, dark leaves, 5 to 6 inches long, are bronze and purple shades all winter. A great companion to other broad-leaved, evergreen shrubs, such as rhododendrons and mountain laurel, especially since its shorter stature does a good job of filling in at their base.

Plant in spring or fall in a partial- to full-shade location. Prefers a loose, well-drained soil, amended with plenty of peat moss or leaf mold. Keep soil consistently moist, but not wet, throughout the growing season. Feed once in spring with an acid-forming fertilizer (sold in garden centers as fertilizer for "acid-lovers"), according to label directions. Prune in spring; along with any dead wood, remove some of the older canes to keep plants vital. A permanent mulch of shredded leaves, peat moss or pine needles is beneficial.

Recommended: 'Lovita', 'Rainbow', 'Scarletta'.

LIATRIS

Blazing Star, Gayfeather

PERENNIAL, ZONE 4

Late summer finds this striking border plant in all its glory. The long, straight spires of purplish or white flowers attract bees; unlike most flowers of this form, they start opening at the top of the spike. Because of the flower's extreme height—3 to 5 feet—and very straight habit of growth, gayfeather is best used as an accent at the rear of any planting. Its lavender tones combine well with hardy asters and late marigolds. When cut, the bloom spikes are long-lasting in arrangements. The narrow grassy leaves grow in a thick tuft.

Plant in spring in a full-sun location, in clumps of three or more, approximately 12 inches apart. Liatris performs well even in hot, dry places. Prefers a loose, well-drained soil. Regular water requirements. No fertilizer necessary. When cutting flowers for arranging, leave some of the stem on the plant. Dig up, divide and replant after about 3 years.

Recommended: 'Alba', 'Floristan Weiss', 'Gracious', 'Kobold', 'September Glory', 'Silvertips', 'White Spire'.

Liatris spicata 'Picador'

LIGULARIA

Golden Ray, Leopard Plant

PERENNIAL, ZONE 5

Bold, dramatic plants, ligularias are best suited for shady sites with moist or boggy soil and cool summer temperatures. The yellow-to-orange, daisy-like flowers brighten the summer garden and readily attract butterflies.

Plant in spring or fall in a partial- to full-shade location. Prefers a loose, well-drained soil, amended with plenty of peat moss or leaf mold. Keep soil consistently moist, but not wet, throughout the growing season. Fertilize once in spring with a liquid, organic fertilizer, according to label directions. Attractive to slugs and snails so be sure to use precautions. Recommended: 'Argentea', 'Aureo-maculata', 'Crispata', 'Desdemona', 'Gregynog Gold', 'Othello', 'The Rocket'.

Ligularia dentata 'Desdemona' (above), a yellow-flowered *Ligularia dentata* 'Desdemona' (top)

LILIUM

Lily

Bulb, Zones 4 or 5

Lilies, in their various forms, have been among the most admired and revered flowers of all time. Flowers show a delightful variety in both shape and color: Some have big cup-shaped blossoms facing the sky or at right angles to the stem, others are trumpet-shaped, or may have their petals curled back. In most, prominent stamens and wonderful fragrance add to the charm of these flowers. Colors range from white to yellow, apricot, orange, pink and crimson, with some varieties attractively spotted with contrasting colors. Long the subject of intensive work by plant breeders, lilies are continually being improved, both in performance and beauty. With proper choice of varieties, lilies may be had in bloom outdoors from June to October. Heights vary from 18 inches to several feet. Most of them are hardy and need not be disturbed for many years.

Plant in spring or fall, ideally where their "heads" can be in the sun and their "feet" in the shade. Will also tolerate a location with morning sun and afternoon shade. To keep diseases to a minimum, choose a planting spot with good air circulation. Lilies demand a loose soil, amended with plenty of peat moss or leaf mold, and perfect drainage. To ensure good drainage, old-timers put a handful of sand under each bulb at planting time. Allow 12 to 18 inches

Lilium 'Thunderbolt'

between tall lilies; slightly less for low growers. Plant lily bulbs three times as deep as their diameter, with the exception of the Madonna lily (*L. candidum*), which should be planted only 1 or 2 inches deep. Tall varieties will require a stake to keep them from flopping over. To avoid inadvertently damaging the lily bulb, drive the stake into position before covering the bulb with soil. Keep soil consistently moist, but not wet, throughout the growing season. Feed once in spring with a timed-release, pelleted fertilizer, according to label directions. A 2-inch-thick mulch of shredded leaves or compost will help keep the soil cool and moist; to avoid rot, keep mulch away from the stem of the lily. Occasionally bothered by borers, narcissus bulb flies, red lily leaf beetles, botrytis blight, root rot or mosaic virus, which causes yellow streaks or mottling on the leaves. Any lilies affected with this virus should be dug up and destroyed immediately. The virus is spread by aphids, so eradicate any aphids at the first sign of attack with an appropriate insecticide, following all label precautions. Let foliage die naturally after flowers fade; do not cut the stems until they have turned completely brown. In cold climates spread evergreen branches around the plants after the ground freezes. As long as the lilies grow and bloom well, do not disturb them.

Recommended: 'Ace', 'Cascade', 'Black Dragon', 'Connecticut King', 'Croft', 'Enchantment', 'Estate', 'Golden Splendor', 'Mrs. R. O. Backhouse', 'Pink Perfection', 'Tetraploid', 'Thunderbolt', 'Tiger Babies', 'White Henryi', 'Yellow Bunting'.

Lilium 'Black Beauty'

LIMONIUM

Sea Lavender, German Statice, Statice

ANNUAL, ALL ZONES; PERENNIAL, ZONE 3

Limonium

Statice is valued for its 2- to 3-foot-tall, branched stems—appearing from a low clump of leathery leaves—which produce attractive clusters of papery flowers. Available in shades of blue, pink, yellow, purple and rose, often with contrasting white corollas. Statice dries easily, retaining its color and form well. In the perennial border, statice contributes clouds of flowers that soften and fill in around other plants. May self-sow.

Plant in spring in a full-sun location; in hot-summer regions, does best with afternoon shade. Tolerates any neutral pH soil, as long as it is well drained. Moderate water requirements. Does not require fertilizer. To avoid fungal diseases, plant in a location with good air circulation.

Recommended: 'Azure', 'Confetti', 'Forever Moonlight'.

LINARIA MAROCCANA

Baby Snapdragon, Toadflax

ANNUAL, ALL ZONES

This little-known, easy-to-grow annual has flowers that look like small snapdragons. It blooms in many bright colors, including crimson, gold, pink, rose and blue; flowers are borne on thin stems. Standard varieties grow 18 to 24 inches tall; dwarf forms, 8 to 10 inches tall. Best grown in masses, Linaria is very free-flowering and is especially appropriate for rock gardens. If you have nimble fingers and patience, the delicate little flowers can be made into diminutive flower arrangements. Performs best in cool weather. May self-sow.

Plant seed in early spring in a full-sun or partially shaded location. Prefers a loose, well-drained soil, amended with plenty of peat moss or leaf mold. Thin seedlings to 4 to 6 inches apart. Moderate water requirements. Fertilize once in spring with a liquid, organic fertilizer, according to label directions.

Recommended: 'Cannon Went', 'Fairy Bouquet', 'Fairy Lights', 'Gemstones', 'Northern Lights'.

Linaria maroccana 'Fantasy Mix'

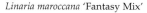

LINUM
Flax
ANNUAL AND PERENNIAL, ZONE 4

Both the annual and perennial forms of flax produce a kind of casual beauty appropriate to wild or naturalized areas of your garden. Easy-to-grow plants are about 2 feet tall and are multibranched with narrow foliage. Delicate, five-petaled flowers are borne very freely in shades of blue, rose, scarlet, yellow and white. Flowers drop their petals after only a day, but are promptly replaced by others the next morning. Self-sows.

Plant seeds or plants in spring or fall in a full-sun or afternoon-shaded location. Tolerant of most any soil, as long as it is well drained. Moderate water requirements. No fertilizer required. To encourage thick new growth, cut back the stems when flax has finished flowering. A 1- to 2-inch mulch of shredded leaves, applied in late autumn, is good insurance in very cold regions.

Recommended: 'Blue Ice', 'Blue Saphyr', 'Cloth and Gold', 'Compactum', 'Gemmel's Hybrid', 'Heavenly Blue', 'Six Hills', 'White Diamond'.

Linum

LIRIOPE

Lily Turf, Liriope

EVERGREEN PERENNIAL, ZONE 5

Popular as a border and edging plant, liriope produces dense clumps of grass-like foliage. From late spring, all through the summer, liriope produces spikes of lavender or white flowers, about 15 inches tall. Liriope is attractive when combined with daylilies.

Plant in spring or fall in a light-to full-shade location, approximately 12 inches apart. In full shade the foliage will be darker green, but in light shade the flower spikes of blue or lilac will be more plentiful. Prefers a loose, well-drained soil. Regular water requirements. Feed once in spring with a liquid, organic fertilizer, according to label directions. After 4 or 5 years, clumps may be divided and replanted.

Recommended: 'Big Blue', 'Lilac Beauty', 'Majestic', 'Monroe's White', 'Silvery Sunproof'.

Liriope platyphylla 'Lilac Beauty'

LOBELIA

Lobelia

ANNUAL, ALL ZONES; PERENNIAL, ZONE 2

With its masses of small, blue or carmine red flowers (some with a contrasting white "eye"), borne all summer long, lobelia is a great favorite for edging beds, borders and rock gardens. The 4- to 6-inch-tall plants spread easily. Trailing kinds are very popular at the edges of container plantings and window boxes. The perennial cardinal flower (*L. cardi-*

Lobelia cardinalis

Lobelia erinus 'Rapid Blue'

nalis) is quite different: It produces stout, 2 $^1/_2$-feet-tall spikes of intense red flowers.

Plant in spring in a full-sun or partially shaded location. Prefers a loose, well-drained soil, amended with plenty of peat moss or leaf mold. Keep soil consistently moist, but not wet, throughout the growing season. Fertilize once or twice during the growing season with a liquid, organic fertilizer, according to label directions. Occasionally bothered by aphids, aster leafhoppers, redbanded leafrollers, wireworms, leafspot or root rot. Control with an appropriate insecticide or fungicide, following all label directions.

Recommended: 'Bee's Flame', 'Blue Cascade', 'Blue Moon', 'Cambridge Blue', 'Cascade Mixed', 'Crystal Palace', 'Hamburgia', 'Paper Moon', 'Queen Victoria', 'Rapid Blue', 'Rosamond', 'Sapphire', 'String of Pearls', 'White Lady'.

LOBULARIA MARITIMA

Alyssum, Sweet Alyssum

ANNUAL, ALL ZONES

Very easy to grow, alyssum is a great annual for impatient gardeners: This spreading plant, 4- to 10-inches-tall, blooms in just 6 weeks after seed is sown outdoors—and it keeps flowering until frost. Largely used for edgings along walks and beds, and for window boxes, the masses of light, dainty flowers, in white, pink and violet tones, are the perfect complement to practically anything they are combined with. Because of its fragrance, this willing performer is sometimes called sweet alyssum. May self-sow.

Plant in spring in a full-sun location, about 6 inches apart. Tolerant of almost any soil, as long as it is well drained. Regular water requirements. Fertilize once or twice during the growing season with a liquid, organic fertilizer, according to label directions. Occasionally bothered by cutworms, aster yellows, root rot or Southern root-knot nematodes. Control with an appropriate insecticide or fungicide, following all label directions. When plants become straggly in the middle of the summer, cut them back to within a few inches of the ground and make an application of fertilizer; plants will put on new growth in no time and bloom until frost.

Recommended: 'Apricot Shades', 'Carpet of Snow', 'Little Gem', 'Oriental Night', 'Pastel Carpet', 'Pink Heather', 'Rosie O'Day', 'Snow Crystals', 'Sweet White', 'Tetra Snowdrift', 'Tiny Tim', 'Violet Queen'.

Lobularia maritima 'Oriental Night'

LONICERA
Honeysuckle
EVERGREEN, SEMI-EVERGREEN, OR DECIDUOUS SHRUB OR VINE, ZONES VARY BY SPECIES

Honeysuckles are unusually sturdy, willing growers that take to almost any soil and climate. They are easy to grow, easy to transplant, hardy over a wide territory and they don't object to heavy pruning. Honeysuckle flowers are small, but showy—simply because they are borne in such abandon. Most have a rich, sweet fragrance that practically says "summertime." Flower color is yellowish, pink, white or red, followed by small red berries, attractive to birds.

Climbing honeysuckle is invaluable not only as a vine but also as a groundcover. It makes such a thick mat that it may overrun a garden, but is especially useful to control erosion on steep banks. When used as a vertical climber, it must have a trellis or other support around which it can wind.

Bush types of honeysuckle need a great deal of space (from 8 to 15 feet tall with a similar spread) and are vigorous, fast growers. When you need a thick hedge or screen in a hurry, the shrub forms of honeysuckle may be your answer. Withstands repeated trimming well.

Plant in spring or fall in a full-sun or partially shaded location. Tolerant of most any soil, as long as it is well drained. Moderate water requirements; once established, tolerates drought. Fertilize once in spring with a liquid, organic fertilizer, according to label directions. Be careful where you plant honeysuckle as a groundcover. It may go wild and smother choicer plants. To prevent this, cut off the ends of the runners. If you want to control the growth of a climbing honeysuckle vine, prune it as soon as the flowers have faded, including some of the oldest branches. If bush types get too thick, thin them out when the flowering season is over.

Lonicera

LUNARIA BIENNIS

Honesty, Money Plant

BIENNIAL, ZONE 4

This old-fashioned favorite is easy to grow—and who can resist a flower called "money plant." It produces beautiful white or purple flowers in spring, followed by large, shiny, translucent seed pods the size of coins later in the summer. Plants grow to a height of about 2 feet, best planted in groups of five or more. It is not really an annual at all, but somewhat unusually, a hardy biennial. Planted in late sum-mer, it "rests" through the cold winter before it goes to work flowering the following spring. Self-sows.

Sow seeds directly in the garden in late summer or start them indoors and transplant them in early fall. They develop heavy roots which hold them through winter, though the tops of the plants disappear until spring. Look for new growth quite early in the spring, and for flowers before summer gets into full swing. Tolerates most any soil, as long as it is well drained. Moderate water needs. No fertilizer required.

Recommended: 'Stella'.

Lunaria biennis

Lupinus

Lupine, Texas Bluebonnet

ANNUAL AND PERENNIAL, ALL ZONES

There are many members of the lupine family, but all have graceful spires of densely packed flowers. Besides the native wildflower of the far West (*L. polyphyllus*), the lupines most often planted by home gardeners are Russell hybrids. These plants produce remarkable flower spikes, from 3 to 5 feet tall, in a wide variety of vivid colors. Soft, green, attractive foliage is a bonus until it dies down in late summer. As befits such great beauty, lupines are somewhat temperamental: They really only succeed in cool, damp conditions, as in New England, the Pacific Northwest, the Upper Midwest, and the higher elevations of the South. That said, given the range of microclimates offered in any home garden, they're worth trying in any region. The stately spires combine well with irises, poppies and delphinium in early summer borders.

Set out lupine plants in early spring or fall, about 18 inches apart, in a full-sun location. Prefers a loose, well-drained soil, amended with plenty of peat moss or leaf mold. Keep soil consistently moist, but not wet, throughout the growing season. Fertilize once in spring with a liquid, organic fertilizer, according to label directions. Occasionally bothered by aphids, whiteflies, leafspot, powdery mildew or rust. Control with an appropriate insecticide or fungicide, following all label directions. Remove seed pods at once, but let the foliage die of its own accord. Where winters are severe, provide a 1-inch layer of evergreen boughs or buckwheat hulls.

Recommended: 'Band of Nobles Mixed', 'Biancaneve', 'Dwarf Gallery Mixed', 'Little Lulu', 'Minarette', 'Russell Hybrids', 'Sunrise'.

Lupinus

LYCHNIS

German Catchfly, Jerusalem Cross, Maltese Cross, Rose Campion

ANNUAL AND PERENNIAL, ZONES VARY BY SPECIES

Easy to grow, undemanding plants, Lychnis have been grown in home gardens for generations. There is considerable variation among the various members of the family, but all are reliable producers of summer color, from late May through July. Although there are dwarf forms that grow no taller than 10 inches, most lychnis grow between 2 and 3 feet tall. Flower color ranges from blue, pink, magenta, crimson, orange, salmon and purple, to pure white. Foliage varies widely by variety, from grasslike *(L. viscaria)* to the silky, almost white leaves of *L. coronaria*, commonly called rose campion.

Plant in spring or fall in a full-sun or partially shaded location. Set several plants in a group, 8 to 15 inches apart. Tolerates almost any soil, but prefers a well-drained one. Moderate to regular water needs. No fertilizer necessary. Every third year, dig up, divide and replant the clump.

Recommended: 'Alba', 'Alpina', 'Angel's Blush', 'Dwarf Form', 'Splendens', 'Splendens Flore pleno', 'Zulu'.

Lychnis x *arkwrightii* 'Vesuvius'

Lychnis chalcedonica

LYSIMACHIA CLETHROIDES

Gooseneck Loosestrife

PERENNIAL, ZONE 3

Quite an unusual plant, the aptly named gooseneck loose-strife is sure to call attention to itself when in flower. Plants grow to about 3 feet tall with a similar spread. In summer, gracefully arched, tapered, 12-inch-long racemes appear at the end of the plant's stems, densely crowded with very small white flowers—all pointing in the same direction. Attractive beside streams, garden ponds or other damp, woodland settings. Can be invasive; plant in bottomless plastic containers (sunk in the soil up to their rims) to control their spread.

Plant in spring or fall in a full-sun or partially shaded location. Prefers a loose, well-drained soil, amended with plenty of peat moss or leaf mold. Keep soil consistently moist, but not wet, throughout the growing season. No fertilizer required.

Lysmachia clethroides (above), *Lysmachia clethroides* flower detail (top)

LYTHRUM VIRGATUM

Purple Loosestrife

PERENNIAL, ZONE 3

Lythrum virgatum 'Rose Queen'

The rosy purple flowers are carried in long spikes from early summer through September, with July and August finding them at their peak, just when garden borders need them. They are used for cutting, too, and combine nicely with delphinium. The vigorous, 3- to 4-foot plants are perfectly hardy anywhere. For best effect, plant in groups of three or more.

Plant in spring or fall in a full-sun location. Prefers a loose, well-drained soil, amended with plenty of peat moss or leaf mold. Keep soil consistently moist, but not wet, throughout the growing season. Fertilize monthly with a liquid, organic fertilizer, according to label directions. Occasionally bothered by mealybugs (cottony white insects) or whiteflies. Control with an appropriate insecticide, following all label precautions.

Lythrum

In many parts of the United States this sturdy and self-reliant perennial has "gone native" and made itself at home along the banks of streams and in low, wet, shaded spots—so much so that planting it has actually been outlawed in some regions where it is most "at home." Any garden having similar growing conditions can take advantage of this willingness to endure poorly drained soil, but lythrum will also grow in sunny locations where soil quality is poor. This ability to thrive almost anywhere can make it a handy plant. But if you're concerned about it becoming a nuisance, favor the (hopefully) sterile hybrids listed below.

MACLEAYA

Plume Poppy

<small>PERENNIAL, ZONE 3</small>

Not for small gardens, nor the faint of heart, these very large perennials make quite a statement. Growing upwards of 7 feet tall, with a spread of 4 feet or more, these are plants that command attention. Foliage looks something like that of the edible fig tree; masses of tiny, pinkish flowers are borne in cloudlike abandon in summer. Both the flowers and seed pods can be used in arrangements. Can become invasive if not controlled.

Plant in spring or fall in a full-sun or partially shaded location, especially in regions with hot summers. Best if grown in a site sheltered from wind, otherwise staking may be necessary. Not particular as to type of soil, as long as it is well drained. Regular water requirements. No fertilizer required.

Recommended: 'Coral Plume'.

Macleaya cordata

MAGNOLIA

Magnolia

DECIDUOUS OR EVERGREEN TREE AND SHRUB,
ZONES VARY BY SPECIES

One of the "all-stars" of any garden, the magnificent blossoms of magnolias are the stuff that memories are made of. Several members of the large magnolia family grow into very large trees, but fortunately there are some types small enough to be included in gardens of modest size, so no gardener need be deprived of their beauty. Flowers range from the large, saucer-shaped blossoms of *M. grandiflora*, to the looser, star-shaped beauties produced by many of the shrub-sized magnolias. Flower color ranges from white, to creamy white, to lavender and purple. Most are delightfully fragrant. Happily, most magnolias do splendidly as specimens planted in the middle of lawns, where they can grow to the full extent of their glory.

Plant in spring or fall in a full-sun or lightly shaded location. Prefers a loose, well-drained soil, amended with plenty of peat moss or leaf mold. Will not tolerate alkaline soil. Keep soil consistently

Magnolia flowers close-up

moist, but not wet, throughout the growing season. Give a magnolia plenty of room, and when it is once established, don't try to move it. No pruning is necessary except possibly to improve the shape of a young tree, a job best done in summer.

Magnolia x *soulangeana, Magnolia grandiflora* (inset)

MALUS
Flowering Crab
DECIDUOUS TREES, ONLY RARELY SHRUB, ZONE 4

Among the most desirable of all small ornamental trees, flowering crabapples contribute greatly to the glory of any garden during "the merry month of May." Reliably hardy and long-lived, crabapples have the endearing quality of providing something of interest in every season. True, crabapples are grown chiefly for their heavenly masses of fragrant, pink, white or red, single, double or semi-double flowers (especially pretty in the bud), but by early fall these flowers have become equally charming little apples—green, yellow, scarlet or crimson, depending on the variety—varying from the size of a cherry to 2 to 2 $^1/_2$ inches in diameter. Larger kinds are good for making jelly, and all are favorite food for wild birds. Some varieties have reddish or bronzy foliage, and some have leaves that change to a brilliant color in the fall.

'Winter Gold' *Malus* berries

Flowering crabapples do well in full-sun or light shade and are not particular about having a sheltered location. They grow in a wide range of soils, and they can stand the fumes and grime of cities. Because they are so hardy and adaptable, they are in great demand, and new kinds are continually being offered.

Plant in spring or fall in a full-sun location. Accepts most garden soil, as long as it is well drained. Regular water requirements. No fertilizer necessary. Occasionally bothered by aphids, borers, Japanese beetles, scale, spider mites and tent caterpillars. Control with an appropriate insecticide, following all label precautions. To avoid diseases, favor disease-resistant varieties. Crabapples may need occasional pruning if they grow too thick.

Prune just after the flowers fade, or in the fall after the fruit is gone, or in late winter before growth starts.

Recommended: 'Adams', 'Callaway', 'Centurion', 'Donald Wyman', 'Indian Summer', 'Molten Lava', 'Pink Perfection', 'Prairie Fire', 'Radiant', 'Red Jewel', 'Selkirk', 'Snowdrift', 'Sugar Tyme', 'Weeping Candied Apple', 'Zumi Calocarpa'.

Malus 'Winter Gold', flowering crab blossoms (inset)

MALVA

Mallow, Musk Mallow

PERENNIAL OR BIENNIAL, ZONE 4

Mallows are valued for their quick, upright growth, from 2 to 4 feet tall, and pink, lavender or white, hollyhock-like, late summer flowers. Their bushy form, long blooming period and drought tolerance more than make up for their relatively short life. Self-sows. Not well adapted to the South or Southwest.

Plant in spring or fall in a full-sun to partially shaded location, especially in regions with hot summers. Tolerant of most any soil, as long as it is well drained. Regular water requirements. Fertilize once in spring with a liquid, organic fertilizer, according to label directions. Relatively pest- and disease-free.

Recommended: 'Alba', *Fastigiata*, 'Mauritiana', 'Pirouette', 'Rosea'.

MALVAVISCUS

Turk's Cap

PERENNIAL, ZONE 7

Malaviscus

Turk's cap is a fast-growing perennial, producing a 4- to 7-foot-tall mounded shrub with soft, lobed leaves. Attractive, drooping, tubular, scarlet flowers never open wide; nevertheless, they are favored by hummingbirds. They are very showy against the evergreen foliage over a long season. Attractive as a singular specimen plant or as a hedge.

Plant in spring or fall in a full-sun, partial-shade, or full-shade location. Tolerates almost any garden soil. Moderate water requirements. No fertilizer necessary. Prune in spring or summer, as necessary, to keep plants busy.

Malva sylvestris

MATTHIOLA
Stock
BIENNIAL OR PERENNIAL, GROWN AS ANNUAL IN ALL ZONES

Plant in early spring in a full-sun location, about 9 inches apart. Prefers a loose, well-drained soil, amended with plenty of peat moss or leaf mold. Keep soil consistently moist, but not wet, throughout the growing season. Fertilize once in spring with a liquid, organic fertilizer, according to label directions.

Recommended: 'Brompton Dwarf Mixed', 'Cinderella', 'Legacy Mixed', 'Ten Weeks Mixed', 'Night Scented', 'Starlight Scentsation'.

Matthiola incana 'Nordic Crimson'

The sweetly purfumed, pastel-colored spikes of stock are a familiar component in florists' arrangements and, while it's possible to grow this flower in the home garden, it's not particularly easy to do it well. The 12- to 15-inch-tall stems are densely packed with rosette-shaped flowers in shades of pink, rose, red, blue, purple and yellow. Desirous of cool growing conditions; unfortunately, if the flower buds of stock are not formed before hot weather sets in, they are not likely to bloom.

Matthiola incana 'Nordic Lilac Rose'

MECONOPSIS BETONICIFOLIA
Himalayan Poppy

PERENNIAL, ZONE 6

Something like the Holy Grail of the plant world, sky blue *Meconopsis* poppies elude the efforts of most home gardeners. Fussy about climate, the so-called Himalayan poppy wants cool conditions common to northern coastal areas such as the Pacific Northwest and coastal Maine. When they get what they want,

Meconopsis betonicifolia

White Meconopsis betonicifolia

Himalayan poppies may grow to 6 feet tall and produce beautiful, silk-like blue poppies with bright yellow stamens in late spring and early summer. The Welsh poppy (*M. cambrica*), with orange or yellow flowers, is much easier to grow—but then again, the poppies aren't blue.

Plant in spring in a partial- or full-shade location. Demands a loose, well-drained soil, amended with plenty of peat moss or leaf mold. Keep soil consistently moist, but not wet, throughout the growing season. Fertilize once or twice with an acid-forming fertilizer (sold in garden centers as fertilizer for "acid-lovers"), according to label directions.

Recommended: 'Crewdson's Hybrids', 'Flore-pleno', 'Frances Perry'.

MERTENSIA
Virginia Bluebells

PERENNIAL, ZONE 3

This old-fashioned favorite is native to the eastern part of this country. Appearing quickly in spring, Virginia bluebells produce 1 $1/2$- to 2-foot-tall leafy plants with a similar spread. Nodding, loose clusters of blue, pink or white, bell-shaped flowers appear in early spring, about the same time as early daffodils—with which they combine beautifully.

Wonderful in shaded, naturalized areas or in woodland gardens. Once flowers fade, plants disappear almost as quickly as they appear, and are gone by midsummer.

Plant in spring in partial- to full-shade location. Prefers a loose, well-drained soil, amended with plenty of peat moss or leaf mold. Keep soil consistently moist, but not wet, throughout the growing season. No fertilizer necessary. Once planted, do not disturb. Plants spread slowly.

Recommended: 'Alba', 'Rubra'.

Mertensia virginica

MIRABILIS JALAPA

Four O'Clocks, Marvel of Peru

ANNUAL, ALL ZONES

Four o'clock blossom close-up

This quick-growing plant is perennial in its native tropical home, but most gardeners treat mirabilis as an annual, growing it from seed. Growing to 3 to 4 feet tall, with a similar spread, mirabilis looks more like a bushy shrub than a perennial. The very fragrant, single, trumpet-shaped flowers open late in the afternoon, or earlier if the day is cloudy, attractively colored in shades of magenta, yellow and white, often streaked and splashed in interesting patterns. They are freely produced from midsummer through fall. Fast and strong growing, mirabilis makes a good low hedge or temporary foundation planting. Four o'clocks need the sun but almost any soil is good enough.

Plant from seed in spring in a full-sun location, about 15 inches apart. Accepts most any garden soil, as long as it is well drained. Moderate water needs. No fertilizer necessary. Occasionally bothered by Japanese beetles. Control with an appropriate insecticide, following all label precautions.

Recommended: 'Broken Colors', '4 O'Clock Special'.

Mirabillis jalapa

MOLUCELLA LAEVIS

Bells-of-Ireland, Shell Flower

ANNUAL, ALL ZONES

Something of a novelty, bells-of-Ireland produces 2-foot-tall spires, tightly packed with shell-shaped, light apple-green, 2-inch flowers. The spikes are charming either alone or in mixed bouquets and are often dried for winter decoration.

Close-up of *Molucella laevis*

Molucella laevis

To dry bells-of-Ireland, cut when the bell-shaped flowers are fully open and strip the foliage off the stem. Hang the flowers upside down in a dark, warm, dry place until they are completely dry. Very long-lasting.

It is easy to grow these plants. Buy a packet of seeds and sow them outdoors when the ground has warmed up. They do not transplant easily. Seedlings can be thinned to stand 12 inch apart.

Plant from seed in spring in a full-sun location. Prefers a loose, well-drained soil, amended with plenty of peat moss or leaf mold. Regular water requirements. For the tallest flower spikes, fertilize monthly with a liquid, organic fertilizer, according to label directions.

MONARDA DIDYMA

Bee Balm

PERENNIAL, ZONE 4

This is a husky perennial, native along rivers and in the woods in the eastern United States. It is very hardy and easy to grow, producing a 2- to 4-foot-tall plant with a spread of 3 to 5 feet. In midsummer, striking, mop-like flowers make a brilliant display, in shades of red, pink and white. If spent flowers are cut off, will continue to bloom for 6 to 8 weeks. Does well in wild gardens, especially near water, and the flowers are good for cutting. It has a shallow root system that soon spreads to form a large clump; will muscle out weaker, neighboring plants if not contained. The flowers and mint-like fragrance of the leaves attract bees and hummingbirds.

Plant in spring or fall in a full-sun or partially shaded location, about 15 inches apart. Prefers a loose, well-drained soil, amended with plenty of peat moss or leaf mold. Keep soil consistently moist, but not wet, throughout the growing season. Fertilize once in spring with a liquid, organic fertilizer, according to label directions. Every second or third autumn, dig up the clump, discard the center portion, and replant sections from around the edge.

Recommended: 'Adam', 'Cambridge Scarlet', 'Croftway Pink', 'Gardenview Scarlet', 'Granite Pink', 'Marshall's Delight', 'Snow White', 'Mahogany', 'Violet Queen' .

Monarda didyma 'Cambridge Scarlet'

MUSCARI
Grape Hyacinth
BULB, ZONE 4

In early spring, this bulb produces little (about 6 inches tall) upright spikes of bells that never quite open. Pure deep blue is the most common color, but grape hyacinths are also available in pink and white forms. Blue varieties are very attractive combined with yellow daffodils. Very hardy and easy to grow in any soil, grape hyacinth asks only to be left alone to multiply and spread freely, preferably in the filtered shade under shrubs or trees where it eventually forms a beautiful blue spring carpet.

Bulbs should be planted just as soon as they can be purchased in the fall. Set them in clusters, 2 to 3 inches deep and 3 to 4 inches apart, in a full-sun or partially shaded location. Accepts almost any garden soil, as long as it is well drained. Regular water requirements during the growing season. No fertilizer needed. After flowers fade, allow foliage to die down naturally.

Recommended: 'Alba', 'Blue Spike', 'Cantab'.

Muscari botryoides (above), Muscari armeniacum (top)

MYOSOTIS
Forget-Me-Not
ANNUAL AND PERENNIAL, ALL ZONES

The modest and dainty blue forget-me-not is familiar in springtime gardens, where it serves as a good, 6- to 12-inch-tall (with a similar spread) groundcover for yellow and white daffodils and other early bulbs. This annual kind (*M. sylvatica*) is also available in pink and white forms. Flowers best while the weather is still cool. When the ground is moist enough, it spreads quickly, and will self-sow, returning to your garden every year.

A perennial form (*M. scorpioides*) grows slightly lower than the annual form, but in all other respects, looks very similar. As a hardy perennial, forget-me-not spreads by creeping roots, returning to the garden in increasing numbers each year.

Seed of annual forget-me-not sown in early spring will bloom just a few weeks after planting. Plant transplants of perennial forms in fall or early spring, 6 inches apart. It prefers a partially shaded location and a loose, well-drained soil. Keep soil consistently moist, but not wet, throughout the growing season. No fertilizer required. Occasionally bothered by green peach aphids, potato flea beetles, botrytis blight or crown rot. Control with an appropriate insecticide or fungicide, following all label directions. Recommended: 'Blue Ball', 'Rosylva', 'Royal Blue Improved', 'Semperflorens', 'Victoria Mixed'.

Myosotis

Myosotis in bloom

NARCISSUS

Daffodil, Jonquil

BULB, ZONE 3

From late March through April these hardy bulbs provide an impressive show—the very essence of spring for many gardeners. All daffodils are known botanically as *Narcissus*. Although it is not a hard-and-fast classification, *Narcissus* with small, very fragrant blooms in clusters and with tubular foliage are called jonquils. Daffodils bloom early enough to be replaced by annuals, which may be planted right on top of—or between—the bulbs. The one essential is that the bulb foliage be allowed to grow and die down naturally without being cut. This may mean an untidy-looking place for a time, but if the bulbs are expected to bloom the following year the growth must be permitted to run its course. Do not tie the foliage into knots, or bind them with rubber bands.

Where there is a grassy, unmowed bank, or an open space under trees where plenty of sunshine filters through, daffodil may be naturalized—that is, planted in great masses at random and allowed to take over the space completely. To achieve a natural-looking pattern, simply scatter the bulbs and plant them where they land.

Fall is the best time to plant all types of narcissus. Set large bulbs 4 to 5 inches deep and about that distance apart; smaller ones only 2 to 4 inches deep. Choose a full-sun or partially shaded location. Narcissus will accept almost any garden soil, as long as it is well drained. Keep soil consistently moist, but not wet, throughout the growing season. Fertilize once, after the flowers fade, with a liquid, organic fertilizer, according to label directions. Occasionally bothered by narcissus bulb flies, basal rot, narcissus mosaic virus or stem nematodes. Control with an appropriate insecticide or fungicide, following all label directions.

Recommended: 'Cantatrice', 'Carbineer', 'Carlton', 'Empress of Ireland', 'February Gold', 'Golden Ducat', 'Ice Follies', 'King Alfred', 'Mount Hood', 'Peeping Tom', 'Silver Chimes', 'Spellbinder', 'Spring Glory', 'Suzy', 'Texas', 'Thalia', 'Trevithian', 'Trousseau', 'Unsurpassable', 'William the Silent', 'Windblown'.

Narcissus 'Fortissima'

NEPETA FAASSENII

Catmint

PERENNIAL, ZONE 3

Catmint grows 1 $^1/_2$ to 2 feet tall with a similar spread, producing a silvery gray mound of foliage. Clusters of tiny lavender or white flowers appear in late spring and early summer. Foliage is highly aromatic. As a low edging, on top of a wall, or in the foreground of a perennial border, this hardy plant is extremely pleasing. The restful color combines well with the brighter colors of summer flowers, and it is not invasive.

Plant in spring in a full-sun location, approximately 12 inches apart. Prefers a loose, well-drained soil, amended with plenty of peat moss or leaf mold. Moderate water needs; will not tolerate wet feet. Fertilize once or twice during the growing season with a liquid, organic fertilizer, according to label directions. When bloom starts to fade in midsummer, cut back the plants; new growth may produce a second wave of blossoms. Catmint will need to be dug up, divided and replanted every few years, in spring. Recommended: 'Dropmore Scarlet', 'Six Hills Giant'.

Nepeta x faassenii

NERIUM OLEANDER

Oleander

EVERGREEN SHRUB, ZONE 8

In regions with mild-winter climates, oleanders are popular and dependable broad-leaved evergreen shrubs that thrive with little care. They look fresh and attractive even through hot weather and difficult surroundings—even as highway or seaside plantings. Oleanders make a graceful, informal flowering hedge and are impressively fast growing. Big, loose clusters of single or double, pink, white, yellow, salmon or red flowers appear in spring and through the summer. Most varieties grow 8 to 12 feet tall, with a 6- to 12-foot spread. Tall-growing varieties can be pruned or sheared; lower-growing dwarf forms are also available.

In cold-winter climates oleanders are grown mostly as container plants. Over the summer it may be used on patio or terrace, or the container may be sunk in the open ground where it gets plenty of sun. Bring indoors to the sunniest window possible for the winter.

White *Nerium oleander* (above), red *Nerium oleander* (top right)

Plant in spring or fall in a full-sun location. Tolerant of a wide range of garden soils. Regular water requirements; once established, oleander is quite drought tolerant. Feed once each spring with a liquid, organic fertilizer, according to label directions. Occasionally bothered by scale. Control with an appropriate insecticide, following all label precautions. Prune to control size and shape after flowers fade.

Recommended: 'Algiers', 'Casablanca', 'Little Red', 'Marrakesh', 'Morocco', 'Mrs. Roeding', 'Petite Pink', 'Petite Salmon', 'Ruby Lace', 'Sister Agnes', 'Tangier'.

NICOTIANA
Flowering Tobacco

TENDER PERENNIAL, USUALLY GROWN AS AN ANNUAL,
ALL ZONES

Elegant-looking plants, nicotiana ranges in height from 1 to 6 feet tall, depending on the variety. All types bear tubular flowers in clusters; most are wonderfully fragrant. Older varieties drooped during the day and didn't open their five-pointed flowers until late afternoon. Now there are greatly improved kinds that not only stay open all day but come in many colors other than the original white, including pink, rose and an unusual lime green. Shorter, hybrid forms of nicotiana are wonderful container plants. Very free-flowering. Older, taller varieties are best grown in informal settings, where their casual grace is noticed.

Plant in spring in a full-sun or partially shaded location. Prefers a loose, well-drained soil, amended with plenty of peat moss or leaf mold. Keep soil consistently moist, but not wet, throughout the growing season. Fertilize once in the spring with a liquid, organic fertilizer, according to label directions. Occasionally bothered by cutworms, Colorado potato beetles, potato flea beetles, downy mildew, leaf spot, powdery mildew, root rot or tobacco mosaic virus. Control

Nicotiana 'Merlin'

with an appropriate insecticide or fungicide, following all label directions. All parts of this plant are poisonous if eaten.

Recommended: 'Domino', 'Dwarf White Bedder', 'Fragrant Cloud', 'Grandiflora', 'Lime Green', 'Nicki', 'Sensation'.

Nicotiana sylvestris (above), *Nicotiana* 'Saratoga Lime' (inset)

NIEREMBERGIA

Cup Flower

ANNUAL, ALL ZONES; PERENNIAL, ZONE 5

The so-called cup flower makes a tidy, compact mound, 6 inches tall with a 10-inch spread. Foliage is so fine as to appear needle-like. By summer, the plants are covered with 1-inch, cup-shaped, blue to violet flowers over a long season. Best used as an edger, in low borders, rock gardens and in window boxes. A creeping perennial form (*N. repens*) produces creamy white flowers and grows only 4 to 6 inches tall; especially good in rock gardens.

Plant in spring in a full-sun or partially shaded location. Prefers a loose, well-drained soil, amended with plenty of peat moss or leaf mold. Regular water requirements. No fertilizer necessary. In cold-winter climates, cover the perennial form with a 1-inch layer of shredded leaves for protection.

Nierembergia frutescens 'Purple Robe' (above), *Nierembergia* 'Mount Blanc' (top)

NIGELLA DAMASCENA
Love-in-a-Mist

ANNUAL, ALL ZONES

Love-in-a-mist is a quaint, but apt name for these old-fashioned flowers. In midsummer, blue, rose or white, $1\,^1/_2$-inch flowers are surrounded by airy, finely cut foliage—the "mist." Flowers are followed by unusual seed pods, favored by dried flower arrangers. Flowers are long-lasting and combine well in mixed bouquets. Easy to grow, love-in-a-mist often self-sows, returning to your garden year after year.

Plant seed in spring or fall, in a full-sun or partially shaded location. Prefers a loose, well-drained soil. Regular water requirements. No fertilizer necessary. Thin seedlings to 5 inches apart. Once established, love-in-a-mist resents being moved.

Nigella damascena

NYMPHAEA
Waterlily

AQUATIC PLANTS, ZONE 4

A large pool is not necessary for all waterlilies, nor must a large assortment be grown in order to enjoy these delightful aquatic flowers of midsummer. Even one or two in a pond contributes unusual charm to any garden during the hottest part of the summer. The pink, yellow, white or blue flowers appear among big, flat leaves; tropical types hold their flowers above the water on upright stems. Both are equally beautiful.

Waterlilies need a sunny area in which to grow and bloom. Hardy varieties require a pool about 2 feet deep, but tender ones need only 10 inches of water over the root of the plant.

Nymphaea 'Mayla'

Nymphaea 'Blue Star'

To grow waterlilies in a pond, secure a wooden box or tub 2 feet square and 1 foot deep. Fill it with good garden soil enriched with a little dry, organic fertilizer. Set one waterlily root in it, cover with soil and then with an inch of gravel or sand; sink the box in the pond. Hardy waterlilies can be put out from May through August, but wait until the temperature of the water is 70 degrees to plant tender varieties.

Hardy waterlilies may be left in the pool all year where winters are not severe. In cold regions, drain the pool, and leave the box on the bottom of the pool, protected by a 4- to 6-inch layer of leaves or straw. Tropical waterlilies are usually replaced each season.

OENOTHERA

Evening Primrose

BIENNIAL AND PERENNIAL, ALL ZONES

Most members of this large family grow wild in different parts of North and South America. Some have flowers that do not open until late in the afternoon and then last only until noon of the next day. The lowest growing are good in rock gardens, while others are attractive planted along the edge of a sunny border, where their clusters of bright, clear yellow, cup-shaped flowers really shine. Evening primroses are rampant growers, blooming continuously through the summer.

Plants are best in groups in full sun. Soil should be light and well drained. Heavy, damp clay is not to their liking. Set out the plants in spring or fall, 8 inches apart.

Plant in spring or fall in a full-sun location, 8 inches apart. Prefers a loose, well-drained soil. Moderate water needs. No fertilizer necessary. Not bothered by pests or diseases. To prolong flowering, keep seed pods removed. About every second year, in early spring or fall, dig up plants, divide and replant immediately.

Recommended: 'Fireworks', 'Yellow River', 'Highlight', 'Summer Solstice', 'Youngii'.

Yellow *Oenothera fruticosa*, Lavender *Oenothera* (right)

ORNITHOGALUM

Star of Bethlehem, Chincherinchee

BULB, ZONE 5

The star-shaped white flowers of this hardy bulb (*O. umbellatum*) are greenish underneath and are born in clusters atop 12-inch stems in late spring. The plant soon spreads to form a large mass and should be used only where there is plenty of space, as in a shrub border, under trees or naturalized in a smemi-wild area. Sun or light shade and ordinary, well-drained garden soil will satisfy this bulb. The grassy foliage dies away in midsummer.

There is also a tender variety (*O. thyrsoides*), the so-called chincherinchee, which is grown outdoors in mild-winter regions. It produces long-lasting clusters of white, 2-inch flowers, with brownish-green centers, atop 2-foot-tall stems. Plant bulbs outdoors in early fall, 2 inches deep and 2 to 3 inches apart. To grow tender varieties indoors, plant several bulbs in 6-inch pots and barely cover with soil. Keep in cool place until well rooted, and then move to a sunny window. When the planting gets too crowded, dig up and divide the bulbs.

Ornithogalum

Ornithogalum unbellatum

OSTEOSPERMUM
African Daisy

PERENNIAL, USUALLY GROWN AS AN ANNUAL, ALL ZONES

Like cape marigold (*Dimorphotheca*, page 95), this annual comes from South Africa. The dark-centered, daisy-shaped flowers, 2 $^1/_2$ to 3 inches in diameter, are borne in great profusion all summer long. Flowers start out purplish-lilac and fade quickly to white. Foliage is grayish-green, producing mat-like growth, 6 to 12 inches tall, spreading 2 to 4 feet in a single season.

Plant in spring in a full-sun location, about 12 inches apart. Prefers a loose, well-drained soil. Regular water requirements; drought resistant once established. Fertilize once in spring with a liquid, organic fertilizer, according to label directions. Cut the flowers freely for use in bouquets and to keep the plants blooming.

Recommended: 'African Queen', 'Burgundy', 'Whirlygig'.

PAEONIA
Peony, Tree Peony

PERENNIAL, DECIDUOUS SHRUB, ZONE 3

Paeonia 'Doreen'

In Japan this is known as the flower of prosperity; in the United States it has been loved since Colonial days. Its hardiness and ability to thrive for 40 to 50 years (or more) in one spot has endeared the peony to home gardeners in all but the warmest parts of the country. While gardeners in the lower South and in southern California will have trouble with peonies, the harshest Canadian winters hold no terrors for this tough beauty.

Peonies produce big, double, semi-double or single flowers in shades of red, pink and white, from late spring through mid-summer. Plants are used as showy specimens beside steps, at a doorway or garden gate, along a driveway, or in mixed plantings with other perennials such as iris, columbine, phlox and daylilies. The foliage is pleasing long after the flowers have gone.

Peonies typically grow 2 to 4 feet tall and die to the ground in late fall.

Osteospermum

Tree peonies are shrubs, not trees, that have had an honored position in China and Japan for centuries. The Chinese call them the "king of flowers." These are very hardy plants, with graceful light green foliage and striking flowers that are larger and earlier than the better known perennial peonies. The plants grow 3 to 6 feet tall and do not die down in autumn, although they do lose their leaves. They require a somewhat protected location, ideally with high shade from nearby trees. The soil must be well drained and enriched with plenty of peat moss, compost or leaf mold.

In cold-winter climates, the best time to plant perennial peonies is September. In warmer areas a month later is preferable. After preparing the ground well, dig a shallow hole, and cover the root with no more than 2 inches of soil (1 inch in warm regions). Planting perennial peonies too deep is a major reason for failure to bloom. Firm the soil well around the root, and water thoroughly. Allow 3 feet between plants.

When buying a tree peony, choose a plant of blooming size, at least 3 years old. Plant in late September or October, at the same depth as in the nursery. Give the roots a covering of straw for the first winter.

Both perennial and tree peonies prefer a full-sun to partially shaded location—particularly afternoon shade for tree peonies grown in hot summer climates. Prefers a loose, well-drained soil, amended with plenty of peat moss, compost or leaf mold. Regular water requirements. Feed once, after flowers fade, with a liquid, organic fertilizer, according to label directions. Occasionally bothered by ants (which can spread disease), four-lined plant bugs, Japanese beetles, oystershell scale, slugs, snails, thrips, anthracnose, botrytis blight, leaf spot, phytophthora blight or root-knot nematodes. Control with an appropriate insecticide or fungicide, following all label directions.

For perennial types, cut off all dead flowers as soon as they fade, but let the foliage grow as long as possible. In late fall, cut the foliage to the ground and destroy. In areas where there are low winter temperatures without much snow, a cover of evergreen branches may be necessary, but generally peonies need no winter protection.

Tree peonies require little or no pruning. Occasionally an extra-cold winter kills the top growth back to the ground. In that case, cut the dead wood back in the spring; the plant will then put out new growth.

Paeonia 'Kansas'

PAPAVER
Poppy

ANNUAL AND PERENNIAL, ZONE 3

Few flowers possess a more carefree beauty than the many types of poppies. Poppies are available in a wide variety of colors: Brilliant orange and red are the colors most often associated with poppies, but pink, white, apricot and coral are also available, most all held proudly aloft on thin, wiry stems, which sway gently in a breeze. Both single- and double-flowered forms are available. All make excellent cut flowers. For the most spectacular—if somewhat short-lived—effect in the garden, mass-plant poppies in large drifts. Replace poppies after they fade with later-blooming annuals, such as marigolds or zinnias, or with summer-flowering bulbs.

The perennial Oriental poppies (*P. orientale*) bloom at the same time as bearded irises and peonies in June, making for a spectacular combination. Oriental poppies are particularly showy because of their immense size, flaming hues and blue-black centers. Extremely long-lived, they disappear each year during the hottest part of the summer and begin to grow again in the fall. During this period, mask the resting poppies by over-planting them with other plants such as phlox or shasta daisies, both to cover the bare spot and to protect the poppy roots.

Iceland poppies (*P. nudicaule*) produce cheerful 2- to 3-inch-diameter flowers, single and double, on strong, slender stems. They can be grown from seed or from transplants available in early spring. Annual kinds grown from seed will bloom over a longer period if the plants are not too close together and if the dead flowers are picked off regularly. In most gardens, they reseed easily and will come up again year after year, without any help from the gardener.

All poppies demand a full-sun location and, once planted, none of them like to be moved. They do well in ordinary soil, as long as it is well drained. Perennial kinds appreciate an application of complete fertilizer and a shovelful or two

Papaver orientale 'Helen Elisabeth'

Carnation-flowered poppies

of organic soil amendment mixed into the ground before planting. If you want to cut the flowers for bouquets, do it while they are still buds. For the longest-lasting flowers, hold the cut end of the poppy stem over a flame to char it—just for a second or two—before plunging it in deep water.

August or September is the best time to plant Oriental poppies, although transplants may be set out in the spring. Provide winter protection with a thick layer of straw or leaves only after the first year of growth; the poppies will be sufficiently established in future years, making winter protection unnecessary.

Sow seed of Iceland and Shirley poppies, preferably in early fall to bloom the following spring, or in very early spring, as soon as the ground can be worked. For easier and more even distribution, mix the extremely fine poppy seed with a little sand, and don't be too generous in scattering it. Thin young plants 10 to 12 inches apart. Because they will not tolerate transplanting, simply throw away the plants you pull out. Once up and growing, don't disturb the roots of any poppies with too-close cultivation, and cut off all dead flowers promptly to ensure maximum bloom.

Poppies have regular to moderate water needs and do not require fertilizer. Occasionally bothered by aphids, four-lined plant bugs, leafhoppers, bacterial blight, powdery mildew or verticillium wilt. Control with an appropriate insecticide or fungicide, following all label directions.

Recommended: (*P. orientale*)—'Brilliant', 'Coral Reef',

Papaver rhoeas

'Minicap Hybrids', 'Pizzicato'; (*P. nudicaule*)—'Champagne Bubbles', 'Garden Gnome Mixed', 'Oregon Rainbows', 'Misato Carnival', 'Red Sails', 'Wonderland Mixed'.

PASSIFLORA
Passionflower
SEMI-EVERGREEN VINE, ZONE 7

This vigorous vine with exotic flowers can cover from 20 to 30 feet in a single season. Fragrant flowers, up to 4 inches across, are borne in great profusion during the summer. Each flower is an intricate work of art, in shades of white, to lavender, pink and deep blue. *P.* x *alatocaerulea* does not produce fruit and is the least attractive of all the passionflowers to the caterpillars of the gulf fritillary butterfly, which cause extensive damage on other forms of this vine. Excellent for covering fences, trellises and the like.

Plant in spring in a full-sun location. Plant it where the tendrils will have a support on which to cling. Accepts any garden soil. Regular to moderate water requirements. No fertilizer necessary. Occasionally bothered by caterpillars. Control with an appropriate insecticide, following all label precautions. After the flowers have gone, thin out the weakest growth. In cold climates plant against a south wall and give the roots some covering over winter.

Recommended: 'Incense' (hardy to Zone 5).

Passiflora 'Incense' (above), *Passiflora incarnata* (top)

PELARGONIUM

Geranium

PERENNIAL, SHRUB, AND SOME ANNUAL, ALL ZONES

Perhaps the most familiar of all garden flowers; there is more to this family than the old-fashioned, red-flowered geranium growing in a terra-cotta pot that everyone—including non-gardeners—seems to know. There are many kinds grown by hobbyists who make a specialty of collecting their favorites. There are those with fragrant leaves, grown primarily for their rose, lemon or other scents rather than their flowers. Others have leaves zoned and variegated and frilled in many combinations. Ivy-leaved geraniums are graceful trailing plants for hanging baskets and window boxes. The so-called "Martha Washington" (*P. domesticum*) geraniums boast large ruffled flowers with dark blotches. Dwarf varieties are very popular, with their fancy colored leaves.

Plant all types of geraniums outdoors after all danger of frost is over. Prefers a loose, well-drained soil. Keep soil consistently moist, but not wet, throughout the growing season. Feed once or twice during the growing season with a liquid, organic fertilizer, according to label directions. Occasionally bothered by aphids, caterpillars, leafrollers, leaftiers, mealybugs, slugs, snails, botrytis blight, cercospera leaf spot, rust, southern root-knot, nematodes, whiteflies, spider mites and tobacco budworms. Control with an appropriate insecticide, following all label precautions. Pinching back the tops will

A pale-pink *Pelargonium*

make them branch more. In warm climates the plants may be left in the ground all year long. In that case they need pruning from time to time.

In late summer, instead of trying to move large plants indoors for winter bloom, take slips and start new plants. Cut off a 5-inch section from a strong branch, strip off the leaves from the end, and push 2 inches deep into a pot of moist, lightweight potting mix. In about a month it will have formed roots and can be brought indoors. It is better not to use a very large pot, for geraniums bloom better when slightly root-bound. Keep the plant in a sunny window. It doesn't need a particularly humid atmosphere nor a great deal of fertilizer. Be a little miserly with water.

Recommended: 'Diamond', 'Elite', 'Multibloom', 'Orange Appeal', 'Orbit', 'Marvick', 'Sprinter'.

Pelargoniums as a border

PENSTEMON

Beard Tongue

PERENNIAL, ZONE 3

Penstemon is a huge family, with many members growing wild, mostly in the Rocky Mountain region and farther west. Some are dwarf growers only a few inches tall, suitable for rock-garden use, while taller ones are grown in perennial borders or as summer annuals. Recent work by plant hybridizers has resulted in a number of beautiful cultivars of great value to flower gardeners. In general, tubular, lipped flowers appear on slender stalks in early summer in a wide variety of colors, from purple, violet, pink, salmon and white, with some stunning bicolored varieties and a few rare yellow types. Penstemon tends to look best planted in groups of three or more. Most make excellent cut flowers.

Plant in spring or fall in a full-sun or partially shaded location, about 12 inches apart. Prefers a loose, well-drained soil, amended with plenty of peat moss or leaf mold. Regular to moderate water needs. No fertilizer necessary. Occasionally bothered by aphids, tobacco budworms, leaf spot, rust or Southern blight. Control with an appropriate insecticide or fungicide, following all label directions. Cut plants back about halfway after initial blooming period to encourage second bloom.

Recommended: 'Alice Hindley', 'Apple Blossom', 'Elfin Pink', 'Evelyn', 'Firebird', 'Garnet', 'Holly White', 'Huntington Pink', 'Midnight', 'Pink Beauty', 'Prairie Dusk', 'Prairie Fire', 'Rose Elf', 'Schooley's Yellow', 'Sour Grapes'.

Penstemon gentianoides

PEROVSKIA
Russian Sage
PERENNIAL, ZONE 5

Relatively new on the home garden scene, Russian sage is a fine-textured, airy shrub with gray foliage, with a haze of tiny purple-blue flowers from summer into fall. Plants produce woody, upright stems, 3 to 4 feet tall, with an equal spread. Attractive when planted in groups of three or more. Russian sage has endeared itself to gardeners as a very low-maintenance plant. Full sun. Average, well-drained soil. Drought tolerant. Must have good winter drainage. Cut back plants in spring to encourage bushy growth.

Plant in spring or fall in a full-sun location. Accepts any soil type, as long as it is well drained. Moderate water needs; once established, Russian sage is extremely heat and drought tolerant. No fertilizer necessary. Cut back plants nearly to the ground in spring, before new growth begins.

Recommended: 'Blue Haze', 'Blue Mist', 'Blue Spire', 'Filagran'.

Perovskia

PETUNIA

Petunia

ANNUAL OR PERENNIAL, ALL ZONES

Petunias are extremely versatile annuals that have made a place for themselves in millions of home gardens around the world. While there are no tall types for planting at the rear of a flower border, that's about petunia's only deficiency. They can be used almost anywhere—as bedding plants, as low edgers for borders, on banks, in containers or hanging baskets and for cutting. The softly perfumed flowers blossom freely until frost, spilling their lovely colors in abandon. Single, double, ruffled and fringed blooms are available on plants that may be bushy or sprawling or trailing. An incredible range of colors includes blue, violet, purple lavender, pink, salmon, red, white, cream and yellow, along with many outstanding bicolors.

Plant in spring in a full-sun or lightly shaded location. Prefers a loose, well-drained soil. Keep

Petunia 'White Storm'

Petunia 'Total Madness'

soil consistently moist, but not wet, throughout the growing season. Fertilize once or twice during the growing season with a liquid, organic fertilizer, according to label directions. Occasionally bothered by caterpillars, Colorado potato beetles, slugs, snails, spotted cucumber beetles, bacterial fasciation, cucumber mosaic virus, dodder, Southern root-knot nematodes. Control with an appropriate insecticide or fungicide, following all label directions. Pick off spent flowers to encourage more blossoms. Cut container-grown petunias back about halfway in midsummer to encourage new growth and a second wave of blossoms. A light application of fertilizer at this time is a good practice.

PHILADELPHUS
Mock Orange
DECIDUOUS SHRUB, ZONE 4

Philadelphus 'Snow Belle'

Although mock orange bushes bloom for only a short while in early summer and are leafless all winter, they are, nonetheless, old-fashioned favorites, loved for their fragrance. All mock oranges produce white flowers, but some are single and others double or semidouble, and some are much more fragrant than others. There are varieties with dense, compact growth only 5 to 7 feet tall, while others are as much as 12 feet in both height and width. Mock oranges are easy to grow and perform well in a variety of settings, from perennial borders to foundation plantings.

Plant in spring or fall in a full-sun to light-shade location. Will accept almost any garden soil, as long as it is well drained. Regular to moderate water needs. No fertilizer required. Low-growing kinds bloom better if they are pruned every year just after the flowering season. Branches that have bloomed should be cut back by half or more. Some of the old canes of larger-growing varieties may be cut back to the ground when the bush gets out of bounds; best time is immediately after the flowers fade.

Recommended: 'Aureus', 'Belle Etoile', 'Buckley's Quill', 'Dwarf Minnesota Snowflake', 'Galahad', 'Glacier', 'Goose Creek', 'Minnesota Snowflake', 'Natchez', 'Virginal'.

PHLOMIS
Jerusalem Sage
PERENNIAL, ZONE 7

This rather unusual plant produces a rounded thicket of upright stems, from $2\,^1/_2$ to 4 feet tall, each stem punctuated with whorls of yellow or purplish-pink flowers spaced along the stems from base to top. Blooms in late spring and early summer. Cut stems back after flowers fade to encourage repeated flowering.

Plant in spring or fall in a full-sun or lightly shaded location. Will accept a variety of soil types, as long as it is well drained. Moderate water needs. No fertilizer necessary.

Phlomis russeliana

PHLOX

Phlox

ANNUAL, PERENNIAL, OR SMALL SHRUB,
ZONES VARY BY SPECIES

Phlox

From early in the season, when rock gardens miraculously spring into color, until the dog days of August, there is some kind of phlox ready to contribute its share of color to the home garden. Phlox is a large and important plant family, native to North America. The word phlox means "flame" in Greek, and the name is justified by the bright colors of the flowers. Flowers vary in size, depending on the variety, but are usually borne in clusters; some have an eye or star-shaped center of a different color, and some varieties are fragrant. Colors range from magenta, pink, lavender, pale blue, rose, red and white. Creeping kinds are extremely showy in rock and wall gardens, but their 3 $\frac{1}{2}$- to 4-foot-tall cousins are just as eye-catching in midsummer borders. Between these extremes are phloxes 12 to 18 inches tall, some glorying in full sun, while others prefer part shade.

Plant perennial types in spring or fall in a full-sun or lightly shaded location. Annual phlox can be planted from seed or transplants in spring. Prefers a loose, well-drained soil, amended with plenty of peat moss or leaf mold. Keep soil consistently moist, but not wet, throughout the growing season. Fertilize once in spring with a liquid, organic fertilizer, according to label directions. Occasionally bothered by phlox plant bugs, nematodes, powdery mildew, Southern blight. Control with an appropriate insecticide and/or fungicide, following all label precautions.

Cut off all flowers as soon as they fade. In late fall cut all the stalks down almost to the ground and destroy them (helps prevent the spread of mildew and other diseases). Every third or fourth year, in fall or early spring, dig up the clump and divide it into smaller pieces. Plant the outside portions and discard the center.

Recommended: 'Alpha', 'Arrowhead', 'Bruce's White', 'Camla', 'David', 'Delta', 'Dirigo Ice', 'Eva Cullum', 'Franz Schubert', 'Fuller's White', 'London Grove', 'Melrose', 'Miss Lingard', 'Omega', 'Rosalinde', 'Sherwood Purple'.

Phlox 'Norah Leigh'

PHYSALIS ALKEKENGI
Chinese Lantern Plant

PERENNIAL, ZONE 3

The orange-red, papery lanterns produced by this easy to grow, 2-foot perennial are unusual and ornamental enough to tempt anyone to plant it. But be careful! Although hardy and fast-growing, it's too fast-growing for some: It spreads like a weed, by means of long creeping underground stems that can take over any area. The bright seed pods hung along the stems are so decorative and long-lasting, however, that if you have plenty of space you might well give up some of it to the Chinese lantern plant. Wait until the lanterns have turned completely orange before you cut them. Alone or with other dried everlastings, they retain their intense color and add a festive touch to harvest-time decorations.

Plant in spring or fall in a full-sun location. Accepts almost any garden soil. Regular water needs. No fertilizer necessary.

Physalis alkekengi

PHYSOSTEGIA
False Dragonhead, Obedient Plant

PERENNIAL, ZONE 2

Physostegia virginiana

This old-fashioned, extremely hardy perennial produces a clump of upright stems, 4 feet tall, with a spread of about 3 feet. Thick spikes of flowers—which look like snapdragons—appear in late summer when other perennials are slowing down. Flower colors include pink, lavender and white. Because it is such a willing grower and spreads so easily, it should not be placed too close to choice plants that could be crowded by it. Good as a cut flower. Dwarf forms are available.

Plant in spring or fall in a full-sun or partially shaded location, about 20 inches apart. Tolerant of any soil type, as long as it is well drained. Regular water requirements. No fertilizer required. Every year or two, dig up the clump in spring, pull it apart, throw away the center and replant the outside pieces immediately.

Recommended: 'Alba', 'Bouquet Rose', 'Summer Snow', 'Variegata', 'Vivid'.

PIERIS JAPONICA

Andromeda, Lily-of-the-Valley Shrub

EVERGREEN SHRUB, ZONE 5

This is a superior evergreen shrub which grows 6 to 10 feet tall, depending on the variety. At its best in woodland settings, most varieties produce brilliant red new growth—so red, the foliage actually looks like flowers. Later in the summer, arching clusters of small white flowers appear and are responsible for this shrub's common name, although its flowers are much more tightly clustered than those of real lily-of-the-valley. The shiny, dark evergreen foliage shows off the white flowers perfectly. If possible, plant lily-of-the-valley shrub where its merits can be appreciated up close.

Pieris japonica 'Brouer's Beauty' (above), *Pieris japonica* flowers (top right)

Plant in spring or fall in a filtered-shade location. Prefers a loose, well-drained, acid soil, amended with plenty of peat moss or leaf mold. Keep soil consistently moist, but not wet, throughout the growing season. Feed once in spring with an acid-forming fertilizer (sold in garden centers as fertilizer for "acid-lovers"), according to label directions. No pruning is needed, but cut off the old flowers before they go to seed.

Recommended: 'Bert Chandler', 'Bright Red', 'Compacta', 'Crispa', 'Forest Flame', 'Karenoma', 'Mountain Fire', 'Snow Drift', 'Spring Snow', 'Variegata'.

PLATYCODON GRANDIFLORUS

Balloon Flower

PERENNIAL, ZONE 3

The buds, not the flowers, of this long-lived, hardy perennial account for its name—they not only look like balloons, but they pop like balloons when pressed between your fingers. Blooming at the height of summer, this 1 ^{1}/$_2$- to 3-foot-tall plant, with a 2-foot spread, is an excellent candidate for the middle ground of a flower border. Plants are well-behaved and stay where they belong without spreading out of bounds. The lavender-blue, open bell-shaped flowers are especially attractive combined with pink and yellow flowers. Double-flowered balloon flowers are available, as well as dwarf ones for rock gardens and the front of a border. Pink and white flowering forms are also available. Balloon flower is a slow starter: It may take two or three years before a clump is at its prime, and it is also one of the last perennials to make its appearance in spring.

Plant in spring in a full-sun or partially shaded location, especially in areas with hot summers. Easy to grow from seed. If planting transplants, set crown of plant right at soil level. Prefers a loose, well-drained soil. Regular water requirements. Fertilize once in spring with a liquid, organic fertilizer, according to label directions. Cut off individual flowers as they fade (not entire stalks). Don't move or disturb the plant, and be careful not to dig around and injure it before it comes up in the spring.

Recommended: 'Baby Blue', 'Fuji White', *P. g. mariesii*.

Platycodon grandiflorus blossom

Platycodon grandiflorus

POLEMONIUM CAERULEUM

Jacob's Ladder

PERENNIAL, ZONE 2

This little-known perennial deserves wider recognition. Plants grow from 9 to 30 inches tall, depending on variety. Lush clumps of finely cut, fern-like foliage produce upright flower stalks in late spring and summer, with loose clusters of bell-shaped flowers, mostly in shades of blue and lavender, some in apricot and yellow. A very attractive, easy-to-grow addition to woodland gardens, it combines well with ferns, hostas and bleeding heart. May self-sow.

Plant in spring or fall in a partially shaded location, about 8 to 12 inches apart. Prefers a loose, well-drained soil, amended with plenty of peat moss or leaf mold. Keep soil consistently moist, but not wet, throughout the growing season. No fertilizer required. When a clump gets too large, dig it up in late summer, separate it into pieces and replant.

Recommended: 'Apricot Delight', 'Blue Pearl', 'Firmament', 'Silver Leaf Form'.

Polemonium caeruleum

POLIANTHES TUBEROSA

Tuberose

<small>TUBEROUS-ROOTED PERENNIAL, ZONE 9</small>

This native of Mexico produces one of the most intensely scented flowers in the plant world. The waxy white, tubular flowers, borne on 2- to 3-foot spikes from July to frost, are particularly fragrant at night. Single-and double-flowered forms are available. A single stem, cut and brought indoors, will perfume an entire room. Although it is not hardy, tuberose can be grown outdoors without any trouble; simply lift the bulb-like, tuberous roots carefully in fall and store in a dry, warm place over the winter. Planting in groups produces the best effect in the garden, preferably where perennials with decorative foliage can help to cover the rather bare stems of the tuberose.

Plant in spring in a full-sun location, after all danger of frost has passed. Prefers a sandy, well-drained soil. Plant in groups of at least three, 2 inches deep and 6 inches apart. Keep soil consistently moist, but not wet, throughout the growing season. No fertilizer necessary.

Recommended: 'The Pearl'.

Polianthes tuberosa

POLYGONATUM

Solomon's Seal

PERENNIAL, ZONE 3

One of the stars of woodland gardens, Solomon's seal sends up gracefully arching, unbranched stems with pointed, oval leaves held out horizontally on either side. Depending on the variety, the stems grow from 3 to 7 feet tall. In late spring and early summer, the plant produces attractive tubular, greenish-white flowers, which dangle from beneath the leaves, spaced along the stem with great precision. Attractive to hummingbirds. Solomon's seal spreads slowly by rhizomatous roots; with enough time, plants gradually form impressive colonies.

Plant in spring or fall in a filtered-shade location. Prefers a loose, well-drained soil, amended with plenty of peat moss or leaf mold. Keep soil consistently moist, but not wet, throughout the growing season. No fertilizer necessary. Recommended: 'Variegatum'.

Polygonatum odoratum 'Variegatum'

POLYGONUM AUBERTII (FALLOPIA)

China Fleece Vine, Silver Lace Vine

EVERGREEN VINE (DECIDUOUS IN COLDER ZONES), ZONE 5

This vine, native to China, is one of the hardest-working plants imaginable. In a single season it can cover an area more than 100 square feet, and do so with very few requirements. In summer and early fall this vigorous plant is a mass of foamy, pinkish-white, fragrant flowers. Useful as a quick screen for wire fences or lattice, or grown horizontally, as a groundcover for banks or hillsides. Even tolerates seaside conditions.

Plant in spring or fall in a full-sun location. Prefers a loose, well-drained soil. Moderate water needs; drought tolerant once established. No fertilizer necessary. Generally pest and disease-free; may be bothered by Japanese beetles where they are a problem. Control with an appropriate insecticide, following all label precautions. Hard pruning—all the way to the ground—in early spring may be necessary to keep this exuberant grower within limits.

Polygonum aubertii

PORTULACA
Mexican Rose, Moss Rose, Rose Moss
ANNUAL, ALL ZONES

This tough annual can be used as a brilliant groundcover, especially on hot, dry, sunny patches where few plants want to grow. Plants grow approximately 6 inches tall with an 18-inch spread and have small, succulent leaves. In late spring, portulaca starts blooming with a profusion of 1-inch, flattened, rose-like flowers in brilliant shades of red, cerise, rose, orange, yellow and white, and just doesn't stop until the first frost in fall. No annual performs quite as well, nor blooms as hard, as portulaca. Often self-sows.

Plant seed or transplants in spring in a full-sun location, after all danger of frost has passed. Accepts almost any soil, even dry, gritty ones. Seed is very fine, so mix it with dry sand and press it into the soil lightly. Moderate water needs. No fertilizer required. In midsummer, portulaca can be sheared back about halfway and fertilized lightly, to encourage a late season show of flowers.

Recommended: 'Afternoon Delight', 'Kariba Mixed', 'Magic Carpet', 'Prize Strain', 'Sundance', 'Sundial Mango', 'Sundial Peppermint', 'Sunkiss', 'Sunglo'.

Portulaca 'Sundial Peach' (above), *Portulaca grandiflora* 'Swan Lake' (top)

POTENTILLA FRUTICOSA

Cinquefoil

PERENNIAL OR SHRUB, ZONE 2

A reliable performer—even in severe Northern climates—potentilla blooms freely all summer long, is neat and slow-growing, and unusually hardy. Some of this family are dwarf perennials with white, crimson or orange-yellow flowers for sunny rock gardens or borders. The shrubby kinds are especially useful in small gardens where they form a compact, 2- to 3-foot-tall (occasionally taller) shrubby plant covered with single yellow flowers like buttercups from early June to October. The small, dense, fern-like leaves are not kept through the winter.

Potentilla atrosanguinea 'Gibson's Scarlet'

Plant in spring or fall in a full-sun location. Accepts most soils, as long as they are well drained. Moderate water needs. Fertilize once in spring with a liquid, organic fertilizer, according to label directions. Generally pest and disease-free, potentilla may be bothered by spider mites in extended periods of hot, dry weather. Control with an appropriate insecticide, following all label precautions. If cosmetic pruning is required, do so in spring.

Recommended: 'Abbotswood', 'Goldfinger', 'Katherine Dykes', 'Klondike', 'Primrose Beauty', 'Sunset', 'Sutter's Gold', 'Tangerine'.

Potentilla fruticosa 'Primrose Beauty'

PRIMULA
Primroses
PERENNIAL, SOMETIMES TREATED AS ANNUAL, ZONE 3

This is a large family of perennials, whose botanical name means "first," indicating their early spring blooming season. An extremely pretty group of flowering plants, primroses require rich, damp soil and a semishaded location in the garden. Think of the coolest coastal regions of the Far West and New England and you'll have a good idea of where primroses are best suited.

Some primroses begin blooming even before the last snow has gone; others appear in April and May. Once the heat of summer arrives, they will abruptly stop blooming and all but disappear from the garden. Many of the species (non-hybrid) forms of primroses have all the charm of wildflowers and come in a splendid array of colors, from yellow, orange and lavender to mahogany, cream, rose and apricot. In some varieties the flowers are carried one to a stem, while in others they appear in a cluster or in tiers along the stem. Leaves grow in a clump at ground level. For maximum show, plant primroses in groups or drifts; they are also lovely when planted in containers.

In general, primroses require cool, moist soil, rich in organic matter, such as leaf mold or peatmoss. In mild-winter climates, plant primroses in late fall or early spring; in cold-winter regions, plant in spring. No fertilizer necessary. Protect newly set-out plants from slugs and snails.

Recommended: 'Concorde', 'Barnhaven', 'Miller's Crimson', 'Pacific', 'Santa Barbara', 'True Blue'.

Primula obconica (above), *Primula japonica* (top)

PRUNUS SERRULATA

Japanese Flowering Cherry

EVERGREEN OR DECIDUOUS SHRUB OR TREE, ZONE 6

These beautiful flowering trees have been cultivated and admired in Japan for centuries. In 1912 the city of Tokyo sent several hundred trees to Washington, D.C., as a goodwill gesture and, ever since, tourists have been making the spring pilgrimage there to see them in bloom.

Among the most colorful and free-flowering of all spring-blooming trees, some kinds of flowering cherries have a broad, spreading form, while others are more upright. The more unusual weeping forms are especially ornamental. No higher than 20 to 30 feet when full-grown. The single or double flowers, white or pink, appear in profusion in midspring, just before or with the leaves; some varieties are fragrant. The double-flowered varieties do not bear fruit. Early-flowering varieties show up best against a background of dark evergreens.

Plant in very early spring or early fall in a full-sun location.

Recommended: 'Akebono', 'Amanogawa', 'Kwanzan' (may be sold as 'Kanzan' or 'Sekiyama'), 'Pink Star', 'Snow Fountains', 'Tai Haku'.

Prunus serrulata 'Sekiyama'

PRUNUS
Flowering Peach

DECIDUOUS FLOWERING FRUIT TREE, ZONE 6

This small ornamental tree, native to the Orient, may not be as popular as the flowering cherry, but it is a lovely tree with dense, rounded growth and plentiful flowers in early spring. Flowers are available in both single and double forms, in shades of pink, white or red. An unusual weeping peach is also available. Attractive in all seasons, the flowering peach grows 15 to 25 feet tall and does not bear fruit.

Spring planting is best in northern areas; in the South, spring or fall.

Recommended: 'Early Double Pink', 'Early Double White', 'Icicle', 'Late Double Red', 'Peppermint Stick'.

Prunus (left), flowering peach blossom (right)

PRUNUS
Flowering Plum

DECIDUOUS FLOWERING FRUIT TREE, ZONE 4

A spring cloud of small pink or white blossoms precedes the foliage on flowering plums, but the primary reason most gardeners grow this tough, compact tree is for its unusual, dark purple foliage. Small fruits follow the flowers and are favored by school children and birds. Because of their compact growth, flowering plums are a good choice for relatively small gardens and make attractive accents for special locations. Flowering plums can endure hot, dry summers

Blossom of Japanese flowering plum

and city growing conditions.

Plant in spring or fall in a full-sun location. Accepts most soils, as long as they are well drained. Regular water requirements. No fertilizer necessary. If suckers come up from the roots, cut them off at once.

PRUNUS GLANDULOSA
Flowering Almond

SHRUB, ZONE 4

No almonds are produced on this dwarf, compact shrub, but its profuse early spring bloom is reason enough for growing it. The little double flowers, pink or white, usually open ahead of the leaves. The flowering branches, studded with bloom, are good for cut-flower arrangements. Because it grows only 4 to 6 feet in height, the flowering almond can be grown in the smallest of gardens, or in containers. Because it typically branches close to the ground, it is best placed in the foreground of beds and borders where it can be easily admired and not crowded.

Plant in early spring or fall in well-drained soil, in full sun or very light shade. Accepts most soils, as long as they are well drained. Regular water requirements. No fertilizer necessary. Little if any pruning should be needed; if necessary, do so just after the flowers fade. Occasionally borers attack branches causing the leaves to wilt. If this happens, cut back the damaged part completely and give the shrub a thorough watering.

Prunus glandulosa

RANUNCULUS

Ranunculus

BULB, ALL ZONES

The showy double and semi-double flowers of ranunculus look almost like small peonies. Each bulb produces multiple stems, from 8 to 24 inches tall, depending on the variety. Available in a wide array of lovely clear colors—yellow, orange, pink, red and white—some have a contrasting center of black stamens. Those labeled "Picotee" have various shades of color on each flower. These tender bulbs are sometimes forced by florists to bloom in the winter. Forced, or

Ranunculus (above), a pink *Ranunculus* (top right)

garden-grown, they make stunning cut flowers. In areas where they are not hardy, they are available as started plants, just like other annuals, for planting in spring. In Zones 8 and 9, plant ranunculus in the fall, along with other spring-flowering bulbs. Whether planted from bulbs in the fall (with the "claws" of the bulbs pointing down), or as transplants in the spring, plant them in rich soil to which plenty of organic soil amendments have been added, in a full-sun location. Excellent drainage is important. No fertilizer is necessary. Protect young plants from slugs and snails. After the bulbs bloom, dig them up and store them in a cool, dry place until the next planting time.

Recommended: 'Bloomingdale', 'Tecolote Giants'.

RATIBIDA

Prairie Coneflower, Mexican Hat

PERENNIAL, ZONE 3

This tough plant, native to the prairies and plains of the southwestern United States, produces somewhat coarse-looking, 2-foot-tall, upright plants and a profusion of daisy-like flowers. Individual plants have about an 18-inch spread when mature. Each blossom has a pronounced center, looking a little like a small pinecone, with a single row of yellow or reddish-brown, drooping petals. A good, low-maintenance perennial for any natural-looking garden, especially in hot, dry regions. May self-sow.

Plant in spring or fall in a full-sun location. Tolerates any well-drained soil. Regular to moderate water. No fertilizer necessary.

Ratibida pinnata

RHODODENDRON

Azalea, Rhododendron

EVERGREEN OR DECIDUOUS SHRUB, RARELY TREE, ZONE 5

Rhododendron

Rhododendrons and azaleas belong in the top rank of flowering shrubs, highly valued for the permanent beauty they bring to home gardens. Azaleas and rhododendrons may be classed together by botanists, but many azaleas lose their foliage in autumn and practically all rhododendrons hold their thick, leathery leaves all year long. Over twenty kinds of rhododendron are native to North America, but many others have been brought from the Himalayas, the Orient and other faraway places. These shrubs are worldwide in origin and have been honored for centuries for their noble forms, handsome foliage and remarkable flowers. In this immense family there are some types as large as trees, while others are small enough for rock gardens. A few varieties are fragrant.

Hybridizers, first in Europe and later in the United States, have devoted a great deal of time and labor to rhododendrons, resulting in the addition of many very fine hybrids. Often these are more desirable than the native kinds and are more adaptable to growing conditions in certain areas.

Rhododendrons grow well in areas where the winters are not excessively cold or the summers unduly dry and hot. They do well in mountainous regions in the Southeast and are very successful in the Pacific Northwest. In the Central States, where both summers and winters are likely to be severe, there is increasing hope that testing will prove the adaptability of certain varieties to that region.

In home gardens, rhododendrons are used as specimen plants, in shrub borders and for screens. Combined with other broad-leaved evergreens they are fine for massing. The heavy, dark green foliage makes a splendid background for smaller perennials and other flowering plants. These shrubs need a somewhat sheltered location with a northern or eastern exposure rather than a southern one. They cannot endure either sharp winds or strong sun in winter. The distant protection of trees is desirable, furnishing high but not dense or continuous shade in summer.

Soil for any member of the rhododendron family should have an acid pH. The surest way to achieve the soil these special plants desire is to mix rotted oak leaves, peat moss and an acid-forming fertilizer (applied according to label instructions) into the soil before planting. For optimum growth, the soil must be consistently moist but well drained. Since the roots are shallow, a 2- to 3-inch mulch of pine needles or peat moss helps to keep the soil cool and damp.

After the soil is prepared, plants in the rhododendron family can be planted in spring or fall. All should be planted with their crowns right at soil level. Water well after planting and, if necessary, provide some artificial shade until the plants have become well established.

Rhododendrons (above), *Rhododendrons* and live oaks (top right)

After flowering, cut off dead flower clusters to keep seeds from forming. No regular pruning is necessary, but any damaged branches may be cut off at the ground in early spring. Fertilize once in spring with an acid-forming fertilizer, according to label directions. Give plants a thorough soaking before winter sets in, especially if fall weather has been dry. In cold-winter climates, a screen of burlap or evergreen branches should be used as winter protection for plants in exposed situations. Leaves rolled up in the winter merely show that the plant is protecting itself from the cold.

Recommended: (Azaleas)—'Chimes', 'Coral Bells', 'Holland', 'Mission Bells', 'Purple Splendor', 'Red Poppy', 'Red Wing', 'Snow', 'Violetta'; (Rhododendrons)— 'America', 'Anah Kruschke', 'Belle Heller', 'Boule de Neige', 'Cheer', 'Cynthia', 'Ignatius Sargent', 'PJM', 'President Lincoln', 'Scintillation'.

ROSA
Rose

DECIDUOUS OR EVERGREEN SHRUB, ZONE 3

It's no contest when it comes to everyone's favorite flower—the rose wins every time. And why not? No flower surpasses the rose for color, superb form and size, and rich fragrance. Flowers range from those scarcely an inch wide to exhibition beauties 6 to 7 inches across. The number of petals in individual blossoms varies from five to more than a hundred. Colors span the rainbow (with the solitary exception of true blue). Among the new varieties are some tinted with lavender, orchid and tan. Perfume is sometimes very pronounced and varied. Plants may be miniatures less than a foot high, stately bushes 3 to 6 feet tall (sometimes more) or climbers that cover the side of a barn.

For practical purposes, roses may be reduced to about half a dozen classes. The long-stemmed, large, shapely flowers so admired for cutting are hybrid teas. These plants grow 2 to 6 feet tall and bloom repeatedly from early summer to late fall. Floribundas are produced both one to a stem and in clusters; they have smaller blooms than hybrid teas, although some are just as well-formed. Bushy and very free-flowering over a long season, floribundas make beautiful hedges. Grandifloras are said to combine the best traits of both hybrid teas and floribundas. Climbers include ramblers

Rosa 'Carefree Wonder' shrub rose

Rosa 'Joseph's Coat'

with small flowers in heavy clusters, blooming in early summer, and large-flowered repeat bloomers. On posts, pillars, trellises and fences they add enormous charm to any garden. Shrub roses are extra hardy but usually not continuous-blooming; many are species forms (non-hybrids) adapted to landscaping like other shrubs. Miniature roses, 8 to 12 inches tall, are excellent in rock gardens, as edgings or in containers. And any desired rose variety may be produced in tree or standard form.

Roses need full sun for at least 6 hours a day, preferably in the morning. As heavy feeders, locate roses where they will have a minimum of competition from nearby shrub or tree roots. Good air circulation is necessary, but exposure to heavy winds should be avoided. As with most plants, drainage is extremely important. Average, fertile garden soil will grow roses, provided it has been amended with plenty of organic soil amendment (compost, rotted manure, peat moss and the like) before the bushes are set out. Do not add fertilizer to the beds until after the roses have been planted,

so each plant can receive individual attention.

In coldest regions, plant roses in early spring; in most other areas, either spring or fall planting is successful. Container-grown roses can be planted at practically any time.

Prune bush roses as the leaf buds start to burst in early spring. Cut out dead branches and weak twigs; also shorten the main canes and eliminate overlapping ones. On ramblers cut back the older canes after the blooming period. Ever-blooming climbers need less pruning; simply cut back the dead flowers to the first leaf bud.

Keep soil consistently moist (like that of a squeezed-out sponge), but not wet, throughout the growing season. Prevent weeds from growing and keep the soil moist by providing it with a 2-inch-thick mulch of shredded leaves, compost, or other locally available organic material.

In early spring scatter some rose fertilizer around the bushes, according to label instructions, and follow with a deep watering. Follow up with a second feeding 6 to 8 weeks later. Don't overfeed.

If rose diseases are prevalent in your area, always favor disease-resistant rose varieties. Keep your eye out for the first sign of attack from any insect or disease; pest problems are the easiest to control when they are minor. Great strides have been made in natural, organic pest and disease controls. Responsible gardeners use the most benign controls first, before resorting to stronger, more toxic remedies. Roses play host to a variety of maladies, including aphids, bristly rose slugs, borers, fuller rose beetles, caterpillars, Japanese beetles, rose midges, scale, spider mites, thrips, brown canker, black spot, botrytis blight, powdery mildew or rust. When using any pest or disease control, read and follow directions explicitly.

In cold regions mound the soil around the plants after the first hard frost. Add a cover of evergreen branches or straw if temperatures are likely to go lower then 10 degrees below zero. Uncover gradually the next spring as new growth begins.

Rosa 'Chrysler Imperial'

RUDBECKIA HIRTA
Gloriosa Daisy

ANNUAL, ALL ZONES; PERENNIAL, ZONE 3

The gloriosa daisy is a very satisfying, easy-to-grow plant, producing masses of cheerful flowers that practically shout "summer." Especially attractive in the landscape when planted in masses, gloriosa daisies also make excellent cut flowers. Flowers are long-lasting, big, sunshine-colored daisies with broad petals, carried on sturdy stems. Most varieties grow in the 2- to 4-foot-tall range, with a spread of 2 feet or so. One exception is the old-fashioned hybrid 'Golden Glow', which grows to more than 6 feet tall with a 4-foot spread. All gloriosa daisies bloom from late summer into fall; perennial varieties are long-lived in the garden. Particularly well adapted to regions with hot, dry summers.

Plant in spring or fall in a full-sun location, about 24 inches apart. Prefers a loose, well-drained soil. Regular to moderate water needs. No fertilizer necessary. Occasionally bothered by brown ambrosia aphids, leafhoppers, powdery mildew or rust. Control with an appropriate insecticide or fungicide, following all label directions.

Recommended: (*R. fulgida*)—'Goldsturm'; (*R. lanciniata*)—'Golden Glow'.

Rudbeckia 'Sonora'

Rudbeckia hirta 'Becky Mix'

SALIX DISCOLOR

Pussy Willow

SHRUB OR SMALL TREE, ZONE 4

Salix discolor

This fast-growing, vigorous shrub deserves a place in more home gardens, just for the sake of having branches to cut for indoor arrangements. Left alone in the garden, pussy willows may reach 20 feet tall, but can be contained much lower with judicious pruning. Bare-looking branches can be brought indoors as early as January, where the warmth will force the familiar, fuzzy catkins into being. It will last several weeks as a cut "flower."

Set plants in the garden in either spring or fall, packing the soil around the roots; water regularly until established. Pussy willows need full sun and fairly moist soil; will tolerate "wet feet." No fertilizer required. It's not unusual for cut branches to produce

roots while in a vase; any rooted cuttings can be transplanted into the garden. Every third or fourth spring, pussy willows should be pruned to within 3 feet or so from the ground to produce the maximum number of catkin-bearing branches.

SALPIGLOSSIS

Painted Tongue

ANNUAL, ALL ZONES

All gardeners should grow salpiglossis at least once, if for no other reason than to see just how intricately patterned and painted a flower can be. Because its form is not especially attractive, salpiglossis doesn't find its way into many beds or flower borders; old-time gardeners relegated it to the cutting garden and admired the long-lasting flowers in arrangements, rather than in the garden. Clusters of graceful, petunia-shaped flowers come in shades of maroon, purple, blue and scarlet, penciled and veined in blended colors, and reach the height of their bloom in July and August. The $2 \frac{1}{2}$- to 3-foot plants like good soil, a location in sun or part shade and a cool growing season with not too much moisture. Plant in spring when all danger of frost has passed. Space plants 6 to 9 inches apart. Pinch out the growing tips of young plants to increase bushiness. Tall kinds may require staking—or better yet, a place sheltered from summer storms. Fertilize once or twice during the growing season with a liquid, organic fertilizer, according to label directions.

Recommended: 'Bolero', 'Friendship', 'Splash'.

Salpiglossis sinuata 'Splash'

SALVIA

Scarlet Sage, Sage

ANNUAL, BIENNIAL, PERENNIAL, SHRUB, ZONES VARY WIDELY

Plant in spring or fall in a full-sun location. Prefers a loose, well-drained soil. Regular water requirements. Fertilize once in spring with a liquid, organic fertilizer, according to label directions.

Recommended: 'Allen Chickering', 'Argentina Skies', 'Blue Hill', 'Brenthurst', 'Dara's Choice', 'East Friesland', 'Figueroa', 'Haematodes', 'Huntington', 'Lady in Red', 'Lubeca', 'May Night', 'Mina', 'Point Sal', 'Purple Rain', 'Rose Queen', 'Turkestanica', 'Victoria', 'Winifred Gilllman'.

Salvia farinacea 'Strata'

Salvia splendens 'Bonfire'

This huge family not only includes some of the all-time favorite flowering plants, but several culinary herbs, as well. Perhaps the best known salvia is the annual salvia splendens, with its familiar spikes of summerlong, scarlet-red flowers. When you move into the perennial forms of salvia, the predominant flower color changes from red to brilliant blue. Two of the best known, blueflowering perennial salvias are *salvia farinacea*, and *S. patens*. And then there is the silver sage, the pineapple sage, autumn sage, purple sage, gentian sage . . . you get the picture. The sage family is a wonderful one for gardeners to explore, especially since its members are so easy to grow.

Sanguinaria
Bloodroot

Perennial, Zone 4

Native to North America, this elegant woodland plant is gradually finding its way into more home gardens. Deeply lobed, gray-green leaves produce 8-inch-tall flower stalks in spring, topped with $1 \frac{1}{2}$-inch white or pinkish single flowers. The essence of simplicity and beauty, bloodroot is most at home in semi-shaded woodland or wildflower gardens. When the stems of this plant are cut, a reddish-orange juice flows out, hence the common name. Foliage goes dormant by mid- to late summer.

Plant in spring or fall in a filtered-sun location. Prefers a loose, well-drained soil, amended with plenty of peat moss or leaf mold. Keep soil consistently moist, but not wet, throughout the growing season. No fertilizer necessary.

Recommended: 'Multiplex'.

Sanguinaria

Sanguinaria canadensis

SANTOLINA CHAMAECYPARISSUS
Lavender Cotton
LOW-GROWING SHRUB, ZONE 6

If you're looking for a low-growing, tidy plant, with finely textured gray-green foliage, santolina is the answer. Santolina produces dense, shrubby plants, to 2 feet tall with a slightly wider spread, but, because they take well to shearing, they can easily be kept to half that height. A favorite for use as a low-growing hedge around formal flower and herb gardens. If left unsheared, santolina sports a multitude of small, button-like, bright yellow flowers in in summer. The foliage is aromatic and easily dried, traits much appreciated

A bed of *Santolina*

Santolina chamaecyparissus

by those making winter arrangements.

Plant in spring or fall in a full-sun location with good air circulation. Prefers a loose, well-drained, even sandy, soil. Moderate water needs. Fertilize once in spring with a liquid, organic fertilizer, according to label directions. Prune after flowering to encourage fresh new growth. Does best in dry climates. Winter mulch is beneficial. In optimum conditions, rarely bothered by pests or diseases; in humid, damp situations, subject to rot and fungus diseases. Control with an appropriate fungicide, following all label precautions.

Recommended: 'Lemon Queen', 'Nana'.

SAPONARIA OFFICINALIS
Bouncing Bet, Soapwort
PERENNIAL, ZONE 4

Saponaria officinalis

Saponaria is a tough plant, growing to 2 feet tall, with dark green foliage. Spreads by underground runners. In midsummer, clusters of red, pink or white flowers are produced in profusion, with a clove-like fragrance, especially at night. Although this plant can be invasive, it's just the thing for difficult, out-of-the-way locations, tumbling over rock wall or banks.

Plant in spring or fall in a full-sun location. Grows in any well-drained soil. Moderate water needs. Does not require fertilizer. Cut back hard after flowering to encourage new growth and repeat bloom.

Recommended: 'Alba', 'Rosea Plena', 'Rubra Plena', 'Splendens'.

SCABIOSA CAUCASICA
Pincushion Flower
PERENNIAL, ZONE 3

This hard-working perennial grows from 1 $^1/_2$ to 3 feet tall, with an 18-inch spread. Foliage is gray-green. Attractive, 2- to 3-inch flowers appear in midsummer and continue blooming right up until frost, mostly in shades of blue, lavender and white. Make excellent cut flowers because of their strong, 2-foot stems and long-lasting quality. In bouquets they combine well with spikes of larkspur and snapdragon.

Plant in early spring in a full-sun location, about 15 inches apart, preferably in groups of three or more. Demands a loose, well-drained soil with a neutral pH; plant so that the crown of the plant is just at soil level. Moderate water needs. Fertilize once in spring with a liquid, organic fertilizer, according to label directions. Always cut off the flowers before they can go to seed. If they get straggly after a few years, dig up the clump in the spring, separate it into smaller parts and replant.

Recommended: 'Ace of Spades', 'Blue Perfection', 'Butterfly Blue', 'Fama', 'Salmon Queen'.

Scabiosa caucasica

SCHLUMBERGERA BRIDGESII

Christmas Cactus, Thanksgiving Cactus

TENDER SHRUB, ALL ZONES (AS AN INDOOR/OUTDOOR PLANT)

Christmas cactus is a popular houseplant with jointed stems and scarlet flowers from about November to January. The exotic, multi-petaled flowers are carried at the very tip of the branches, often in great numbers. Plants can become large specimens—more than 2 feet tall with a spread of 3 feet—and live for many years.

Once all danger of frost has passed, move your Christmas cactus outdoors for the summer. Leave it in its pot and find a sheltered spot with filtered sunlight. Moderate water needs during the summer. Feed monthly with a diluted (about one-half strength) solution of liquid fertilizer. Bring the plant indoors before cold weather, and let it stay rather dry for a month to 6 weeks to help trigger its winter bloom season. Keep soil evenly moist while the cactus is in bloom. Indoors, these sturdy plants prefer a sunny window. To start a new plant, cut off a section of a stem and let it dry in the open air for several days, then simply insert it into damp potting soil. Cutting will produce roots in 2 to 3 weeks.

Schlumbergera bridgesii

SCILLA SIBERICA
Siberian Squill
BULB, ZONE 3

This spring-flowering bulb blooms early in the season, right when a gardener's spirits are in need of a little lift. From a cluster of narrow strap-shaped leaves, scilla produces several flower stalks, 4 to 8 inches tall, each with three intensely blue flowers. A real knockout when planted in large, natural-looking drifts in woodland settings.

Plant scilla in fall about 2 to 3 inches deep and 4 inches apart. Best in a filtered-shade location and in a loose, well-drained soil, enriched with plenty of peat moss and leaf mold. Keep soil consistently moist during the growing season. Leave foliage to die down naturally. Scilla are best left undisturbed to establish themselves.

A small planting of *Scilla siberica* (above), *Scilla siberica* (top)

Sedum

Stonecrop

SUCCULENT PERENNIAL, ZONE 3

This very large family of easy-to-grow plants includes many home garden favorites. The sedum family is so diverse, however, that beyond a few basic generalizations, all that can be truthfully said is that it is a group of rugged "individualists." The foliage of sedum plants is unusually thick, smooth and fleshy; and in some varieties it is decidedly gray or bluish, often tinted pink or purple or edged with lighter green. Many kinds, including the popular *sedum spurium* 'Dragon's Blood', are evergreen trailers, forming carpets of delightful, thick leaves covered with bloom in their season. Leaves may be in rosettes or on longer, arching stems. These plants are very hardy, and probably nothing is easier to establish in a garden. In fact, some members of the tribe are a nuisance because they crowd out everything else. The low growers make a fine carpet in sunny rock gardens and are easily grown between paving blocks and in pockets in a stone wall. Very easy to grow, these plants may be started at practically any season.

Taller kinds, with upright growth from 18 to 30 inches, with a similar spread, are epitomized by the very popular *sedum telephium* 'Autumn Joy'. With dense, spreading growth and blunt, fleshy leaves, these sedums produce masses of large, tight clusters of very tiny flowers in shades of pink and rose. Bloom is over a long period from late summer through fall.

All sedums require a full-sun location. They can tolerate almost any soil type, as long as it has perfect drainage. Sedums can stand dry conditions better than most plants. No fertilizer is necessary. Tall varieties may require dividing and replanting if they grow too large. In general, sedums are remarkably free of pests and diseases, but may occasionally be bothered by aphids, scale, root rot or Southern blight. Control with an appropriate insecticide or fungicide, following all label directions.

Sedum 'Autumn Joy'

SIDALCEA

Checkerbloom, Miniature Hollyhock

PERENNIAL, ZONE 5

Sidalcea malviflora 'Party Girl'

Sidalcea malviflora planted with phlox

These wildflowers—which have received a lot of attention from plant breeders lately—deserve wider popularity. Think of a short, thinner, more graceful version of hollyhock, and you'll have a good idea of what sidalcea looks like. From a low clump of rounded leaves, 2- to 3-foot-tall flower spikes emerge in early summer. Flowers, 1 to 2 inches across, stud the stems, in rich shades of red and pink. Best when planted in naturalized areas in large groups.

Plant in spring or fall in a full-sun or partially shaded location, particularly in hot-summer regions. Prefers a loose, well-drained soil. Regular water needs. No fertilizer required. Divide clumps every 2 or 3 years.

Must have good winter drainage. Particularly susceptible to Japanese beetles. Cut back faded flower stems for repeat bloom. Staking may be necessary. Does best in cool, dry climates.

Recommended: 'Elsie Heugh', 'Loveliness', 'Party Girl.'

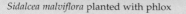

SMILACINA
False Solomon's Seal
PERENNIAL, ZONE 3

Native to woodlands across much of North America, false Solomon's seal is one of those wild plants with natural elegance. It produces single, arching stems from 1 to 3 feet tall, with matching pairs of pointed leaves on either side of the stem. In spring, fluffy clusters of fragrant, ivory flowers appear at the ends of the stems, followed by purple-spotted, red berries in the fall. Leaves of false Solomon's seal turn yellow in fall.

Plant in spring or fall in a partially shaded location. Prefers a loose, well-drained soil, amended with plenty of peat moss or leaf mold. Keep soil consistently moist, but not wet, throughout the growing season. No fertilizer required.

Smilacina racemosa and ostrich fern (above), delicate *Smilacina racemosa* flowers (top)

SOLIDAGO

Goldenrod

PERENNIAL, ZONE 4

Goldenrod just can't seem to get past the incorrect notion that its flowers cause hay fever—they don't. And, yes, a few of the more than 100 species of goldenrod are rather unruly weeds, but what large family doesn't have a few less-than-respected members? Largely due to the efforts of European plant breeders, new, improved cultivars of goldenrod are appearing in our garden centers and catalogs, so perhaps the tide will finally turn in favor of this easy-to-grow, good-looking perennial. Most newer varieties grow in the 2-foot range with a similar spread; others may grow to 5 feet or more. Foliage is medium green and finely cut; plume-shaped clusters of tiny golden yellow flowers appear in mid- to late summer, in great profusion. As beautiful in traditional flower borders as it is naturalized in a meadow planting.

Plant in spring or fall in a full-sun location. Prefers a loose, well-drained soil. Moderate water needs. Fertilizer not necessary.

Recommended: 'Fireworks', 'Golden Fleece', 'Golden-mosa', 'Golden Thumb', 'Cloth of Gold', 'Strahlenkrone'.

Solidago rugosa 'Fireworks', *Solidago* 'Goldstrahl' (inset)

SPIGELIA

Indian Pink, Pinkroot

PERENNIAL, ZONE 6

Native to woodlands in the southeastern portion of the U. S., spigelia has retained all of its innocent charm. Growing 1 to 2 feet tall, it produces thin stems topped with upward-facing, trumpet-shaped flowers—remarkably, yellow on the inside and red on the outside. Bloom season is early summer. Equally beautiful in formal flower borders or naturalized in woodland settings. Best planted in groups of seven or more. All parts of the plants are poisonous if eaten.

Plant in spring or fall in a partially shaded location; protection from hot afternoon sun is important. Prefers a loose, well-drained soil, amended with plenty of peat moss or leaf mold, with a slightly acid pH. Keep soil consistently moist, but not wet, throughout the growing season. Fertilize once in spring with an acid-forming fertilizer (sold in garden centers as fertilizer for "acid-lovers").

Spigelia marilandica (left), flower close-up (right)

SPIRAEA
Spiraea Bridal Wreath
DECIDUOUS SHRUB, ZONE 3

Popular among generations of home gardeners, today's spiraea continues to embody old-fashioned charm. These sturdy shrubs fall in the medium-height class and are of the easiest culture, lasting many, many years. They are completely hardy and have attractive foliage even when not in bloom. Two very different types of spiraea exist: the so-called "bridal wreath" type, which grows to 6 feet tall with an equal spread, producing elegantly arching stems completely covered with tiny white blossoms in spring, and the shrub types, represented by the popular 'Anthony Waterer' variety, growing between 2 and 3 feet tall, with an equal spread, producing upright stems topped with tight clusters of tiny pink, red or white flowers in summer.

Plant in spring or fall in a full-sun or lightly shaded location. Accepts most any garden soil, as long as it is well drained. Moderate water needs. Fertilize once in spring with a liquid, organic fertilizer, according to label directions. Occasionally bothered by mealybugs (cottony white insects) or whiteflies. Cut away any dead branches in early spring. If the plants start to get out of bounds, trim them after the blooming period. Try to retain the natural shape of the plant, and allow new shoots to grow up to replace the older ones.

Recommended: 'Anthony Waterer', 'Coccinea', 'Crispa', 'Dolchica', 'Goldflame', 'Grefsheim', 'Limemound', 'Little Princess', 'Magic Carpet', 'Neon Flash', 'Shirobana', *S. japonica* var. *albiflora*, 'Snowmound'.

Spiraea

SPREKELIA

Aztec Lily, Jacobean Lily, St. James Lily

BULB, ZONE 8

This bulb, a native of Mexico, produces narcissus-like foliage and then, in summer, 1-foot-tall stems topped with graceful, velvety crimson flowers that look more like an orchid than a lily. If planted in the ground, they look best in natural-looking drifts. Because they are tender, most gardeners opt for growing sprekelia in containers.

If grown in containers, fill the containers with a lightweight soil mix, and plant bulbs, 5 inches deep, in early spring. Place the containers in a warm, sunny, protected location; water regularly and feed monthly with a complete liquid fertilizer, mixed at one-half the recommended strength. Enjoy the plants while they are in bloom; after flowers fade, gradually taper off on water and let the foliage die down naturally. Move the pots to a dry, cool location for the winter. They need not be repotted every year. Move back outdoors the following spring and begin watering and fertilizing again.

In mild-winter regions, plant sprekelia bulbs in the garden, as soon as the soil has warmed, in late spring. Choose a full-sun location. Prefers a loose, well-drained soil, amended with plenty of peat moss or leaf mold. Keep soil consistently moist, but not wet, throughout the growing season. Fertilize

Sprekelia formosissima

monthly with a liquid, organic fertilizer, at one-half the recommended strength. After flowers fade, let foliage die down naturally. No need to lift the bulbs, as long as your climate is relatively mild.

Sprekelia

STOKESIA LAEVIS

Stokes' Aster

PERENNIAL, ZONE 5

This perennial, native to the Southeastern United States, deserves wider popularity. Very easy to grow, stokesia is a valuable addition to late summer borders, where it puts forth 10- to 24-inch-tall erect stems sporting 3-inch-wide, multipetaled flowers in shades of blue, pink or white. With its stiff stems, stokesia also makes a good cut flower. Late-flowering annuals make good companion plants.

Plant in spring in a full-sun location, spaced 12 to 15 inches apart. Prefers a loose, well-drained soil, but tolerates even poor soil. Regular water needs. No fertilizer necessary. Where winters are likely to bring alternate freezing and thawing, provide a protecting cover of straw or evergreen branches.

Recommended: 'Bluestone', 'Blue Danube', 'Klaus Jelitto', 'Silver Moon', 'Wyoming'.

Stokesia laevis 'Silver Moon'

Stokesia laevis 'Cyanea'

SYRINGA

Lilac

DECIDUOUS SHRUB, ZONE 3

The longtime popularity of lilacs has as much to do with their dependability as it does their beauty and ethereal fragrance. Lilacs are rapid growers, reaching 10 to 12 feet in height, and carrying their single or double flowers in large clusters in late spring. Colors run from deep reddish-purple through shades of lavender, blue, pink and white. They are perfectly hardy in the northern United States and into Canada. For an informal hedge around a garden, for a screen or as a single specimen plant, there is nothing more enjoyable than lilacs. Blooming at the same time as tulips, the two flowers are often combined for magnificent spring bouquets.

Plant in spring or fall in a full-sun location. Accepts a wide variety of soils, as long as they are well drained, with a nearly neutral pH. No fertilizer is necessary. Generally pest and disease free, lilacs are sometimes bothered by scale. Control with an appropriate insecticide, following all label precautions.

Cut off all dead flowers so that seed cannot form. In order to keep the bush from growing so tall that you cannot see or reach the flowers, cut out weak shoots and most of the suckers that grow around the base of the plant. If all the suckers are permitted to grow, the number of flowers will be reduced. If a neglected plant has grown overly tall and lanky, cut it down almost to the ground in early spring, and feed with a complete fertilizer; within two or three years it will have recovered to the point where it will begin blooming again.

Because plant breeders in France worked so hard and accomplished so much in the improvement of the common old-fashioned lilac (*S. vulgaris*), the varieties they created have come to be called "French Hybrids." The flower heads of these hybrids are larger, the color range more extensive and the fragrance pronounced.

Recommended: 'Blue Boy', 'Charles Joly', 'Chiffon', 'Lavender Lady', 'Ludwig Spaeth' 'Miss Ellen Wilmott', 'President Lincoln', 'Sensation', 'William Robinson'.

Syringa vulgaris (above), *Syringa* x *hyacinthiflora* 'Lamartine' (inset)

TAGETES

Marigold

ANNUAL AND PERENNIAL, ZONES VARY BY SPECIES

In the world of annual flowers, marigolds certainly rank near the top in terms of popularity, usefulness and sheer ability to produce great quantities of beautiful flowers. Marigolds are undemanding, always reliable and unceasing in their production of bloom from July until the first hard frosts of fall. In terms of beauty, they can certainly hold their own in a mixed planting with such perennials as hardy asters and chrysanthemums.

Marigolds' familiar cushions of tightly packed petals range from lemon and gold through all the shades of yellow and orange, to brown and mahogany, to nearly white. Some have flowers hardly less spectacular than show chrysanthemums; others are looser-petaled, like carnations; while various kinds have full crested centers surrounded by guard petals. Heights run from dwarf, 6 inches, up to the standard varieties, which can grow to 4 feet. They make good cut flowers; the more you cut, the more they'll produce. Indoors they are very long lasting as cut flowers.

Plant in spring in a full-sun location. Prefers a loose, well-drained soil. Regular water requirements. No fertilizer necessary. Occasionally attacked by aphids, earwigs, Japanese beetles, leafrollers, leaftiers, slugs, snails, tarnished plant bugs, aster yellows, botrytis blight, Southern blight or wilt or stem rot. Control with an appropriate insecticide or fungicide, following all label directions.

Recommended: 'Aurora', 'Bonanza', 'Galore', 'Golden Gem', 'Guys and Dolls', 'Hero', 'Inca', 'Janie', 'Lady', 'Perfection', 'Snowbird', 'Sophia', 'Ursula'.

Tagetes 'Tangerine Gem' (above), *Tagetes* 'Bonanza Bolero' (top)

THALICTRUM

Meadow Rue

PERENNIAL, ZONE 4

Meadow rue is right at home in woodland gardens. The base leaves are finely cut, and look a little like columbine foliage. In late spring and summer, it sends up 2- to 3-foot-tall flower stems, topped by large, airy clusters of small flowers in shades of rose, lilac, yellow and white. Beautiful when planted in front of a darker background planting.

Also makes unusual cut flowers. For best effect, plant in groups of three or more, allowing 2 feet between them.

Plant in spring or fall in a lightly shaded location. Prefers a loose, well-drained soil, amended with plenty of peat moss or leaf mold. Keep soil consistently moist, but not wet, throughout the growing season. No fertilizer necessary. Occasionally, but not every year, plants may have to be dug up, divided and replanted in spring.

Recommended: 'Hewitt's Double', 'Illuminator', 'Purpureum', 'Roseum', 'White Cloud'.

Thalictrum

THERMOPSIS

Bush Pea, False Lupine

PERENNIAL, ZONE 4

As its common name suggests, thermopsis flowers resemble lupines. These easy-to-grow perennials have silver-green foliage and produce erect stalks, from 3 to 6 feet tall (depending on the species), with about a 3-foot spread. In late spring the stalks are crowned with 12-inch-long spikes of pea-like, yellow flowers, which are good for cutting. Long-lived, thermopsis has deep, drought-resistant roots. Although it spreads slowly, it does spread, so be careful where you plant it.

Plant in spring or fall in a full-sun to partially shaded location. Prefers a loose, well-drained soil, amended with plenty of peat moss or leaf mold; tolerates poor soil. Keep soil consistently moist, but not wet, throughout the growing season. Staking may be necessary with a windy site or when grown in shade. No fertilizer necessary.

Newly budding *Thermopsis caroliniana* (left), *Thermopsis caroliniana* (right)

THUNBERGIA

Black-Eyed Susan Vine, Clock Vine,
Orange Clock Vine, Sky Flower

TENDER VINE, ZONE 9

In mild-winter climates, where they are adapted, these rapid-growing vines scramble to a considerable height on porches and arbors. They are tender, twining climbers that grow wild in the tropics of Asia and Africa. The leaves, pointed at the tip, grow as much as 6 to 8 inches long. Although there is considerable variation between the species, all thunbergias produce very showy flowers—from the pale lavender-blue flowers of the sky flower (*T. grandiflora*), the orange, yellow or white flowers with black centers of the black-eyed Susan vine (*T. alata*), to the intensely orange, tubular flowers of the orange clock vine (*T. gregorii*).

Plant in spring or fall in a full-sun location. Prefers a loose, well-drained soil, amended with plenty of peat moss or leaf mold. Keep soil consistently moist, but not wet, throughout the growing season. Fertilize once or twice during the growing season with a liquid, organic fertilizer, according to label directions.

Thunbergia grandiflora

TIARELLA

Foamflower, False Mitrewort, Sugar-Scoop

PERENNIAL, ZONE 3

These woodland beauties form 6- to 12-inch-tall clumps of lobed leaves, with a slightly larger spread. Late spring sees the arrival of 8- to 16-inch-tall, thin flower spikes adorned with clusters of small white or pinkish flowers. Flowers last for 6 weeks or more. Foliage turns yellow and red in fall. In

Tiarella cordifolia blankets a landscape, flowers close-up (top right)

a location it likes, tiarella can spread rapidly by underground rhizomes.

Plant in spring or fall in a partially shaded location. Prefers a loose, well-drained soil, amended with plenty of peat moss or leaf mold. Keep soil consistently moist, but not wet, throughout the growing season. No fertilizer necessary.

Recommended: 'Dunvegan', 'Eco Red Heart', 'Oakleaf', 'Slickrock'.

TIGRIDIA PAVONIA

Tiger Flower, Mexican Shell Flower

BULB, ZONE 8

Called tiger flower for its spotted flowers, or Mexican shell flower because of its origin, this tender bulb is grown like gladiolus. The huge blooms are sometimes 6 inches across, on stiff stems 2 to $2\,1/2$ feet tall. They have three large petals of yellow, orange, pink or white, with three smaller spotted ones at the center—a distinctive and unusual combination. Each slender stem produces several buds in a tight cluster. Each flower lasts only one day, but is immediately replaced by another over a period of several weeks from mid-July on.

In late spring, when frost is over, plant in groups of at least five, 4 inches deep and 6 inches apart. Choose a full-sun or partially shaded location. Prefers a loose, well-drained soil, amended with plenty of peat moss or leaf mold. Keep soil consistently moist, but not wet, throughout the growing season. Fertilize every 2 weeks throughout the growing season with a liquid, organic fertilizer, diluted to one-half the recommended strength. Occasionally bothered by spider mites. Control with an appropriate insecticide, following all label precautions. When the foliage dies down, dig up the bulbs and store them in a dry, frost-free place over winter.

Tigridia pavonia

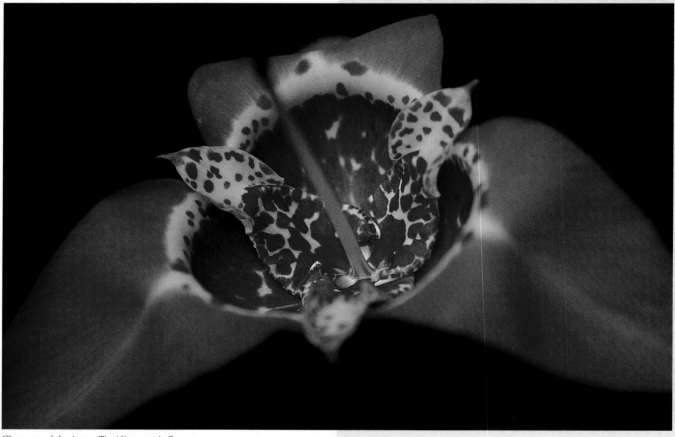

Close-up of the inner *Tigridia pavonia* flower

TITHONIA ROTUNDIFOLIA

Mexican Sunflower

ANNUAL, ALL ZONES

Fast and easy to grow, this is a robust annual with large, coarse leaves. Plants may grow to 6 feet or more, with a spread of 4 feet. Produces wonderful, big, bold daisy-like flowers, 3 to 4 inches across, either brilliant, deep orange or yellow. This plant may be a relic of the ancient civilization of

Tithonia

the Incas, for it is also known as golden flower of the Incas and it grows wild in Mexico and Central America. Because it is so sturdy and tall, it should not be tried in a small garden, but in a large garden for background planting, or where a space filler is needed, it can be very useful. The flowers, blooming in late summer, right through the first frost in fall, are fine for cutting. As an added benefit, both butterflies and hummingbirds love the flowers.

Plant from seed in spring, as soon as all danger of frost has passed. Space plants 3 to 4 feet apart. Tolerates most soil types, as long as soil is well drained. Regular water requirements. No fertilizernecessary.

Recommended: 'Goldfinger', 'Sundance', 'Torch'.

TRACHYMENE COERULEA

Blue Lace Flower

ANNUAL, ALL ZONES

This miniature version of the wild Queen Anne's lace makes a decorative cut flower, excellent and extremely long-lasting as a filler in bouquets. In the garden the soft lavender-blue color is too delicate to call attention to itself. The 2 $1/2$-inch flowers have been called "little lace umbrellas," an apt referrence to their shape and texture. Plants grow about 2 feet tall.

Sow seed in spring where the plants are to stand, and thin to 9 inches apart. Pinch out the tips of young plants to make them branch more.

Plant seeds in spring or fall in a full-sun location; thin seedlings to about 9 inches apart. Pinch out growing tips to produce bushy plants when seedlings are about 6 inches tall. Prefers a loose, well-drained soil. Keep soil consistently moist, but not wet, throughout the growing season. No fertilizer necessary.

Trachymene 'Blue Lace'

TRILLIUM
Wake Robin
PERENNIAL, ZONE 4

Trillium grandiflorum

In early spring, these unusual woodland treasures appear like three-pointed stars on the forest floor. From a clump of foliage, trilliums produce 8- to 24-inch-tall flower stems, each topped with a whorl of three pointed leaves and a single, three-petaled flower, either reddish-maroon, brownish-purple, yellow or white in color. Given the right conditions, trillium will spread slowly, by means of underground rhizomes, establishing an impressive colony.

Plant in spring or fall in a partially shaded, cool location. Plant rhizomes 2 to 4 inches deep. Prefers a loose, well-drained soil, amended with plenty of peat moss or leaf mold. Keep soil consistently moist, but not wet, throughout the growing season. No fertilizer necessary. Foliage goes dormant by late summer.

Recommended: 'Flore-pleno'.

TROLLIUS
Globe Flower
PERENNIAL, ZONE 3

This shade-loving hardy perennial actually succeeds in soil too heavy and damp for many other flowers. Found growing naturally in damp meadows, this 18- to 36-inch-tall plant is slow to spread. Orange and yellow globe flowers, produced in May, June and into July, are like big, waxy buttercups. Flowers are long lasting when cut.

Plant in spring in a full-sun or partially shaded, cool location. Space plants 2 feet apart. Tolerant of a wide variety of soil types. Keep soil consistently moist throughout the growing season. No fertilizer necessary. Remove spent flowers to encourage continued bloom.

Recommended: 'Earliest of All', 'Golden Queen', 'Lemon Queen'.

Trollius 'Golden Queen'

TROPAEOLUM MAJUS
Nasturtium
ANNUAL AND PERENNIAL, ALL ZONES

Very vigorous and dependable, nasturtiums have been loved by generations of gardeners the world over. In borders, beds and window boxes, their red, orange and yellow blooms are always cheery and colorful. Varieties with double and semi-double, fragrant flowers are relatively recent developments. They may be cut freely for informal bouquets, attractive when paired with their own round, light green leaves. Trailing varieties do well when grown on a trellis or allowed to wander down a bank or wall. All nasturtiums need full sun, but hot, sticky summers are not to their liking; They bloom right up until frost.

The seeds are large, and it is easy to space them 10 inches apart when planting. Cover them to a depth of three times their own diameter. Don't plant, however, until frost is over and the ground is warm. They need sun, tolerate most any soil, and should not be given fertilizer (which will produce foliage at the expense of flowers). Occasionally bothered by caterpillars, potato flea beetles, serpentine leafminers or bacterial wilt. Control with an appropriate insecticide or fungicide, following all label directions.

Tropaeolum majus 'Tiptop Apricot' (above), nasturtium as a vine (top)

TULIPA

Tulip

BULB, ZONE 4

One of the most beloved of all garden flowers—the world over—tulips of some kind may be had over a period of about 5 or 6 weeks in the spring, from late April through May. They are the most colorful of all the spring-flowering bulbs, and fortunately they are extremely easy to grow.

There are more than a dozen classes of tulips, some more distinctive than others. Best know are the Darwins with their large cups, 2- to 3-foot stems, and dazzling solid colors at the peak of the tulip season. Breeder tulips are late blooming, with large oval to roundish flowers, on stems up to 3 feet tall. Triumph tulips arrive in midseason

Double tulip (above), *Tulipa* 'Princess Irene' (top)

Tulipa

flowers may begin to grow smaller; if this is the case, dig the bulbs after the foliage has turned yellow, dry them in the shade, and then store them in a cool dry room until fall planting time. Tulips should not be planted repeatedly in the same spot. In the very coldest climates a winter covering of leaves is advisable.

UVULARIA

Bellwort, Merrybells

PERENNIAL, ZONE 4

These elegant-looking perennials are about as graceful as woodland plants can be. Erect stems, about 2 feet tall, arch gently toward the tips. Nodding, narrow, bell-shaped yellow flowers are produced along the stems in spring. Uvularia is most at home in woodland gardens and naturalized settings. Plants spread slowly by rhizomatous roots. Be sure to plant uvularia where their beauty can be admired up close.

Plant in spring or fall in a partially shaded to full-shade location. Prefers a loose, well-drained soil, amended with plenty of peat moss or leaf mold, with a slightly acid pH. Keep soil consistently moist, but not wet, throughout the growing season. No fertilizer necessary.

but are not so tall as the Darwins. Cottage varieties have more slender, light-colored blooms, and lily-flowered have flared, pointed petals.

Parrot tulips are probably the most easily recognized of all because of their twisted, slashed petals flecked green on the outside. Double late tulips are also called peony-flowered because of their shape. Single early and double early varieties are especially good for forcing indoors and for mass planting. Rembrandts, Bizarre and Bybloems are the "broken" tulips with striped and streaked flowers, so popular in the early days in Holland. It is known now that a virus disease is responsible for the breakdown of the colors. Earliest of all tulips to bloom are the species or botanical varieties (non-hybrid forms). These last for many years and are much used in rock gardens.

Plant tulip bulbs in the fall, in a full-sun location in a well-drained soil, improved with plenty of compost or other organic soil amendment. Regular water requirements. Fertilizer is not necessary if the soil is of average richness. In regions with cold winters the best planting time is early October; in milder climates, the bulbs may go into the ground from late October through November. Average planting depth is 6 inches (in very light soil, 8 inches is better), and about 6 inches should be allowed between bulbs. Damage from rodents is avoided by placing the bulbs in a wire enclosure before planting them. Occasionally bothered by aphids, bulb mites, two-spotted spider mites, cucumber mosaic virus or tulip breaking virus. Control with an appropriate insecticide or fungicide, following all label directions.

Tulip bulbs may be left in the ground for several years before being taken up and replanted. Whether lifted or not, allow the leaves to ripen completely—the foliage must never be cut off before it has died down as this is what supplies the nutrients to the bulbs for the following year's growth. After 3 to 5 years in the same location the tulip

Uvularia grandiflora

VERBASCUM
Mullein
BIENNIAL, ZONE 5

Quite unlike any other plants, the *Verbascum* family produces very distinctive plants, most with furry, gray-green leaves. Despite their roadside heritage (many are considered weeds), these are stately plants, worthy of more attention. Especially attractive in rock gardens. Most members of the *Verbascum* family start as big clumps of woolly leaves. By early summer, the clumps will have produced flower stalks, anywhere from 1 to 6 feet tall, covered with shallow, saucer-shaped flowers. Colors range from yellow, purple, pink, cream and white. Most types will self-sow.

Plant in early spring or fall in a full-sun location. Not picky about soil type, as long as it is well drained. Moderate water requirements; drought tolerant, once established. No fertilizer required.

Recommended: 'Album', 'Arctic Summer', 'Letitia', 'Pink Domino'.

Verbascum olympicum

VERBENA
Verbena
PERENNIAL, SOME GROWN AS ANNUAL, ZONE 7

Verbena

Verbenas are hard-working perennials, putting on a profuse, continuous, colorful display of blossoms from June to frost, even in hot, dry places. Individual clusters of flowers are 2 to 3 inches in diameter, available in a wide range of colors, from white through rose to scarlet, lavender, blue and deep violet, some with distinctive white "eyes." Generally low-growing (from 6 to 18 inches tall), verbenas are good for holding a bank or for planting in either a sunny porch box or a rock garden.

Plant in spring in a full-sun location with good air circulation. Prefers a loose, well-drained soil. Moderate water needs. No fertilizer necessary. Occasionally bothered by aphids, spider mites, verbena leafminers, whiteflies or mildew. Control with an appropriate insecticide and/or fungicide, following all label precautions. Cut the plants back after they bloom the first time, to prolong their flowers until October.

Recommended: 'Alba', 'Flame', 'Homestead Purple', 'Romance', 'Showtime Trinidad', 'Sissinghurst', 'Taylortown Red'.

VERONICA
Speedwell

PERENNIAL, ZONE 3

Veronica 'Sunny Border Blue'

The many forms of veronica are attractive in both mixed perennial plantings and rock and wall gardens. These hardy plants range in height from ground-hugging 4-inch-tall varieties, to shrubby, upright growers to 30 inches tall. Widely admired for their flowers in many shades of blue; pink, rose and white varieties are also available. The showy spike form of the flowers makes them good candidates for indoor arrangements. Easy to grow, veronica looks best when planted in groups of three or more.

In rock gardens, low-growing kinds are very useful, with flowers in nesting little spires that give a bit of height. Excellent also as a groundcover, these drought-resistant plants need good drainage. Their scientific name, *Veronica*, is prettier than the common one. Plant in groups of three for a nice effect, in early fall or spring, leaving 12 to 15 inches between plants.

Plant in spring or fall in a full-sun location. Prefers a loose, well-drained soil. Regular water requirements. No fertilizer necessary. Occasionally bothered by chalcedon checkerspot butterflies, foxglove aphids, downy mildew, leaf spot, powdery mildew or rust. Control with an appropriate insecticide or fungicide, following all label directions.

Cut back the flower stalks after the color fades. Every third or fourth spring the tall kinds should be dug up, divided into smaller clumps and replanted immediately.

Recommended: 'Crater Lake Blue', 'Goodness Grows', 'Icicle', 'Minuet', 'Red Fox', 'Sarabande', 'Sunny Border Blue', 'Variegata'.

VERONICASTRUM
Culver's Root, Bowman's Root, Blackroot

PERENNIAL, ZONE 3

This native to the eastern United States grows to an impressive 5 to 7 feet tall, producing a multi-branched, shrubby plant. By mid- to late summer, the ends of the branches produce several 9-inch-long tapered spikes of pale blue, white or pink flowers. Beautiful in woodland settings or at the back of mixed flower borders. May be slow to establish.

Plant in spring or fall in a full-sun or partially shaded location. Prefers a loose, well-drained soil, amended with plenty of peat moss or leaf mold. Keep soil consistently moist, but not wet, throughout the growing season. No fertilizer necessary.

Veronicastrum virginicum 'Roseum'

VIBURNUM
Viburnum

<small>DECIDUOUS OR EVERGREEN SHRUB, SMALL TREE, ZONE 4</small>

Viburnum plicatum 'Newport'

The viburnums are one of the most important of all shrub groups. They are among the basic plants depended on for permanent garden beauty throughout the year, season after season. There are many fine members of the family—including the beloved "snowball" viburnum (*V. carlcephalum*)—each offering something special in the way of plant growth, flowers, foliage or fruit—and most often a combination of several attractive features.

Some are almost tree-like in growth, while others are rather low and compact. Some have foliage that colors brilliantly before it falls; the kinds that lose their leaves are hardy as far north as New England. Others are semi-ever-green, or completely evergreen in the South. All are sturdy and dense growing. Many are planted especially for their red or blue or black berries, which are borne in great abundance. Flowers are a white or creamy white to pinkish, in clusters of varying size and shape but always decorative in May and early June; some are fragrant.

Viburnums give rich returns for a small outlay of labor and expense. They are not at all hard to grow in average garden soil, in the sun or in light shade. They will give satisfaction wherever used.

Plant in spring or fall in a full-sun location. Tolerates a variety of soil types, as long as they are well drained. Regular water requirements. Fertilize once in spring with a liquid, organic fertilizer, according to label directions. Pruning young plants just after they bloom will encourage them to grow bushy. Older specimens need not be pruned every year, but if they get too large, some of the old canes may be cut back to the ground following the blooming season.

Viburnum carlcephalum

VINCA MAJOR AND VINCA MINOR

Myrtle, Periwinkle

PERENNIAL, ZONE 7

In either sun or shade, vincas are very fine evergreen groundcovers, good-looking all year round. The two vincas are very similar in appearance, except that *V. major* will mound to 1 to 2 feet in height, while *V. minor* only grows to about 6 inches tall. In spring, little single blue flowers are sprinkled through the dark, glossy leaves. Vines quickly cover the ground with a neat carpet; anywhere the stems come into contact with the soil, they take root, making them good candidates for keeping a slope from washing away.

Plant in spring or fall in a full-sun location. Prefers a loose, well-drained soil. Keep soil consistently moist, but not wet, throughout the growing season. No fertilizer is necessary. No trimming is necessary.

Recommended: 'Atropurpurea', 'Aureola', 'Bowles Variety', 'Miss Jekyll', 'Reticulata', 'Sterling Silver', 'Variegata'.

Vinca major 'Variegata' (above), *Vinca minor* 'Bowelsii' (top)

VIOLA
Viola, Violet, Pansy

PERENNIAL, SOME TREATED AS ANNUAL, ALL ZONES

Viola cornuta 'Purple Showers'

The viola clan contains some of the most charming members of the flower garden, including pansies, violas and violets. Members of the viola family are very hardy and so easy to grow that they may be used in many places. As a groundcover under shrubs, as an edging along a path, in sun or shade, and as clumps in a rock garden, violas—whatever the variety—are always welcome.

The largest flowered of the viola family are pansies (*V.* x *wittrockiana*). With their velvety-textured flowers, often like charming uplifted faces, in many rich colors and combinations of colors, they are nearly impossible for any gardener to resist.

Even the smallest garden has room for half a dozen pansy plants. In the shade of a doorway shrub they give a friendly touch. With early spring bulbs and perennials they contribute colors that blend with anything. In small arrangements—even in fair-sized ones—pansies are delightful. And the best way to keep plants blooming is to pick the flowers every day.

Cool, early spring weather is the best growing time. Pansies love cool, moist, rich soil and a somewhat shaded spot. The high protection of nearby shrubs or perennials is ideal. It pays to prepare the bed carefully by adding rotted or dried cow manure or commercial fertilizer before planting. Hot summers are harder on pansies than cold winter. They can stand moderate cold if the ground is well drained. Occasionally bothered by slugs, snails or leaf spot. Control with an appropriate insecticide or fungicide, following all label directions.

Recommended: 'Clear Sky Primrose', 'Jolly Joker', 'Lavender Shades', 'Lilac Frost', 'Silver Wings', 'Spanish Sun', 'True Blue'.

Like pansies, the smaller-flowered violas (*V. cornuta*) need rich moist soil. Although long, hot, dry summers are not to their liking, they bloom better in warm weather than pansies do. Set out the plants in early spring, about 4 inches apart, and water well. Pick off the flowers as they fade so that seed does not form and stop bloom production. Cut back the plants lightly in summer, and water thoroughly in hot, dry weather.

It cannot be said too often that pansies and violas must be picked and picked and picked. Once allowed to go to seed, the plants will stop blooming. If plants get leggy in hot weather, cut them back about halfway to encourage another round of flowering.

Recommended: 'Better Times', 'Columbine', 'Etain', 'Mt. Spokane', 'Whiskers'.

Violets (*V. odorata*) are said to be shy and shrinking, but that does not describe them at all. Individual blossoms of wild violets may appear modest; however, the plants are so durable and hardy that one type or another grows wild on every continent except South America, from the Middle East to Japan and Australia. Many of them may be cultivated successfully in semi-wild gardens and in shady spots under trees and shrubs.

Set out the plants in early spring in well-prepared soil, and water deeply. Never let violets suffer from lack of water in summer. Pick the flowers freely.

Recommended: 'Freckles', 'Red Giant', 'Royal Robe', 'White Czar'.

Viola x *wittrockiana* 'Crown Rose'

WEIGELA

Weigela

DECIDUOUS SHRUB, ZONE 5

Popular for its ease of growth, weigela make a vigorous, wide-spreading shrub; standard-sized weigela will grow to 10 feet tall with an 8-foot spread. Thankfully, dwarf forms exist, growing no taller or wider than 4 feet, putting them into the realm of most home gardens. Weigela comes into spectacular bloom in late spring, with the shrubs literally covered with white, pink or rose flowers all along the branches, which sweep to the ground. Foliage remains attractive until it drops in the fall.

Plant in spring or fall in a full-sun location. Accepts almost any soil, as long as it is well drained. Regular water needs. No fertilizer necessary. Severely cold winters may kill some of the canes; if so, prune them back in early spring to renew growth. After the blooming season, cut back some of the older branches and any that are thin and twiggy.

Recommended: 'Bristol Red', 'Candida', 'Foliis Purpureis', 'Java Red', 'Minuet', 'Newport', 'Pink Delight', 'Red Prince', 'Variegata'.

Weigela florida 'Foliis Purpureis' (above), *Weigela florida* 'Rosea' (top)

WISTERIA

Wisteria

DECIDUOUS VINE, ZONE 5

This long-lived, hardy vine is as sturdy as it is decorative. Known chiefly for its beautiful blue, purple, pink or white hanging flower clusters, which on some varieties produce flowers that grow to an astonishing length—20 inches or more. As anyone who has ever seen them in full bloom will tell you, wisteria is an outstanding addition to any home garden. Wisteria grows so vigorously that it must be given plenty of space and very sturdy support. Often they are planted where they can climb over a porch roof. They are twining rather than clinging. They may also be trained into a single-stemmed tree form, beautiful as specimens in lawns.

Big old specimens with thick, twisted trunks often survive even when neglected. Wisteria require only average garden soil and a full-sun location; southern or western exposures are preferable. Feed once in very late autumn, after the leaves have dropped with a complete fertilizer, following label directions. Pruning time is early summer. Cut back the newest shoots as they grow, leaving only three or four buds. If wisteria does not bloom well, harder pruning is necessary.

Wisteria floribunda 'Royal Purple'

XERANTHEMUM

Immortelle

PERENNIAL, GROWN AS AN ANNUAL, ALL ZONES

Xeranthemum 'Rollei'

One of the best flowers for drying, xeranthemum has been largely forgotten by contemporary gardeners. A big producer of star-shaped flowers in shades of pink, lilac and white, it is also a very easy plant to grow from seed. Flowers are produced in late summer on wiry, but strong, 24-inch-tall stems, perfect for arranging.

Plant seed in spring, after all danger of frost has passed, in a full-sun location. Keep soil moist until seeds have germinated. Prefers a loose, well-drained, even sandy soil. Moderate water requirements. No fertilizer necessary.

Recommended: 'Lilac Stars'.

YUCCA FILAMENTOSA

Adam's Needle

PERENNIAL OR SHRUB, ZONE 5

If you're looking for something unusual, Adam's needle may fill the bill. This plant produces a very big cluster of

Yucca filamentosa

stiff evergreen leaves as much as 2 $^1/_2$ feet long, each shaped like a sword, with a sharp spine at the tip. Clusters of creamy white, bell-shaped flowers, fragrant at night, are borne on amazing 6- to 7-foot stalks in July and August. This is not a plant for a small garden where every foot of space is valuable, but it has its place in large plantings as a distinctive accent.

Plant in spring or fall in a full-sun location. Prefers a loose, well-drained, even sandy soil. Moderate water needs. No fertilizer necessary. Cut off the flower stalk when the blooms have faded.

Recommended: 'Bright Edge', 'Concava Variegata', 'Garland Gold', 'Ivory Tower'.

ZANTEDESCHIA

Calla Lily

BULB, ZONE 8

One of the most simple and classic flowers of all, the calla lily has enduring beauty. Although cream-white flowers are by far the most popular, yellow and pink kinds are now available. The flowers bloom in the spring on sturdy, 3-foot-tall stems and are long lasting, both in the garden and in arrangements. The arrow-shaped foliage is produced in a clump, 2 feet tall with a similar spread, lending the garden a lush, tropical look. Some calla varieties have foliage that is spotted or flecked, white or silver.

Plant tubers in spring in a full-sun or partially shaded location, 4 to 6 inches deep. Prefers a loose, well-drained soil, amended with plenty of peat moss or leaf mold. Keep soil consistently moist, but not wet, throughout the growing season. No fertilizer necessary. In cold-winter climates, dig the tubers after the foliage has faded and store in a cool, dry place over winter. Replant the following spring.

Recommended: 'Childsiana', 'Green Goddess', 'Hercules', 'Minor'.

Zantedeschia

ZEPHYRANTHES

Fairy Lily, Zephyr Lily

BULB, ZONE 7

Although not on a par with gladiolus in popularity, this summer-flowering bulb is grown in much the same way outdoors. It needs light, well-drained soil and complete sun. This is a profuse bloomer with grasslike leaves and showy pink, yellow or white flowers on 8- to 10-inch stems.

Plant outdoors in the spring after all danger of frost is past. Set the bulbs about 2 to 3 inches deep and 3 to 4 inches apart. Regular water requirements. No fertilizer is necessary. In warm regions, plant in early fall. Where winters are mild, bulbs may be left in the ground. In cold-winter climates, dig them up after frost and store in sand in a cool, frostproof place over winter. Replant the following spring.

Recommended: 'Alamo', 'Apricot Queen', 'Prairie Sunset', 'Ruth Page'.

ZINNIA

Zinnia

ANNUAL AND PERENNIAL, ALL ZONES

Nothing beats zinnias for a dependable riot of color in the garden all through hot weather and for countless, effortless arrangements for indoors. Easy to grow from seed, zinnias are the beginning gardener's standby. And with new varieties being introduced every year, it is impossible for anyone to become bored with the numerous possibilities they offer.

Zinnias grow quickly and bloom from midsummer to frost. When many other plants are listless in the heat of summer, zinnias are at their best. They are coarse plants—many of them massive—with tough foliage and stiff stems. Some grow as tall as 3 feet, but others are much lower. Flowers, too, vary from immense 5- to 6-inch heads to dainty little buttons. Whatever your need, there's a zinnia to fill it. Both in the garden and in bouquets it is important to combine zinnias with other bold flowers rather than fragile ones.

Plant in spring in a full-sun location. Prefers a loose, well-drained soil. Regular water requirements. Fertilize once or twice during the growing season with a liquid, organic fertilizer, according to label directions. Occasionally bothered by Japanese beetles, mildew or zinnia blight. Control with an appropriate insecticide or fungicide, following all label precautions.

Recommended: 'Border Beauty', 'Burpee California Giants', 'Dreamland', 'Old Mexico', 'Persian Carpet', 'Peter Pan', 'Ruffles', 'State Fair', 'Thumbelina', 'Zenith'.

Zinnia 'Golden Sun' (above), *Zephyranthes candida* (top)

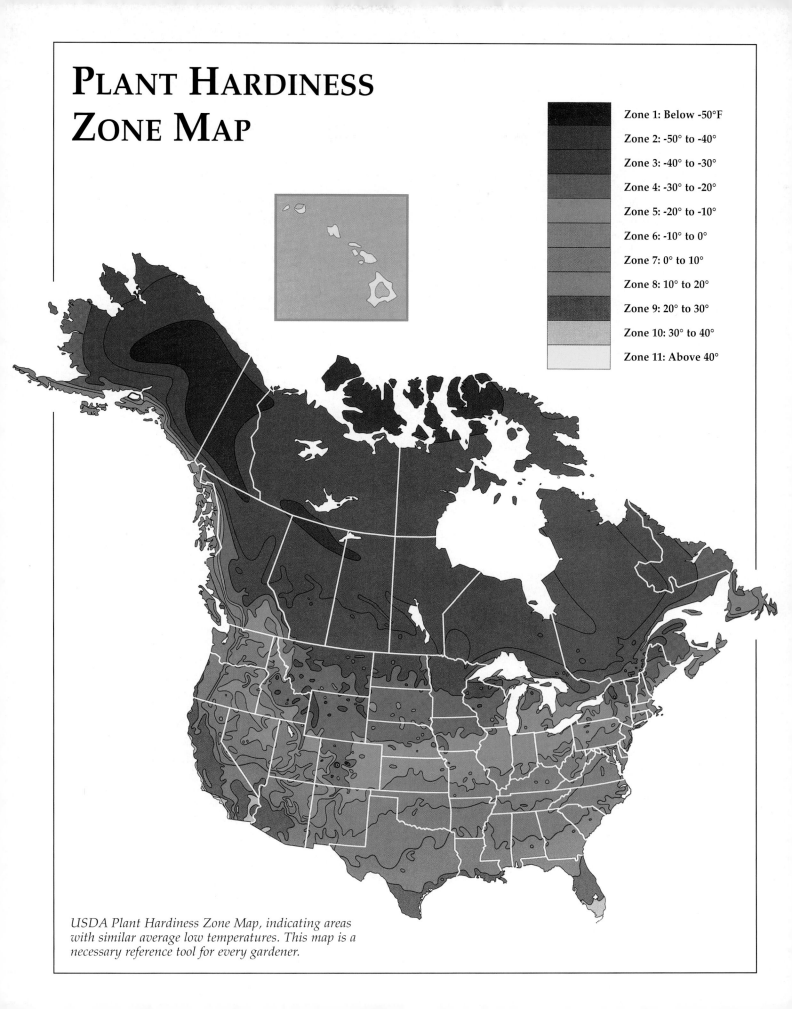

PLANT HARDINESS ZONE MAP

Zone 1: Below -50°F
Zone 2: -50° to -40°
Zone 3: -40° to -30°
Zone 4: -30° to -20°
Zone 5: -20° to -10°
Zone 6: -10° to 0°
Zone 7: 0° to 10°
Zone 8: 10° to 20°
Zone 9: 20° to 30°
Zone 10: 30° to 40°
Zone 11: Above 40°

USDA Plant Hardiness Zone Map, indicating areas with similar average low temperatures. This map is a necessary reference tool for every gardener.

Common Name Cross-Reference Chart

If you know a common name of the flower you're interested in, look it up here. You'll find that name, the flower's botanical (latin) name, and the page you can locate it on. If you can't find what you think is a common name here, that common name might be the same as the botanical name; try the Botanical Name Cross-Reference Chart on page 253.

Aaron's Beard, see *Hypericum calycinum*, page 132

Abelia, see *Abelia*, page 10

Acanthus, see *Acanthus*, page 11

Acidanthera, see *Gladiolus callianthus*, page 119

Adam's Needle, see *Yucca filamentosa*, page 247

African Daisy, see *Dimorphotheca*, page 95

African Daisy, see *Osteospermum*, page 180

Alkanet, see *Anchusa*, page 25

Alyssum, see *Lobularia maritima*, page 151

Amaranth, see *Amaranthus*, page 22

Amaryllis, see *Hippeastrum*, page 127

Andromeda, see *Pieris japonica*, page 192

Anemone, see *Anemone*, page 26

Aster, see *Aster*, page 38

Astilbe, see *Astilbe*, page 39

Autumn Crocus, see *Colchicum*, page 70

Avens, see *Geum*, page 117

Azalea, see *Rhododendron*, page 208

Aztec Lily, see *Sprekelia*, page 226

Baby's Breath, see *Gypsophila*, page 120

Baby Snapdragon, see *Linaria maroccana*, page 147

Bachelor's Buttons, see *Centaurea*, page 57

Balloon Flower, see *Platycodon grandiflorus*, page 194

Baptisia, see *Baptisia*, page 40

Barrenwort, see *Epimedium*, page 99

Basket Flower, see *Hymenocallis*, page 131

Beard Tongue, see *Penstemon*, page 186

Bear's Breeches, see *Acanthus*, page 11

Beauty Bush, see *Kolkwitzia amabilis*, page 139

Bee Balm, see *Monarda didyma*, page 167

Begonia, see *Begonia*, page 41

Belladonna Lily, see *Amaryllis belladonna*, page 23

Bellflower, see *Campanula*, page 51

Bells-Of-Ireland, see *Molucella laevis*, page 166

Bellwort, see *Uvularia*, page 239

Bittersweet, see *Celastrus scandens*, page 55

Black-Eyed Susan Vine, see *Thunbergia*, page 232

Blackroot, see *Veronicastrum*, page 241

Black Snakeroot, see *Cimicifuga*, page 64

Blanket Flower, see *Gaillardia*, page 112

Blazing Star, see *Liatris*, page 144

Bleeding Heart, see *Dicentra*, page 92

Bloodroot, see *Sanguinaria*, page 215

Bluebeard, see *Caryopteris*, page 54

Blue Bottle, see *Centaurea*, page 57

Blue Lace Flower, see *Trachymene coerulea*, page 235

Blue Mist Shrub, see *Caryopteris*, page 54

Blue Spiraea, see *Caryopteris*, page 54

Boneset, see *Eupatorium*, page 104

Bottlebrush, see *Callistemon*, page 47

Bougainvillea, see *Bougainvillea*, page 43

Bouncing Bet, see *Saponaria officinalis*, page 217

Bowman's Root, see *Veronicastrum*, page 241

Bridal Wreath, see *Spiraea*, page 225

Bugbane, see *Cimicifuga*, page 64

Bugloss, see *Anchusa*, page 25

Bush Pea, see *Thermopsis*, page 231

Busy Lizzie, see *Impatiens walleriana*, page 133

Butterfly Bush, see *Buddleia*, page 44

Butterfly Weed, see *Asclepias tuberosa*, page 37

Caladium, see *Caladium*, page 45

Calendula, see *Calendula*, page 46

California Poppy, see *Eschscholzia californica*, page 103

Calla Lily, see *Zantedeschia*, page 247

Calliopsis, see *Coreopsis*, page 74

Camellia, see *Camellia*, page 50

Candytuft, see *Iberis sempervirens*, page 132

Canna, see *Canna*, page 53

Cape Forget-Me-Not, see *Anchusa*, page 25

Cape Marigold, see *Dimorphotheca*, page 95

Cardinal Climber, see *Ipomoea quamoclit*, page 134

Carpet Bugle, see *Ajuga reptans*, page 16

Catmint, see *Nepeta faassenii*, page 171

Checkerbloom, see *Sidalcea*, page 221

Checkered Lily, see *Fritillaria meleagris*, page 110

China Aster, see *Callistephus chinensis*, page 48

China Fleece Vine, see *Polygonum aubertii (Fallopia)*, page 198

Chincherinchee, see *Ornithogalum*, page 179

Chinese Forget-Me-Not, see *Cynoglossum*, page 83

Chinese Lantern Plant, see *Physalis alkekengi*, page 191

Chinese Woolflower, see *Celosia*, page 56

Christmas Cactus, see *Schlumbergera bridgesii*, page 218

Christmas Rose, see *Helleborus*, page 123

Chrysanthemum, see *Dendranthema grandiflorum*, page 88

Cinquefoil, see *Potentilla fruticosa*, page 200

Clarkia, see *Clarkia*, page 65

Clematis, see *Clematis*, page 66

Clock Vine, see *Thunbergia grandiflora*, page 232

Cockscomb, see *Celosia*, page 56

Coleus, see *Coleus* and *Solenostemon*, page 71

Colewort, see *Crambe*, page 78

Columbine, *Aquilegia*, page 31

Coneflower, see *Echinacea purpurea*, page 96

Coral Bells, see *Heuchera*, page 125

Coral Vine, see *Antigonon leptopus*, page 29

Coreopsis, see *Coreopsis*, page 74

Cornflower, see *Centaurea*, page 57

Corn Lily, see *Ixia*, page 136

Cosmos, see *Cosmos*, page 77

Cottage Pink, see *Dianthus plumarius*, page 90

Cranesbill, see *Geranium*, page 115

Crape Myrtle, see *Lagerstroemia indica*, page 140

Crocus, see *Crocus*, page 81

Crown Imperial, see *Fritillaria imperialis*, page 110

Culver's Root, see *Veronicastrum*, page 241

Cup-And-Saucer Vine, see *Cobaea scandens*, page 69

Cup Flower, see *Nierembergia*, page 175

Cupid's Dart, see *Catananche caerulea*, page 54

Cyclamen, see *Cyclamen*, page 82

Cypress Vine, see *Ipomoea quamoclit*, page 134

Daffodil, see *Narcissus*, page 170

Dahlia, see *Dahlia*, page 84

Dame's Rocket, see *Hesperis*, page 125

Daphne, see *Daphne*, page 86

Daylily, see *Hemerocallis*, page 124

Delphinium, see *Delphinium*, page 87

Desert Candle, see *Eremurus*, page 99

Deutzia, see *Deutzia*, page 87

Dogwood, see *Cornus*, page 74

Dusty Miller, see *Artemisia*, page 36

Dutchman's Pipe, see *Aristolochia* Spp., page 134

English Daisy, see *Bellis perennis*, page 42

European Pasque Flower, see *Anemone*, page 26

Evening Primrose, see *Oenothera*, page 178

Fairy Lily, see *Zephyranthes*, page 248

False Dragonhead, see *Physostegia*, page 191

False Indigo, see *Baptisia*, page 40

False Lupine, see *Thermopsis*, page 231

False Mitrewort, see *Tiarella*, page 232

False Solomon's Seal, see *Smilacina*, page 222

False Starwort, see *Boltonia*, page 42

Farewell-To-Spring, see *Clarkia*, page 65

Fiberous Begonia, see *Begonia*, page 41

Flag, see *Canna*, page 53

Flax, see *Linum*, page 148

Fleabane, see *Erigeron*, page 101

Floss Flower, see *Ageratum houstonianum*, page 15

Flowering Almond, see *Prunus glandulosa*, page 205

Flowering Crab, see *Malus*, page 160

Flowering Peach, see *Prunus*, page 203

Flowering Plum, see *Prunus*, page 204

Flowering Quince, see *Chaenomeles*, page 60

Flowering Tobacco, see *Nicotiana*, page 174

Foamflower, see *Tiarella*, page 232

Forget-Me-Not, see *Myosotis*, page 169

Forsythia, see *Forsythia*, page 108

Fountain Butterfly Bush, see *Buddleia*, page 44

Four O'Clocks, see *Mirabilis jalapa*, page 165

Foxglove, see *Digitalis*, page 94

Foxtail Lily, see *Eremurus*, page 99

Fraxinella, see *Dictamus*, page 93

Freesia, see *Freesia*, page 109

Fringe Tree, see *Chionanthus virginicus*, page 61

Fuchsia, see *Fuchsia*, page 111

Fumaria, see *Corydalis*, page 76

Funkia, see *Hosta*, page 128

Gardenia, see *Gardenia*, page 114

Gas Plant, see *Dictamnus*, page 93

Gaura, see *Gaura*, page 115

Gayfeather, see *Liatris*, page 144

Geranium, see *Pelargonium*, page 185

Gerbera, see *Gerbera jamesonii*, page 116

German Catchfly, see *Lychnis*, page 155

German Statice, see *Limonium*, page 147

Gladiolus, see *Gladiolus*, page 118

Globe Flower, see *Trollius*, page 236

Globe Thistle, see *Echinops*, page 97

Gloriosa Daisy, see *Rudbeckia hirta*, page 212

Gloriosa Lily, see *Gloriosa rothschildiana*, page 119

Glory-Of-The-Snow, see *Chionodoxa*, page 62

Goatsbeard, see *Aruncus*, page 36

Golden Chain Tree, see *Laburnum*, page 140

Godetia, see *Clarkia*, page 65

Golden Cup, see *Hunnemannia fumariifolia*, page 129

Golden Marguerite, see *Anthemis tinctoria*, page 28

Golden Ray, see *Ligularia*, page 145

Goldenrod, see *Solidago*, page 223

Golden Trumpet, see *Allamanda*, page 19

Gooseneck Loosestrife, see *Lysimachia clethroides*, page 156

Grape Hyacinth, see *Muscari*, page 168

Grass Pink, see *Dianthus plumarius*, page 91

Guinea Hen Flower, see *Fritillaria meleagris*, page 110

Hardy Amaryllis, see *Amaryllis belladonna*, page 23

Hawthorn, see *Crataegus*, page 79

Heath, see *Erica*, page 100

Heather, see *Erica*, page 100

Helen's-Flower, see *Helenium autumnale*, page 120

Heliopsis, see *Heliopsis*, page 122

Heliotrope, see *Heliotropium*, page 123

Hibiscus, see *Hibiscus rosa-sinensis*, page 126

Himalayan Poppy, see *Meconopsis betonicifolia*, page 163

Hollyhock, see *Alcea rosa*, page 18

Honesty, see *Lunaria biennis*, page 153

Honeysuckle, see *Lonicera*, page 152

Hyacinth, see *Hyacinthus*, page 130

Hydrangea, see *Hydrangea*, page 130

Immortelle, see *Xeranthemum*, page 246

Impatiens, see *Impatiens walleriana*, page 133

Indian Pink, see *Spigelia*, page 224

Indian Turnip, see *Arisaema*, page 33

Iris, see *Iris*, page 135

Italian Bugloss, see *Anchusa*, page 25

Jack-In-The-Pulpit, see *Arisaema*, page 33

Jacobean Lily, see *Sprekelia*, page 226

Jacob's Ladder, see *Polemonium caeruleum*, page 195

Japanese Anemone, see *Anemone*, page 26

Japanese Flowering Cherry, see *Prunus serrulata*, page 202

Japanese Sweet Shrub, see *Clethra*, page 68

Japonica, see *Camellia*, page 50

Jasmine, see *Jasminum*, page 136

Jerusalem Cross, see *Lychnis*, page 155

Jerusalem Sage, see *Phlomis*, page 189

Joe Pye Weed, see *Eupatorium*, page 104

Jonquil, see *Narcissus*, page 170

Joseph's Coat, see *Amaranthus*, page 22

Judas Tree, see *Cercis*, page 59

Kafir Lily, see *Clivia miniata*, page 69

Kalanchoe, see *Kalanchoe*, page 137

Kerria, see *Kerria japonica*, page 138

Lady Bells, see *Adenophora*, page 14

Lady's Mantle, see *Alchemilla*, page 19

Lantana, see *Lantana*, page 141

Larkspur, see *Consolida ambigua*, page 72

Lavender, see *Lavandula*, page 142

Lavender Cotton, see *Santolina chamaecyparissus*, page 216

Lavatera, see *Lavatera trimestris*, page 143

Leopard Plant, see *Ligularia*, page 145

Leopard's Bane, see *Doronicum*, page 95

Leucothoe, see *Leucothoe*, page 144

Lilac, see *Syringa*, page 228

Lily, see *Lilium*, page 146

Lily-Of-The-Nile, see *Agapanthus*, page 14

Lily-Of-The-Valley, see *Convallaria majalis*, page 73

Lily-Of-The-Valley Shrub, see *Pieris japonica*, page 192

Lily Turf, see *Liriope*, page 149

Liriope, see *Liriope*, page 149

Lobelia, see *Lobelia*, page 150

Love-In-A-Mist, see *Nigella damascena*, page 176

Love-Lies-Bleeding, see *Amaranthus*, page 22

Lupine, see *Lupinus*, page 154

Magic Lily, see *Amaryllis belladonna*, page 23

Magnolia, see *Magnolia*, page 159

Mallow, see *Malva*, page 161

Maltese Cross, see *Lychnis*, page 155

Marguerite, see *Chrysanthemum frutescens*, page 63

Marigold, see *Tagetes*, page 229

Marvel Of Peru, see *Mirabilis jalapa*, page 165

Meadow Rue, see *Thalictrum*, page 230

Meadow Saffron, see *Colchicum*, page 70

Merrybells, see *Uvularia*, page 239

Mexican Daisy, see *Erigeron*, page 101

Botanical Name Cross-Reference Chart

> *If you know the botanical (latin) name of a plant, look it up here. You'll find that name, the common name(s) the plant is also known by, and the page you can locate it on.*

Abelia, see Abelia, page 10

Acanthus, see Acanthus and Bear's Breeches, page 11

Achillea, see Yarrow, page 12

Aconitum, see Monkshood, page 13

Adenophora, see Lady Bells, page 14

Agapanthus, see Lily-Of-The-Nile, page 14

Ageratum houstonianum, see Floss Flower, page 15

Ajuga reptans, see Carpet Bugle, page 16

Albizia julibrissin, see Mimosa and Silk Tree, page 17

Alcea rosea, see Hollyhocks, page 18

Alchemilla, see Lady's Mantle, page 19

Allamanda, see Golden Trumpet, page 19

Allium, see Ornamental Onion, page 20

Alstroemeria, see Peruvian Lily, page 21

Amaranthus, see Amaranth, Joseph's Coat, Love-Lies-Bleeding, Summer Poinsettia and Tassel Flower, page 22

Amaryllis belladonna, see Belladonna Lily, Hardy Amaryllis, Magic Lily and Naked Lady, page 23

Ammobium alatum, see Winged Everlasting, page 23

Anaphalis, see Pearly Everlasting, page 24

Anchusa, see Alkanet, Bugloss, Cape Forget-Me-Not, Summer Forget-Me-Not and Italian Bugloss, page 25

Anemone, see Anemone, European Pasque Flower, Japanese Anemone, Pasque Flower, Poppy-Flowered Anemone, Scarlet Anemone and Windflowers, page 26

Anthemis tinctoria, see Golden Marguerite, page 28

Antigonon leptopus, see Coral Vine, Queen's Wreath and Rosa De Montana, page 29

Antirrhinum majus, see Snapdragon, page 30

Aquilegia hybrids, see Columbine, page 31

Arabis, see Rock Cress, page 32

Arisaema, see Jack-In-The-Pulpit, Indian Turnip, page 33

Aristolochia Spp., see Dutchman's Pipe, page 34

Armeria, see Sea Pink and Thrift, page 35

Artemisia, see Dusty Miller, page 36

Aruncus, see Goatsbeard, page 36

Asclepias tuberosa, see Butterfly Weed, page 37

Aster, see Aster, Michaelmas Daisy, New England Aster, New York Aster, page 38

Astilbe, see Astilbe, page 39

Baptisia, see Baptisia and False Indigo, page 40

Begonia, see Begonia, Fibrous Begonia, Tuberous Begonia and Wax Begonia, page 41

Bellis perennis, see English Daisy, page 42

Boltonia, see False Starwort, page 42

Bougainvillea, see Bougainvillea, page 43

Buddleia, see Butterfly Bush, Fountain Butterfly Bush and Summer Lilac, page 44

Caladium, see Caladium, page 45

Calendula, see Calendula and Pot Marigold, page 46

Callistemon, see Bottlebrush, page 47

Callistephus chinensis, see China Aster, page 48

Calluna vulgaris, see Scotch Heather, page 49

Camassia, see Camass and Camassia, page 49

Camellia, see Camellia and Japonica, page 50

Campanula, see Bellflower, page 51

Campsis, see Trumpet Creeper and Trumpet Vine, page 52

Canna, see Canna and Flag, page 53

Caryopteris, see Blue Mist Shrub, Bluebeard and Blue Spiraea, page 54

Catananche caerulea, see Cupid's Dart, page 54

Celastrus scandens, see Bittersweet, page 55

Celosia, see Cockscomb and Chinese Woolflower, page 56

Centaurea, see Bachelor's Buttons, Blue Bottle, Cornflower and Ragged Robin, page 57

Centranthus ruber, see Red Valerian, page 58

Cercis, see Redbud and Judas Tree, page 59

Chaenomeles, see Flowering Quince, page 60

Chionanthus virginicus, see Fringe Tree, page 61

Chionodoxa, see Glory-Of-The-Snow, page 62

Chrysanthemum coccineum, see Painted Daisy and Pyrethrum, page 62

Chrysanthemum frutescens, see Marguerite and Paris Daisy, page 63

Chrysanthemum maximum, see Shasta Daisy, page 63

Cimicifuga, see Bugbane and Black Snakeroot, page 64

Clarkia, see Clarkia, Farewell-To-Spring, Godetia and Mountain Garland, page 65

Clematis, see Clematis, Old Man's Beard, Traveler's Joy and Virgin's Bower, page 66

Cleome hasslerana, see Spider Flower, page 67

Clethra, see Japanese Sweet Shrub, Pepperbush, Summersweet and Sweet Pepperbush, page 68

Clivia miniata, see Kafir Lily, page 69

Cobaea scandens, see Cup-And-Saucer Vine, page 69

Colchicum, see Meadow Saffron and Autumn Crocus, page 70

Coleus, see Coleus, page 71

Consolida ambigua, see Larkspur, page 72

Convallaria majalis, see Lily-Of-The-Valley, page 73

Coreopsis, see Coreopsis and Calliopsis, page 74

Cornus, see Dogwood, page 74

Corydalis, see Fumaria, page 76

Cosmos, see Cosmos, page 77

Cotinus coggygria, see Smoke Tree and Purple Fringe Tree, page 78

Crambe, see Colewort and Sea Kale, page 78

Crataegus, see Hawthorn, page 79

Crocosmia, see Montbretia, page 80

Crocus, see Crocus, page 81

Cyclamen, see Cyclamen, page 82

Cynoglossum, see Chinese Forget-Me-Not, page 83

Dahlia, see Dahlia, page 84

Daphne, see Daphne, page 86

Delphinium, see Delphinium, page 87

Dendranthema grandiflorum, see Chrysanthemum, page 88

Deutzia, see Deutzia, page 89

Dianthus barbatus, see Sweet William, page 90

Dianthus plumarius, see Cottage Pink, Grass Pink and Pink, page 91

Dicentra, see Bleeding Heart, page 92

Photo Credits

David Cavagnaro: pp. cover, 1, 21, 25, 34, 35, 47 both, 63, 89, 92, 93, 95, 97, 98 both, 129, 134, 155, 156 both, 158, 169, 186, 189, 204-205, 205, 215, 221, 222 both, 230, 231, 239, 255; **Dency Kane:** pp. 2, 3(3), 4, 6, 7(2), 10, 11, 12, 13, 16 both, 18, 19, 22, 25, 26 both, 27 both, 30, 31 both, 32, 33, 36, 37, 38, 39, 40, 42 both, 43, 45, 46, 49, 51, 52, 54, 55, 58, 59, 62, 64 both, 66, 68, 69 both, 70, 73, 75, 77, 78, 85, 86, 89, 91 both, 92, 96 both, 99, 100, 102, 104, 108 both, 110 both, 113, 115 both, 116, 120, 121, 124, 125 both, 126, 128, 130, 131, 132, 135, 136, 137, 140, 142 both, 143, 144, 145, 146 both, 147, 148, 149, 150 both, 151, 152, 155, 157, 159, 160(2), 162, 167, 169, 170, 175, 178, 179 both, 182, 183, 185, 187, 188, 189, 190 both, 191 both, 192-193, 193, 195, 197, 200 both, 201 both, 202, 207(2), 208, 210, 212 both, 213, 214, 217, 223, 224, 225, 227, 228 both, 229, 231, 232-233, 233, 236, 237, 238, 242, 243, 244 both, 245 both, 246, 252; **Bill Adams:** pp. 3(5), 6, 7, 14, 15, 17, 19, 22, 23, 29 both, 30, 35, 36, 37, 38, 39, 41 both, 44 both, 46, 48, 50, 51, 53, 54, 56 both, 57, 61, 65, 66, 67 both, 71, 72, 74, 77, 78, 79, 80, 83, 84, 84-85, 87, 94 both, 102, 103, 105, 107, 111, 114, 118, 119, 120, 121, 122, 123, 126, 127, 128, 132, 133, 134, 135, 139, 141, 143, 144, 145, 147, 153, 154, 157, 159, 161 both, 163 both, 165 both, 166, 172-173, 173, 174, 177 both, 178, 183, 184, 185, 188, 194 both, 196, 199, 203 both, 206-207, 208, 209, 211 both, 213, 226, 227, 229, 232, 234 both, 235 both, 238, 240, 241 both, 246, 247, 248, 252; **Joseph DeSoise:** pp. 6, 12, 20, 33, 59, 60, 61, 74, 74-75, 81, 105, 111, 112-113, 119, 123, 130, 138, 140, 159, 160, 168, 174, 180, 181, 184, 219, 220, 239, 240, 242, 247, 248; **Bill Johnson:** pp. 11, 13, 17, 34, 40, 55, 72, 73, 79, 82, 88 both, 107, 117, 138, 166, 175, 176, 218, 243; **Saxon Holt:** pp. 14, 28, 83, 90, 139, 216, 221; **Rosalind Creasy:** pp. 20, 21, 63, 70, 80, 101 both, 216; **Netherland Flower Bulb Information Center:** pp. 23, 49, 76, 99, 109, 136, 168, 219, 226; **Walter Chandoha:** pp. 24, 62, 95, 122, 127, 131, 137, 171, 198, 215, 236; **Amy Sumner:** pp. 57, 81, 106, 237; **National Garden Bureau:** pp. 133, 174, 199; **NAOG Garden Archive:** p. 141; **Derek Fell:** pp. 164, 180; **All-America Selections:** p. 214; ©**Kate Boykin:** p. 224.